PROBLEMS AND PERSPECTIVES IN HISTORY
EDITOR: HUGH F. KEARNEY

A full list of titles in this series
will be found on the back cover of this book

PROBLEMS AND PERSPECTIVES IN HISTORY

EDITOR: H. F. KEARNEY, M A, PH D

The New Deal

The New Deal

John Major

LECTURER IN HISTORY
UNIVERSITY OF HULL

BARNES & NOBLE, Inc.
NEW YORK
PUBLISHERS & BOOKSELLERS SINCE 1873

Published in the United States in 1967
by Barnes & Noble, Inc.
105 Fifth Avenue, New York

© John Major 1967
First published 1967

Printed in Great Britain by Richard Clay (The Chaucer Press), Ltd.,
Bungay, Suffolk

To Rosemary

Editor's Foreword

'Study problems in preference to periods' was the excellent advice given by Lord Acton in his inaugural lecture at Cambridge. To accept it is one thing, to put it into practice is another. In fact, in both schools and universities the teaching of history, in depth, is often hindered by certain difficulties of a technical nature, chiefly to do with the availability of sources. In this respect, history tends to be badly off in comparison with literature or the sciences. The historical equivalents of set texts, readings or experiments, in which the student is encouraged to use his own mind, are the so-called 'special periods'. If these are to be fruitful, the student must be encouraged to deal in his own way with the problems raised by historical documents and the historiography of the issues in question and he must be made aware of the wider perspectives of history. Thus, if the enclosure movement of the sixteenth century is studied, the student might examine the historiographical explanations stretching from More's *Utopia* and Cobbett to Beresford's *Lost Villages of England*. At the same time he might also be dealing with selected documents raising important problems. Finally he might be encouraged to realize the problems of peasantries at other periods of time, including Russia and China in the nineteenth and twentieth centuries. In this particular instance, thanks to Tawney and Power, *Tudor Economic Documents*, the history teacher is comparatively well off. For the other special periods the situation is much more difficult. If, however, the study of history is to encourage the development of the critical faculties as well as the memory, this approach offers the best hope. The object of this series is to go some way towards meeting these difficulties.

The general plan of each volume in the series will be similar, with a threefold approach from aspects of historiography, documents and editorial consideration of wider issues, though the structure and balance between the three aspects may vary.

A broad view is being taken of the limits of history. Political history will not be excluded, but a good deal of emphasis will be placed on economic, intellectual and social history. The idea has in fact grown out of the experience of a group of historians at the University of Sussex, where the student is encouraged to investigate the frontier areas between his own and related disciplines.

H. KEARNEY

Contents

AUTHOR'S NOTE

I regret that it was not possible to reproduce material from two important histories of the Roosevelt years. They are D. W. Brogan's *The Era of Franklin D. Roosevelt*, Yale University Press, 1950, and E. E. Robinson's *The Roosevelt Leadership 1933–1945*, Lippincott, New York, 1955.

Acknowledgements

We are grateful to the following for permission to reproduce copyright material:

George Allen & Unwin Ltd for material from *Freedom and Culture* by J. Dewey and *The American Democracy: A Commentary and an Interpretation* by H. J. Laski; George Allen & Unwin Ltd and The Macmillan Company of New York for material from *The Method of Freedom* by W. Lippman; American Economic Association for material from 'Fiscal Policy in the Thirties: A Reappraisal' by E. Carey Brown, published in the *American Economic Review*; Appleton-Century-Crofts for material from *Documents of American History* edited by H. S. Commager; *The Atlantic Monthly* for material from 'Roosevelt Through European Eyes' by Isaiah Berlin, published in issue July 1955; G. Bell & Sons Ltd for material from *Recovery: The Second Effort* by Arthur Salter; G. Bell & Sons Ltd and Harcourt, Brace & World Inc. for material from *The Acquisitive Society* by R. H. Tawney, Copyright 1920 by Harcourt, Brace & World Inc. Renewed 1948 by R. H. Tawney; the author and *The New York Times* for material from 'Can We Afford Disarmament?' by Emile Benoit, published in an issue 28 April 1963, © 1963 by The New York Times Company; A. & C. Black Ltd for material from *Full Recovery or Stagnation?* by A. H. Hansen: Basil Blackwell & Mott Ltd for material from *Maturity and Stagnation in American Capitalism*, by J. Steindl; the author's agents and Houghton Mifflin Company for material from *From The Morgenthau Diaries* by John M. Blum; The Bodley Head Ltd for material from *The Aspirin Age* by Isabel Leighton and *The Decline of American Capitalism* by L. Corey; Jonathan Cape Ltd and Alfred A. Knopf Inc. for material from *The American Political Tradition* by Richard Hofstadter, Copyright 1948 by Alfred A. Knopf Inc., and *The Age of Reform* by Richard Hofstadter, Copyright 1955 by Richard Hofstadter; Columbia University Press for an extract from *The Battle for Democracy, 1935* by R. G. Tugwell; Constable & Co. Ltd and Harcourt, Brace & World Inc. for material from *Middletown in Transition* by Robert S. and Helen M. Lynd, Copyright 1937 by Harcourt, Brace

& World Inc. Renewed 1965 by Robert S. and Helen M. Lynd; the author for material from *A Generation On Trial* by Alistair Cooke; the Cresset Press for material from *Wall Street Under Oath* by F. Pecora; André Deutsch Ltd for material from *Witness* by Whittacker Chambers; The Devin–Adair Co. for material from *The Roosevelt Myth* by John Flynn; Doubleday & Company Inc. for material from *The Democratic Roosevelt* by Rexford Guy Tugwell, Copyright © 1957 by Rexford Guy Tugwell, *The Nine Old Men* by Drew Pearson and Robert S. Allen, copyright 1936 by Doubleday and Company Inc., and *The Blue Eagle, From Egg to Earth* by Hugh S. Johnson, Copyright 1935 by the Curtiss Publishing Company; Mr Dale D. Drain, co-executor of the Estate of Edith B. Wilson for material from *The New Freedom* by W. Wilson; the Proprietors of *The Economist* for material from issues 3 October and 21 November 1936; the proprietors of *The Evening Star– The Sunday Star* for material from *Washington Star*, 6 June 1932; Farrar, Staus & Giroux Inc. for material from *The Responsibility of Peoples* by Dwight Macdonald (published in the U.S.A. under the title *Memoirs of a Revolutionist*); the proprietors of *Fortune* for material from 'No One Has Starved' published in issue September 1932; the Proprietors of *The Guardian* for material from issue dated 17 July 1964; Hamish Hamilton Ltd and Atheneum Publishers for material from *The Politics of Socialism* (Planning for Freedom) by R. H. S. Crossman, Coyyright © 1950, 1963 and 1965 by R. H. S. Crossman; Hamish Hamilton and Houghton Mifflin Company for material from *American Capitalism* and *The Great Crash* by J. K. Galbraith; Harcourt Brace & World Inc. for material from *Writers on the Left* by Daniel Aaron, *The Liberal Tradition in America* by Louis Hartz, Copyright 1955 by Louis Hartz, and *Behind the Ballots* by James Farley; Harper & Row, Publishers, Inc., for material from *Since Yesterday* by Frederick Lewis Allen, *The Future of American Politics* by Samuel Lubell, *Franklin D. Roosevelt and The New Deal, 1932–1940* by W. E. Leuchtenburg, Copyright © by William E. Leuchtenburg, and *Out of our Past* by Carl N. Degler, Copyright © 1959 by Carl N. Degler; Rupert Hart-Davis Ltd for material from *Essays in Persuasion* by J. M. Keynes; Rupert Hart-Davis Ltd and Harcourt, Brace & World Inc. for material from *The American Presidency* by Clinton Rossiter, Copyright © 1956 by Clinton Rossiter; William Heinemann Ltd and Houghton Mifflin Company for material from *The Coming of the New Deal* by A. M. Schlesinger; Messrs R. Hofstadter and D. Bell for material from '*The Pseudo-Conservative Revolt*' by R. Hofstadter from *The Radical Right* edited by D. Bell; Hollis & Carter and The Macmillan Co, of New York for material from *The Memoirs of Herbert Hoover: The Great Depression 1929–1941* by Herbert Hoover, Copyright 1952 by Herbert Hoover; Holt, Rinehart & Winston Inc. for material from *Depression Decade 1929–1941* by Broadus Mitchell, Copyright 1947 by Broadus Mitchell; Houghton Mifflin Company for material from *The Lean Years* by I. Bernstein, *Paths of American Thought* and *The Politics of Hope* by A. M. Schlesinger, Jnr, and *The Revolt of the Conservatives* by Wolfskill; the author, Hamish Hamilton Ltd and Harper & Row, Publishers, for material from *Roosevelt, An American Study* by Gerald Johnson; the author for material from *Life, Liberty and Property* by Alfred Winslow Jones; the author for material from *Louisiana Hayride* by Harnett Kane; the trustees of the Estate of the late Lord Keynes, Macmillan & Co Ltd, The Macmillan Company of Canada Ltd and Harcourt, Brace & World Inc. for material from *The General Theory of Employment, Interest and Money* by John Maynard Keynes; Alfred A. Knopf Inc. for material from *Beckoning Frontiers* by M. Eccles and *The Struggle for Judicial Supremacy* by R. H. Jackson; the author for material from *The Roosevelt Revolution* by E. K. Lindley; The London School of Economics & Political Science for material from 'The Decline of Liberalism' by H. J. Laski from *The Hobhouse Memorial Lectures 1930–1940*; Louisiana State University Press for material from *Economic Growth in the United States* by S. H. Slichter; McGraw-Hill Book Company for material from *Business Cycles* by J. A. Schumpeter, Copyright © 1964, by McGraw-Hill Book Company; Macmillan & Co. Ltd, St Martin's Press Inc. and the Macmillan Company of Canada for material from *The Life of John Maynard Keynes* by R. F. Harrod; The Macmillan Co. of New York for material from *The New Imperative* and *Interpretations 1933–1935* by Walter Lippmann, the latter title Copyright 1936 by Walter Lippmann, *The Socialist Party of America* by D. Shannon, Copyright © D. Shannon 1955, *The Other America* by M. Harrington, Copyright © M. Harrington 1962, and *Monopoly in America* by W. Adams, and H. M. Gray, Copyright W. Adams and H. M. Gray 1955; the author for *After Seven Years* by Raymond Moley; the author, Wm. Collins Sons & Co. Ltd and Random House Inc. for material from *The Thirties 1930–1940 in Great Britain* by Malcolm Muggeridge; the Proprietors of *The New Republic* for material from 'The New Deal In Review' published in issue 20 May 1940, copyright 1940, Harrison-Blaine of New Jersey Inc., and for material from 'Intellectuals and New Deals' by A. A. Berle, Jnr, and 'The Future of

xi

ACKNOWLEDGEMENTS

Relief' by H. L. Hopkins © 1964 and © 1937 Harrison-Blain of New Jersey Inc., respectively; the proprietors of *Newsweek* for material from 'The Great and Good Society' published in issue 22 November 1965, Copyright Newsweek Inc., November 1965; New York State School of Industrial and Labor Relations, Cornell University, for material from *Conflict Within the AFL* by James O. Morris (Cornell Studies in Industrial and Labor Relations, Vol. X (1958); the Proprietors of *The New York Times* for material from issues 1 April 1937 and 12 January 1939 and 24 November 1966, Copyright 1937, 1939 and 1966 (respectively) by The New York Times Company; Odhams Books Ltd for material from *Great Contemporaries* by Winston S. Churchill; University of Oregon Books for material from *New Deal Mosaic* by L. G. Seligman and E. E. Cornwell, Jnr; Oxford University Press for material from *Survey of International Affairs 1933/34* by Professor A. J. Toynbee (published under the auspices of the Royal Institute of International Affairs), and *Liberalism* by L. T. Hobhouse (Home University Library 21); The Passfield Trustees for material from *A Constitution for the Socialist Commonwealth of Great Britain* by Sidney and Beatrice Webb; A. D. Peters & Co. for material from *TVA-Adventure in Planning* by Sir Julian Huxley, published by Chatto & Windus Ltd; the author and Harper & Row, Publishers, Inc., for material from *The Roosevelt I knew* by Frances Perkins; Prentice-Hall Inc. for material from *Social Darwinism: Selected Essays* of William Graham Sumner by Stow Persons, Copyright 1963, and *Theodore Roosevelt: The New Nationalism*, ed. William E. Lauchtenburg, © 1961; *The Political Quarterly* for an extract from 'The Experimental Roosevelt' from issue in 1950; Princeton University Press for material from *The New Deal and the Problem of Monopoly* by E. W. Hawley, and *The Invasion from Mars* by H. Cantril; G. P. Putnam's Sons for material from *Liberalism and Social Action* by J. Dewey; Random House Inc. for material from *The Public Papers and Addresses of Franklin D. Roosevelt*, Vols. I & II, ed. Samuel I. Rosenman, Copyright 1938 by Franklin Delano Roosevelt and renewed 1965 by Elliott Roosevelt, Hon. James Roosevelt and Franklin Delano Roosevelt, Jnr; William Reeves Booksellers Ltd for material from *Manifesto of the Communist Party* by K. Marx and F. Engels; the editor and the Trustees of the Estate of the late Franklin D. Roosevelt for material from various volumes of *The Public Papers and Addresses of Franklin D. Roosevelt* (edited by Samuel I. Rosenman); the author, Hutchinson & Co. Ltd and Harper & Row, Publishers, Inc., for material from *This I Remember*

ACKNOWLEDGEMENTS

by Eleanor Roosevelt; the author, Rupert Hart-Davis Ltd and Harper & Row, Publishers, Inc., for material from *Working with Roosevelt* by Samuel Rosenman; Routledge & Kegan Paul Ltd for material from *The Politics of Democratic Socialism* by E. F. M. Durbin and *Progress in Poverty* by H. George; the author for material from *Personality in Politics* by Sir Arthur Salter; Charles Scribner's Sons for material from *Boot Straps* by Tom M. Girdler; Martin Secker & Warburg Ltd and Harcourt, Brace & World Inc. for material from *Roosevelt: The Lion and the Fox* by J. M. Burns, Copyright 1956 by James Mac-Gregor Burns; the author and Harper & Row, Publishers, Inc., for material from *The White House Papers of Harry L. Hopkins* by Robert E. Sherwood (published in the U.S.A under the title *Roosevelt and Hopkins*); Simon & Schuster, Inc. for material from *We Saw It Happen*, ed. H. W. Baldwin and S. Stone; The Statesman and Nation Publishing Co. Ltd for material from 'America: The Sick Giant' by Paul Johnson, published in the *New Statesman*, 17 July 1964; Mrs Celia Strachey for material from *The Nature of Capitalist Crisis* and *A Programme for Progress* by John Strachey; the proprietors of *St Paul Dispatch* for material quoted from Mid-Western press reports of September, 1939; the editor of *Survey* for material from 'Toledo: A City the Auto Ran Over' by B. Amidon; Syracuse University Press for material from *Minister of Relief: Harry Hopkins and the Depression* by Searle F. Charles (1963); D. Van Nostrand Company Inc. for material from *Roosevelt Through Foreign Eyes*, ed. N. Halasz, Copyright © 1961 by D. Van Nostrand Company Inc.; The Viking Press Inc. for material from *Ideas for the Ice Age* by Max Lerner, Copyright 1941 by Max Lerner, and *The Story of the C.I.O* by B. Stolberg, Copyright 1938 by The Viking Press Inc. (All Rights Reserved); the Executors of H. G. Wells for material from *The New America: The New World* by H. G. Wells; George Weidenfeld & Nicolson Ltd and Simon & Schuster Inc. for material from *The Secret Diary of Harold L. Ickes. Vols. I & II* by Harold L. Ickes; John Wiley & Sons Inc. for material from *The Psychology of Social Movements* by H. Cantril and *Presidential Power* by R. E. Neustadt; the author for material from *The Shores of Light* by Edmund Wilson; The Regents of the University of Wisconsin for material from *Agricultural Discontent in the Middle West, 1900–1939* by Theodore Saloutos and John D. Hicks (The University of Wisconsin Press), and Yale University Press for material from *The Twilight of the Supreme Court* by E. S. Corwen, *As Steel Goes* by R. R. R. Brooks and *The Folklore of Capitalism* by T. Arnold.

xiii

ACKNOWLEDGEMENTS

While every effort has been made to trace the owners of copyrights, in a few cases this has proved impossible–and we would welcome any information that would enable us to do so.

Introduction:
The Challenge to
Laissez-Faire

This book is about the crisis faced by liberalism in the United States during the 1930s. This crisis was to shake the basic assumptions of liberalism as a social, political and economic system in the very country where that system had seemed unassailable. It lasted throughout the decade and we shall try to trace the varying reactions of some of the principal figures involved—as far as possible in their own words—as the situation changed and developed.

The significance of the breakdown was not confined to America. Its repercussions were worldwide, and to place the experience of the United States in historical perspective one needs to look first at the challenges to liberalism, and especially to liberal laissez-faire economics, which had appeared over the previous century, in America and elsewhere. The first extracts deal with the 1840s when laissez-faire was fighting to establish itself as the creed of the future in the teeth of a severe depression. The next two come from the 1880s, when laissez-faire had triumphed, only to harden into an accepted dogma, and they represent the extreme doctrinaire view of a liberal society. At the same time such an uncompromising liberalism was coming under fire on both sides of the Atlantic and the following twelve pieces illustrate the attacks made by democratic critics of the liberal establishment. The final three extracts date from the aftermath of the First World War, when a new and altogether different challenge was rising from men who had deliberately rejected liberal solutions and chosen to refashion their states on revolutionary lines. They display the major alternatives facing democratic society in Europe and America on the eve of the great depression.

The New Order

1. *Thomas Carlyle, a romantic conservative, was horrified at the consequences of the disruptive new economics; this he wrote in 1843.*

Let inventive men consider, Whether the Secret of this Universe, and of Man's Life there, does, after all, as we rashly fancy it, consist in making money? There is One God, just, supreme, almighty: but is Mammon the name of him?–With a Hell which means 'Failing to make money', I do not think there is any Heaven possible that would suit one well; nor so much as an Earth that can be habitable long! In brief, all this Mammon-Gospel, of Supply-and-Demand, Competition, Laissez-faire, and Devil take the hindmost, begins to be one of the shabbiest Gospels ever preached; or altogether the shabbiest...

... were the Corn-Laws ended tomorrow, there is nothing yet ended; there is only room for all manner of things beginning. The Corn-Laws gone, and Trade made free, it is as good as certain this paralysis of industry will pass away. We shall have another period of commercial enterprise, of victory and prosperity; during which, it is likely, much money will again be made, and all the people may, by the extant methods, still for a space of years, be kept alive and physically fed. The strangling bands of Famine will be loosened from our necks; we shall have room again to breathe; time to bethink ourselves, to repent and consider! A precious and thrice-precious space of years; wherein to struggle as for life in reforming our foul ways; in alleviating, instructing, regulating our people; seeking, as for life, that something like spiritual food be imparted them, some real governance and guidance be provided them! It will be a priceless time. For our new period or paroxysm of commercial prosperity will and can, on the old methods of 'Competition and Devil take the hindmost,' prove but a paroxysm: a new paroxysm,–likely enough, if we do not use it better, to be our last.

'Past and Present', in *Sartor Resartus, Lectures on Heroes, Chartism, Past and Present*, Chapman and Hall, London, 1895, pp. 213, 214–15

2. *Karl Marx and Friedrich Engels were communist revolutionaries dedicated to the violent overthrow of liberalism. Their Manifesto was published on the eve of the 1848 revolutions.*

Modern bourgeois society with its relations of production, of exchange and of property, a society that has conjured up such gigantic means of production and exchange, is like a sorcerer, who is no longer able to control the powers of the nether world whom he has called up by his spells. For many a decade past the history of industry and commerce is but the history of the revolt of modern productive forces against modern conditions of production, against the property relations that are the conditions for the existence of the bourgeoisie and of its rule. It is enough to mention the commercial crises that by their periodical return put on its trial, each time more threateningly, the existence of the entire bourgeois society. In these crises a great part not only of the existing products, but also of the previously created productive forces, are periodically destroyed. In these crises there breaks out an epidemic that, in all earlier epochs, would have seemed an absurdity – the epidemic of over-production. Society suddenly finds itself put back into a state of momentary barbarism; it appears as if a famine, a universal war of devastation had cut off the supply of every means of subsistence; industry and commerce seem to be destroyed; and why? Because there is too much civilization, too much means of subsistence, too much industry, too much commerce. The productive forces at the disposal of society no longer tend to further the development of the conditions of bourgeois property; on the contrary, they have become too powerful for these conditions, by which they are fettered, and so soon as they overcome these fetters, they bring disorder into the whole of bourgeois society, endanger the existence of bourgeois property. . . . The conditions of bourgeois society are too narrow to comprise the wealth created by them. And how does the bourgeoisie get over these crises? On the one hand by enforced destruction of a mass of productive forces; on the other, by the conquest of new markets, and by the more thorough exploitation of the old ones. That is to say, by paving the way for more extensive and more destructive crises, and by diminishing the means whereby crises are prevented.

The weapons with which the bourgeoisie felled feudalism to the ground are now turned against the bourgeoisie itself.

But not only has the bourgeoisie forged the weapons that bring death to itself; it has also called into existence the men who are to wield those weapons – the modern working classing – the proletarians. . . .

. . . What the bourgeoisie . . . produces, above all, is its own grave-diggers. Its fall and the victory of the proletariat are equally inevitable.

Manifesto of the Communist Party, Progress Publishers, Moscow, n.d., pp. 51–3, 64

3. *John Stuart Mill, the son of one of the early apostles of laissez-faire, and himself a liberal, became uneasy about some of the manifestations of liberal economics. Here he writes about his feelings, and those of the woman who was to become his wife, in the 1840s.*

In those days I had seen little further than the old school of political economists into the possibilities of fundamental improvement in social arrangements. Private property, as now understood, and inheritance, appeared to me, as to them, the *dernier mot* of legislation: and I looked no further than to mitigating the inequalities consequent on these institutions, by getting rid of primogeniture and entails. The notion that it was possible to go further than this in removing the injustice–for injustice it is, whether admitting of a complete remedy or not–involved in the fact that some are born to riches and the vast majority to poverty, I then reckoned chimerical, and only hoped that by universal education, leading to universal restraint on population, the portion of the poor might be made more tolerable. In short, I was a democrat, but not the least of a Socialist. We were now much less democrats than I had been, because so long as education continues to be so wretchedly imperfect, we dreaded the ignorance and especially the selfishness and brutality of the mass: but our ideal of ultimate improvement went far beyond Democracy, and would class us decidedly under the general designation of Socialists. While we repudiated with the greatest energy that tyranny of society over the individual which most Socialist systems are supposed to involve, we yet looked forward to a time when society will no longer be divided into the idle and the industrious, when the rule that they who do not work shall not eat, will be applied not to paupers only, but impartially to all; when the division of the produce of labour, instead of depending, as in so great a degree it now does, on the accident of birth, will be made by concert on an acknowledged principle of justice; and when it will no longer either be, or be thought to be, impossible for human beings to exert themselves strenuously in procuring benefits which are not to be exclusively their own, but to be shared with the society they belong to. The social problem of the future we considered to be, how to unite the greatest individual liberty of action, with a common ownership in the raw material of the globe, and an equal participation of all in the benefits of combined labour . . . These considerations did not make us overlook the folly of premature attempts to dispense with the inducements of private interest in social affairs, while no substitute for them has been or can be provided: but we regarded all existing institutions and social arrangements as being (in a phrase I once heard from Austin) 'merely provisional', and we welcomed with the greatest pleasure and interest all socialistic experiments by select individuals (such as the Co-operative Societies), which, whether they succeeded or failed, could not but operate as a most useful education of those who took part in them, by cultivating their capacity of acting upon motives pointing directly to the general good, or making them aware of the defects which render them and others incapable of doing so.

Autobiography, Columbia University Press, New York, 1948, pp. 161–2, 163–4

Liberalism Absolute

4. Herbert Spencer was the high priest of what might be called total liberalism, which categorically rejected any governmental interference with social processes.

That abundant crops now grow where once only wild berries could be gathered, is due to the pursuit of individual satisfactions through many centuries. The progress from wigwams to good houses has resulted from wishes to increase personal welfare; and towns have arisen under like promptings. Beginning with traffic at gatherings on occasions of religious festivals, the trading organization, now so extensive and complex, has been produced entirely by men's efforts to achieve their private ends. Perpetually Governments have thwarted and deranged the growth, but have in no way furthered it; save by partially discharging their proper function and maintaining social order. So, too, with those advances of knowledge and those improvements of appliances, by which these structural changes and these increasing activities have been made possible. It is not the State which made possible extended navigation by a developed astronomy; it was not the State which made the discoveries in physics, chemistry, and the rest, which guide modern manufacturers; it was not the State which devised the machinery for producing fabrics of every kind, for transferring men and things from place to place, and for ministering in a thousand ways to our comforts. The world-wide transactions conducted in merchants' offices, the rush of traffic filling our streets, the retail distributing system which brings everything within easy reach and delivers the necessaries of life daily to our doors, are not of governmental origin. All these are results of the spontaneous activities of citizens, separate or grouped. Nay, to these spontaneous activities Governments owe the very means of performing their duties. Divest the political machinery of all those aids which Science and Art have yielded it – leave it with those only which State-officials have invented; and its functions would cease. The very language in which its laws are registered and the orders of its agents daily given, is an instrument not in the remotest degree due to the legislator; but is one which has unawares grown up during men's intercourse while pursuing their personal satisfactions.

'The Sins of Legislators', from *The Man versus the State*, Williams and Norgate, London, 1888, pp. 62–3

5. *William Graham Sumner was the American Spencer. This extract is taken from an essay written in the late 1880s.*

If this poor old world is as bad as they say, one more reflection may check the zeal of the headlong reformer. It is at any rate a tough old world. It has taken its trend and curvature and all its twists and tangles from a long course of formation. All its wry and crooked gnarls and knobs are therefore stiff and stubborn. It we puny men by our arts can do anything at all to straighten them, it will only be by modifying the tendencies of some of the forces at work, so that, after a sufficient time, their action may be changed a little and slowly the lines of movement may be modified. This effort, however, can be at most only slight, and it will take a long time. In the meantime spontaneous forces will be at work, compared with which our efforts are like those of a man trying to deflect a river, and these forces will have changed the whole problem before our interferences have time to make themselves felt. The great stream of time and earthly things will sweep on just the same in spite of us. It bears with it now all the errors and follies of the past, the wreckage of all the philosophies, the fragments of all the civilizations, the wisdom of all the abandoned ethical systems, the debris of all the institutions, and the penalties of all the mistakes. It is only in imagination that we stand by and look at and criticize it and plan to change it. Everyone of us is a child of his age and cannot get out of it. He is in the stream and is swept along with it. All his sciences and philosophy come to him out of it. Therefore the tide will not be changed by us. It will swallow up both us and our experiments. It will absorb the efforts at change and take them into itself as new but trivial components, and the great movement of tradition and work will go on unchanged by our fads and schemes. The things which will change it are the great discoveries and inventions, the new reactions inside the social organism, and the changes in the earth itself on account of changes in the cosmical forces. These causes will make of it just what, in fidelity to them, it ought to be. The men will be carried along with it and be made by it. The utmost they can do by their cleverness will be to note and record their course as they are carried along, which is what we do now, and is that which leads us to the vain fancy that we can make or guide the movement. That is why it is the greatest folly of which a man can be capable, to sit down with a slate and pencil to plan out a new social world.

'The Absurd Effort to Make the World Over', in *Social Darwinism. Selected Essays of William Graham Sumner*, Prentice-Hall, New Jersey, 1963, pp. 179–80

The Attack in Britain

6. *The Oxford philosopher Thomas Hill Green is now recognized as one of the pioneers of a 'new liberalism' which held that governments must sometimes intervene to protect individuals from the free play of economic forces.*

We shall probably all agree that freedom, rightly understood, is the greatest of blessings; that its attainment is the true end of all our efforts as citizens. But when we thus speak of freedom, we should carefully consider what we mean by it. We do not mean merely freedom from restraint or compulsion. We do not mean merely freedom to do as we like irrespectively of what it is that we like. We do not mean a freedom than can be enjoyed by one man or one set of men at the cost of a loss of freedom to others. When we speak of freedom as something to be so highly prized, we mean a positive power or capacity of doing or enjoying something worth doing or enjoying, and that, too, something that we do or enjoy in common with others. We mean by it a power which each man exercises through the help or security given him by his fellow-men, and which he in return helps to secure for them. When we measure the progress of a society by its growth in freedom, we measure it by the increasing development and exercise on the whole of those powers of contributing to social good with which we believe the members of the society to be endowed; in short, by the greater power on the part of the citizens as a body to make the most and best of themselves. . . .

7

. . . Our modern legislation then with reference to labour, and education, and health, involving as it does manifold interference with freedom of contract, is justified on the ground that it is the business of the state, not indeed directly to promote moral goodness, for that, from the very nature of moral goodness, it cannot do, but to maintain the conditions without which a free exercise of the human faculties is impossible. . . .

. . . the question is whether without these laws the suffering classes could have been delivered quickly or slowly from the condition they were in. Could the enlightened self-interest or benevolence of individuals, working under a system of unlimited freedom of contract, have ever brought them into a state compatible with the free development of the human faculties? No one considering the facts can have any doubt as to the answer to this question. Left to itself, or to the operation of casual benevolence, a degraded population perpetuates and increases itself. Read any of the authorized accounts, given before royal or parliamentary commissions, of the state of the labourers, especially of the women and children, as they were in our great industries before the law was first brought to bear on them, and before freedom of contract was first interfered with in them. Ask yourself what chance there was of a generation, born and bred under such conditions, ever contracting itself out of them.

'Liberal Legislation and Freedom of Contract', from *Works of Thomas Hill Green*, ed. R. L. Nettleship, Longmans, London, 1889, vol. iii, pp. 370–1, 374, 376

7. L. T. Hobhouse represents the younger 'new liberals' who came into their own during the Liberal régime of 1906–14. This passage comes from a book published in 1911.

We are apt to assume uncritically that the wages earned by the labour of an adult man ought to suffice for the maintenance of an average family, providing for all risks. It ought, we think, to cover not only the food and clothing of wife and children, but the risks of sickness, accident, and unemployment. It ought to provide for education and lay by for old age. If it fails we are apt to think that the wage earner is not self-supporting. Now, it is certainly open to doubt whether the actual addition to wealth made by an unskilled labourer denuded of all inherited property would equal the cost represented by the sum of these items.

But here our further principle comes into play. He ought not to be denuded of all inherited property. As a citizen he should have a certain share in the social inheritance. This share should be his support in the times of misfortune, of sickness, and of worklessness, whether due to economic disorganization or to invalidity and old age. His children's share, again, is the State-provided education. These shares are charges on the social surplus. It does not, if fiscal arrangements are what they should be, infringe upon the income of other individuals, and the man who without further aid than the universally available share in the social inheritance which is to fall to him as a citizen pays his way through life is to be justly regarded as self-supporting.

The central point of Liberal economics, then, is the equation of social service and reward. This is the principle that every function of social value requires such remuneration as serves to stimulate and maintain its effective performance; that every one who performs such a function has the right, in the strict ethical sense of that term, to such remuneration and to no more; that the residue of existing wealth should be at the disposal of the community for social purposes. Further, it is the right, in the same sense, of every person capable of performing some useful social function that he should have the opportunity of so doing, and it is his right that the remuneration that he receives for it should be his property, *i.e.* that it should stand at his free disposal enabling him to direct his personal concerns according to his own preferences. These are rights in the sense that they are conditions of the welfare of its members which a well-ordered State will seek by every means to fulfil. But it is not suggested that the way of such fulfilment is plain, or that it could be achieved at a stroke by a revolutionary change in the tenure of property or the system of industry. It is, indeed, implied that the State is vested with a certain overlordship of property in general and a supervisory power over industry in general, and this principle of economic sovereignty may be set side by side with that of economic justice as a no less fundamental conception of economic Liberalism. For here, as elsewhere, liberty implies control. But the manner in which the State is to exercise its controlling power is to be learnt by experience and even in large measure by cautious experiment. We have sought to determine the principle which should guide its action, the ends at which it is to aim. The systematic study of the means lies rather within the province of economics; and the teaching of history seems to be that progress is more continuous and secure when men are content to deal with problems piecemeal than when they seek to destroy root and branch in order to erect a complete system which has captured the imagination.

Liberalism, Oxford University Press, New York, 1964, pp. 107–8

8. *At the same time (and especially after 1918) a more radical alternative—socialism—was making itself felt. Thus Sidney and Beatrice Webb.*

This Dictatorship of the Capitalist is directed fundamentally to one end —the extraction of the largest attainable income for the owners of the land and capital in the form of interest, profit and rent. The economic result in Great Britain—and we believe that much the same is true of other countries of advanced industrialism—is a great waste of productive power through misdirection and internecine competition, and also an inequality so gross that the manual-working wage-earners, comprising two-thirds of the population, obtain for their maintenance much less than half of the community's net product annually, most of them living, accordingly, in chronic penury and insecurity. Nine-tenths of all the accumulated wealth belongs to one-tenth of the population. The continued existence of the functionless rich—of persons who deliberately live by owning instead of by working, and whose futile occupations, often licentious pleasures and inherently insolent manners, undermine the intellectual and moral standards of the community —adds insult to injury. This may seem a harsh condemnation; but how many of the healthy adults who 'live by owning' work as continuously, consume as little of the product of the labour of others, and bear themselves as modestly towards the community, as the common run of professional men and women?

But the central wrong of the Capitalist System is neither the poverty of the poor nor the riches of the rich: it is the power which the mere ownership of the instruments of production gives to a relatively small section of the community over the actions of their fellow-citizens and over the mental and physical environment of successive generations. Under such a system personal freedom becomes, for large masses of the people, little better than a mockery. The tiny minority of rich men enjoy, not personal freedom only, but also personal power over the lives of other people; whilst the underlying mass of poor men find their personal freedom restricted to the choice between obeying the orders of irresponsible masters intent on their own pleasure or their own gain, or remaining without the means of subsistence for themselves and their families. At the same time this inequality in power between the wealthy class and the mass of the community corrupts also the political organization of the community and the newspaper press, and makes it impossible for the National Government and even the Municipality or other form of Local Government (with their twin functions of defence against aggression and the promotion of the permanent interests of the community, and especially the particular type of civilization that it desires) to be or to become genuine Democracies.

What the Socialist aims at is the substitution, for this Dictatorship of the Capitalist, of government of the people and for the people, in all the industries and services by which the people live. Only in this way can either the genuine participation of the whole body of the people in the administration of its own affairs, and the people's effective consciousness of consent to what is done in its name, ever be realized. This application of Democracy to industry, though it has its own inherent value as an unique educational force, is in the eyes of the Socialist also a means to an end, namely, a more equitable sharing of the national product among all members of the community, in order that there should be available for all the members of the community the largest attainable measure of personal freedom. Hence the purpose of Socialism is twofold: the application of Democracy to industry and the adoption by this Socialist Democracy of the principle of maximizing equality in 'life, liberty and the pursuit of happiness'.

A Constitution for the Socialist Commonwealth of Great Britain, Longmans, London, 1920, pp. xi–xiii

9. *R. H. Tawney, the historian, gave socialism a rare eloquence and humanity; this indictment of capitalism was first published in 1921.*

The secret of its triumph is obvious. It is an invitation to men to use the powers with which they have been endowed by nature or society, by skill or energy or relentless egotism or mere good fortune, without enquiring whether there is any principle by which their exercise should be limited. It assumes the social organization which determines the opportunities which different classes shall in fact possess, and concentrates attention upon the right of those who possess or can acquire power to make the fullest use of it for their own self-advancement. By fixing men's minds, not upon the discharge of social obligations, which restricts their energy because it defines the goal to which it should be directed, but upon the exercise of the right to pursue their own self-interest, it offers unlimited scope for the acquisition of riches, and therefore gives free play to one of the most powerful of human instincts.

To the strong it promises unfettered freedom for the exercise of their strength; to the weak the hope that they too one day may be strong. Before the eyes of both it suspends a golden prize, which not all can attain, but for which each may strive, the enchanting vision of infinite expansion. It assures men that there are no ends other than their ends, no law other than their desires, no limit other than that which they think advisable. Thus it makes the individual the centre of his own universe, and dissolves moral principles into a choice of expediencies. And it immensely simplifies the problems of social life in complex communities. For it relieves them of the necessity of discriminating between different types of economic activity and different sources of wealth, between enterprise and avarice, energy and unscrupulous greed, property which is legitimate and property which is theft, the just enjoyment of the fruits of labour and the idle parasitism of birth or fortune, because it treats all economic activities as standing upon the same level, and suggests that excess or defect, waste or superfluity, require no conscious effort of the social will to avert them, but are corrected almost automatically by the mechanical play of economic forces. . . .

That obsession by economic issues is as local and transitory as it is repulsive and disturbing. To future generations it will appear as pitiable as the obsession of the seventeenth century by religious quarrels appears to-day; indeed, it is less rational, since the object with which it is concerned is less important. And it is a poison which inflames every wound and turns each trivial scratch into a malignant ulcer. Society will not solve the particular problems of industry which afflict it, until that poison is expelled, and it has learned to see industry itself in the right perspective. If it is to do that, it must rearrange its scale of values. It must regard economic interests as one element in life, not as the whole of life. It must persuade its members to renounce the opportunity of gains which accrue without any corresponding service, because the struggle for them keeps the whole community in a fever. It must so organize its industry that the instrumental character of economic activity is emphasized by its subordination to the social purpose for which it is carried on.

The Acquisitive Society, Bell, London, 1927 edn, pp. 33–4, 241–2

10. *It was the more clinical thinking of the Liberal economist John Maynard Keynes, however, which was to have the greatest influence in the thirties and later, both in Britain and abroad. This essay was written in 1926.*

It is *not* true that individuals possess a prescriptive 'natural liberty' in their economic activities. There is *no* 'compact' conferring perpetual rights on those who Have or on those who Acquire. The world is *not* so governed from above that private and social interest always coincide. It is *not* so managed here below that in practice they coincide. It is *not* a correct deduction from the Principles of Economics that enlightened self-interest always operates in the public interest. Nor is it true that self-interest generally *is* enlightened; more often individuals acting separately to promote their own ends are too ignorant or too weak to attain even these. Experience does *not* show that individuals, when they make up a social unit, are always less clear-sighted than when they act separately. . . .

. . . Many people, who are really objecting to Capitalism as a way of life, argue as though they were objecting to it on the ground of its inefficiency in attaining its own objects. Contrariwise, devotees of Capitalism are often unduly conservative, and reject reforms in its technique, which might really strengthen and preserve it, for fear that they may prove to be the first steps away from Capitalism itself. Nevertheless a time may be coming when we shall get clearer than at present as to when we are talking about Capitalism as an efficient or an inefficient technique, and when we are talking about it as desirable or objectionable in itself. For my part, I think that Capitalism, wisely managed, can probably be made more efficient for attaining economic ends than any alternative system yet in sight, but that in itself it is in many ways extremely objectionable. Our problem is to work out a social organization which shall be as efficient as possible without offending our notions of a satisfactory way of life.

The next step forward must come, not from political agitation or premature experiments, but from thought. We need by an effort of the mind to elucidate our own feelings. At present our sympathy and our judgment are apt to be on different sides, which is a painful and paralysing state of mind. In the field of action reformers will not be successful until they can steadily pursue a clear and definite object with their intellects and their feelings in tune. There is no party in the world at present which appears to me to be pursuing right aims by right methods. Material Poverty provides the incentive to change precisely in situations where there is little margin for experiments. Material Prosperity removes the incentive just when it might be safe to take a chance. Europe lacks the means, America the will, to make a move. We need a new set of convictions which spring naturally from a candid examination of our own inner feelings in relation to the outside facts.

'The End of Laissez-Faire', in *Essays in Persuasion*, Macmillan, London, 1931, pp. 312, 320–2

The Attack in America

11. *Henry George was that oddity, an American socialist. Here are his observations on the consequences of the depression of the 1870s, the first serious depression to strike the modern American industrial economy. He wrote this in 1879.*

. . . unpleasant as it may be to admit it, it is at last becoming evident that the enormous increase in productive power which has marked the present century and is still going on with accelerating ratio, has no tendency to extirpate poverty or to lighten the burdens of those compelled to toil. It simply widens the gulf between Dives and Lazarus, and makes the struggle for existence more intense. The march of invention has clothed mankind with powers of which a century ago the boldest imagination could not have dreamed. But in factories where labour-saving machinery has reached its most wonderful development, little children are at work; wherever the new forces are anything like fully utilized, large classes are maintained by charity or live on the verge of recourse to it; amid the greatest accumulations of wealth, men die of starvation, and puny infants suckle dry breasts; while everywhere the greed of gain, the worship of wealth, shows the force of the fear of want. The promised land flies before us like the mirage. The fruits of the tree of knowledge turn as we grasp them to apples of Sodom that crumble at the touch. . . .

. . . This association of poverty with progress is the greatest enigma of our times. It is the central fact from which spring industrial, social and political differences that perplex the world, and with which statesmanship and philanthropy and education grapple in vain. From it come the clouds that overhang the future of the most progressive and self-reliant nations. It is the riddle which the Sphinx of Fate puts to our civilization, and which not to answer is to be destroyed. So long as all the increased wealth which modern progress brings goes but to build up great fortunes, to increase luxury, and make sharper the contrast between the House of Have and the House of Want, progress is not real and cannot be permanent. The reaction must come. The tower leans from its very foundations, and every new story (*sic*) but hastens the final catastrophe. To educate men who must be condemned to poverty is but to make them restive; to base on a state of most glaring social inequality political institutions under which men are theoretically equal, is to stand a pyramid on its apex.

Progress and Poverty, Kegan Paul, London, 1926 edn, pp. 5, 6–7

12. *Laissez-faire, in short, was not producing the expected results in America. The small man, far from prospering, was being crushed by 'Big Business' and it was the Federal government in Washington which was called on to redress the balance. The government reacted but with laws which were little more than cynical gestures. Here is part of the Interstate Commerce Act of 1887. Though for many years a dead letter it set crucial precedents, especially for the New Deal.*

Be it enacted . . ., That the provisions of this act shall apply to any common carrier or carriers engaged in the transportation of passengers or property wholly by railroad, or partly by railroad and partly by water when both are used, under a common control, management, or arrangement, for a continuous carriage or shipment, from one State or Territory of the United States, or the District of Columbia, to any other State or Territory of the United States, or the District of Columbia, or from any place in the United States to an adjacent foreign country, or from any place in the United States through a foreign country to any other place in the United States, and also to the transportation in like manner of property shipped from any place in the United States to a foreign country and carried from such place to a port of transshipment, or shipped from a foreign country to any place in the United States and carried to such place from a port of entry either in the United States or an adjacent foreign country: *Provided, however,* That the provisions of this Act shall not apply to the transportation of passengers or property, or to the receiving, delivering, storage, or handling of property, wholly within one State, and not shipped to or from a foreign country from or to any State or Territory as aforesaid.

. . . All charges made for any service rendered or to be rendered in the transportation of passengers or property as aforesaid, or in connection therewith, or for the receiving, delivering, storage, or handling of such property, shall be reasonable and just; and every unjust and unreasonable charge for such service is prohibited and declared to be unlawful. . . .

Sec. 11. . . . a Commission is hereby created and established to be known as the Inter-State Commerce Commission, which shall be composed of five Commissioners, who shall be appointed by the President, by and with the advice of the Senate. . . .

Sec. 12. . . . the Commission . . . shall have authority to inquire into the management of the business of all common carriers subject to the provisions of this act, and shall keep itself informed as to the manner and method in which the same is conducted, and shall have the right to obtain from such common carriers full and complete information necessary to enable the Commission to perform the duties and carry out the objects for which it was created. . . .

Sec. 13. . . . any person, firm, corporation, or association, or any mercantile, agricultural, or manufacturing society, or any body politic or municipal organization complaining of anything done or omitted to be done by any common carrier subject to the provisions of this act in contravention of the provisions thereof, may apply to said Commission by petition, which shall briefly state the facts; whereupon a statement of the charges thus made shall be forwarded by the Commission to such common carrier, who shall be called upon to satisfy the complaint or to answer the same in writing within a reasonable time, to be specified by the Commission. . . . If there shall appear to be any reasonable ground for investigating said complaint, it shall be the duty of the Commission to investigate the matters complained of in such manner and by such means as it shall deem proper. . . .

Sec. 16. . . . whenever any common carrier, . . . shall violate or refuse or neglect to obey any lawful order or requirement of the Commission in this act named, it shall be the duty of the Commission, and lawful for any company or person in such order or requirement, to apply, in a summary way, by petition, to the circuit court of the United States sitting in equity in the judicial district in which the common carrier complained of has its principal office, or in which the violation or disobedience of such order or requirement shall happen, alleging such violation or disobedience as the case may be; and the said court shall have power to hear and determine the matter, on such short notice to the common carrier complained of as the court shall deem reasonable. . . .

Documents of American History, ed. H. S. Commager, 7th edn, Appleton-Century-Crofts, New York, 1963, vol. i, pp. 579, 581-2

13. *Washington was also prevailed on to fight business monopolies and assumed powers equally empty but just as portentous; here the instrumentality was the Sherman Anti-Trust Act of 1890. The monopoly issue was to dominate American politics for the next half-century and like the Interstate Commerce Act, the Sherman Act was to be a supremely important source of inspiration for New Dealers.*

Be it enacted

Sec. 1. Every contract, combination in the form of trust or otherwise, or conspiracy, in restraint of trade or commerce among the several States, or with foreign nations, is hereby declared to be illegal. Every person who shall make any such contract or engage in any such combination or conspiracy, shall be deemed guilty of a misdemeanor, and, on conviction thereof, shall be punished by fine not exceeding five thousand dollars, or by imprisonment not exceeding one year, or by both said punishments, in the discretion of the court.

Sec. 2. Every person who shall monopolize, or attempt to monopolize, or combine or conspire with any other person or persons, to monopolize any part of the trade or commerce among the several States, or with foreign nations, shall be deemed guilty of a misdemeanor, and, on conviction thereof, shall be punished by fine not exceeding five thousand dollars, or by imprisonment not exceeding one year, or by both said punishments, in the discretion of the court. . . .

Sec. 8. . . . the word 'person,' or 'persons,' wherever used in this act shall be deemed to include corporations and associations existing under or authorized by the laws of either the United States, the laws of any of the Territories, the laws of any State, or the laws of any foreign country.

Ibid., vol. i, pp. 586-7

14. *Anti-business legislation was worthless because the government was so largely the creature of industrial interests. During the 1890s the Populists, mostly agrarian radicals from the West, tried and failed to seize power and*

make government the champion of the underdog. Here is part of the preamble to their platform for the presidential campaign of 1892.

We have witnessed for more than a quarter of a century the struggles of the two great political parties for power and plunder, while grievous wrongs have been inflicted upon the suffering people. We charge that the controlling influences dominating both these parties have permitted the dreadful conditions to develop without serious effort to prevent or restrain them. Neither do they now promise us any substantial reform. They have agreed together to ignore, in the coming campaign, every issue but one. They propose to drown the outcries of a plundered people with the uproar of a sham battle over the tariff, so that capitalists, corporations, national banks, rings, trusts, watered stock, the demonetization of silver and the oppressions of the usurers may all be lost sight of. They propose to sacrifice our homes, lives and children on the altar of mammon; to destroy the multitude in order to secure corruption funds from the millionaires.

Assembled on the anniversary of the birthday of the nation, and filled with the spirit of the grand general and chief who established our independence, we seek to restore the government of the Republic to the hands of the 'plain people,' with which class it originated. We assert our purposes to be identical with the purposes of the National Constitution; to form a more perfect union and establish justice, insure domestic tranquillity, provide for the common defence, promote the general welfare, and secure the blessings of liberty for ourselves and our posterity. . . .

. . . We believe that the power of government in other words, of the people–should be expanded . . . as rapidly and as far as the good sense of an intelligent people and the teachings of experience shall justify, to the end that oppression, injustice, and poverty shall eventually cease in the land.

Ibid., vol. i, p. 594

15. *Between 1901 and 1917, after the political failure of Populism, the urban Progressive movement stood in the vanguard of reform. Theodore Roosevelt, President from 1901 to 1909, represented the wing of Progressivism that became prepared to recognize the fact of big business but which was determined to ensure that the Federal government controlled it. In this he was a forerunner*

of the First New Deal. This passage is taken from a celebrated speech at Osawatomie, Kansas, on 31 August 1910.

I stand for the square deal. But when I say that I am for the square deal, I do not mean merely that I stand for fair play under the present rules of the game, but that I stand for having those rules changed so as to work for a more substantial equality of opportunity and of reward for equally good service. . . . The true friend of property, the true conservative, is he who insists that property shall be the servant and not the master of the commonwealth, who insists that the creature of man's making shall be the servant and not the master of the man who made it. The citizens of the United States must effectively control the mighty commercial forces which they have themselves called into being . . .

. . . Combinations in industry are the result of an imperative economic law which cannot be repealed by political legislation. The effort at prohibiting all combination has substantially failed. The way out lies, not in attempting to prevent such combinations, but in completely controlling them in the interest of the public welfare. . . .

. . . We are face to face with new conceptions of the relations of property to human welfare, chiefly because certain advocates of the rights of property as against the rights of men have been pushing their claims too far. The man who wrongly holds that every human right is secondary to his profit must give way to the advocate of human welfare, who rightly holds that every man holds his property subject to the general right of the community to regulate its use to whatever degree the public welfare may require it.

But I think we may go still further. The right to regulate the use of wealth in the public interest is universally admitted. Let us admit also the right to regulate the terms and conditions of labor, which is the chief element of wealth, directly in the interest of the common good. The fundamental thing to do for every man is to give him a chance to reach a place in which he will make the greatest possible contribution to the common good. Understand what I say here. Give him a chance, not push him up if he will not be pushed. Help any man who stumbles; if he lies down, it is a poor job to carry him; but if he is a worthy man, try your best to see that he gets a chance to show the worth that is in him. No man can be a good citizen unless he has a wage more than sufficient to cover the bare cost of living, and hours of labor short enough so that after his day's work is done he will have time and energy to bear his share in the management of the community, to help in carrying the general load. We keep countless men from being good citizens by the conditions of life with which we surround them. We need comprehensive workmen's compensation acts, both state and national laws to regulate child labor and work for women, and, especially, we need in our common schools not merely education in book learning, but also practical training for daily life and work . . .

. . . I do not ask for overcentralization; but I do ask that we work in a spirit of broad and far-reaching nationalism when we work for what concerns our people as a whole. We are all Americans. Our common interests are as broad as the continent. I speak to you here in Kansas exactly as I would speak in New York or Georgia, for the most vital problems are those which affect us all alike. The national government belongs to the whole American people, and where the whole American people are interested, that interest can be guarded effectively only by the national government. The betterment which we seek must be accomplished, I believe, mainly through the national government.

The American people are right in demanding that New Nationalism, without which we cannot hope to deal with new problems. The New Nationalism puts the national need before sectional or personal advantage. It is impatient of the utter confusion that results from local legislatures attempting to treat national issues as local issues. It is still more impatient of the impotence which springs from overdivision of governmental powers, the impotence which makes it possible for local selfishness or for legal cunning, hired by wealthy special interests, to bring national activities to a deadlock. This New Nationalism regards the executive power as the steward of the public welfare. It demands of the judiciary that it shall be interested primarily in human welfare rather than in property, just as it demands that the representative body shall represent all the people rather than any one class or section of the people.

The New Nationalism, Prentice-Hall, New Jersey, 1961 edn, pp. 26, 27, 29, 33–4, 36

16. *Woodrow Wilson, who was President from 1913 to 1921, represented the opposing wing of Progressivism which aimed at breaking up big business monopoly and making things easier for the small businessman. Just as the New Nationalism foreshadowed the First New Deal, so Wilson's New Freedom anticipated much of the Second. This extract dates from 1912.*

The organization of business has become more centralized, vastly more centralized, than the political organization of the country itself. Corporations have come to cover greater areas than states; have come to live under a greater variety of laws than the citizen himself, have excelled states in their budgets and loomed bigger than whole commonwealths in their influence over the lives and fortunes of entire communities of men. Centralized business has built up vast structures of organization and equipment which overtop all states and seem to have no match or competitor except the federal government itself.

What we have got to do,–and it is a colossal task not to be undertaken with a light head or without judgement,–what we have got to do is to disentangle this colossal 'community of interest'. No matter how we may purpose dealing with a single combination in restraint of trade, you will agree with me in this, that no single, avowed, combination is big enough for the United States to be afraid of; but when all the combinations are combined and this final combination is not disclosed by any process of incorporation or law, but is merely an identity of personnel, or of interest, then there is something that even the government of the nation itself might come to fear,–something for the law to pull apart, and gently, but firmly and persistently, dissect. . . .

. . . When we undertake the strategy which is going to be necessary to overcome and destroy this far-reaching system of monopoly, we are rescuing the business of this country, we are not injuring it; and when we separate the interests from each other and dismember these communities of connection, we have in mind a greater community of interest, a vaster community of interest, the community of interest that binds the virtues of all men together, that community of mankind which is broad and catholic enough to take under the sweep of its comprehension all sorts and conditions of men; that vision which sees that no society is renewed from the top but that every society is renewed from the bottom. Limit opportunity, restrict the field of originative achievement, and you cut out the heart and root of all prosperity. . . .

. . . we must put heart into the people by taking the heartlessness out of politics, business, and industry. We have got to make politics a thing in which an honest man can take his part with satisfaction because he knows that his opinion will count as much as the next man's, and that the boss and the interests have been dethroned. Business we have got to untrammel, abolishing tariff favors and railroad discrimination, and credit denials, and all the forms of unjust handicaps against the little man. Industry we have got to humanize,—not through the trusts, —but through the direct action of law guaranteeing protection against dangers and compensation for injuries, guaranteeing sanitary conditions, proper hours, the right to organize, and all the other things which the conscience of the country demands as the workingman's right. We have got to cheer and inspirit our people with the sure prospects of social justice and due reward, with the vision of open gates of opportunity for all.

The New Freedom, Doubleday, Page, New York, 1913, pp. 187–8, 190, 291–2

17. *In the same year, a book was published which suggested a third approach— that businessmen themselves could find the solution, in co-operation with government. Here too we see one of the major aspects of the First New Deal foreshadowed.*

The following [provisions] have to do with the formation of associations to help trade conditions, and which would be useful in applying the principles of the new code. In fact, without associations it would be impossible for a federal commission to enforce the proposed provisions which are general in character. Only the parties engaged in a trade or industry are in a position to work out the details, and formulate the rules necessary to compel obedience. The public does not realize how eager the best businessmen are to do some of these very things, how gladly they would 'blacklist' the manufacturer or dealer who resorts to tricky or unfair practices, but the law as it stands does not permit them to get together and act as a unit; the following suggestions are made to meet this condition:

Remove all restrictions upon the organization of associations and combinations to control occupations, trades and industries; on the contrary directly encourage such organizations, encourage men to do for themselves the things that should be done, but under the following conditions:

(*a*) Each association shall file its articles of agreement and the details of its organization with the proper federal department.

(*b*) Its meetings shall be open to any representative of the government who, in the performance of his duties, wishes to attend, and he shall have power to examine all records, files and papers, and to question officers and members regarding not only the transactions of the association, but their own acts in furtherance of the objects of the association.

(c) Power in the federal commission, upon complaint of any party, to review the acts of the association, if necessary revise and fix prices and conditions of purchases and sales, award damages, enforce penalties, dissolve the association.

(d) Power, also, to require publicity and to name conditions under which representatives of (a) employees, (b) parties who sell to members of the association, and (c) customers, may attend the meetings of the association.

With these broad general provisions the country would have nothing to fear from combinations however large. Their influence would be beneficial, and each would work out for its own occupation, trade or industry such rules as would be necessary for compliance with the letter and spirit of the new code.

A. J. EDDY, *The New Competition* (1912), McClurg, Chicago, 1917 edn, pp. 355–6

The Totalitarians

18. *Benito Mussolini and the Fascists came to power in Italy in 1922 and contemptuously rejected the 'outgrown ideologies' of nineteenth-century liberalism.*

. . . Granted that the XIXth century was the century of socialism, liberalism, democracy, this does not mean that the XXth century must also be the century of socialism, liberalism, democracy. Political doctrines pass; nations remain. We are free to believe that this is a century of authority, a century tending to the 'right', a Fascist century. If the XIXth century was the century of the individual (liberalism implies individualism) we are free to believe that this is the 'collective' century, and therefore the century of the State . . .

. . . The key-stone of the Fascist doctrine is its conception of the State, of its essence, its functions, and its aims. For Fascism the State is absolute, individuals and groups relative. Individuals and groups are admissable in so far as they come within the State. Instead of directing the game and guiding the material and moral progress of the community, the liberal State restricts its activities to recording results. The Fascist State is wide awake and has a will of its own . . .

. . . It is not reactionary but revolutionary, for it anticipates the solution of certain universal problems which have been raised elsewhere, in the political field by the splitting-up of parties, the usurpation of power by parliaments, the irresponsibility of assemblies; in the economic field by the increasingly numerous and important functions discharged by trade-unions and trade associations with their disputes and ententes, affecting both capital and labour; in the ethical field by the need felt for order, discipline, obedience to the moral dictates of patriotism.

Fascism desires the State to be strong and organic, based on broad foundations of popular support. The Fascist State lays claim to rule in the economic field no less than in others; it makes its action felt throughout the length and breadth of the country by means of its corporative, social, and educational institutions, and all the political, economic, and spiritual forces of the nation, organized in their respective associations, circulate within the State. . . .

. . . Never before have the peoples thirsted for authority, discipline, order, as they do now. If each age has its doctrine, then innumerable symptoms indicate that the doctrine of our age is Fascist. That it is vital is shown by the fact that it has aroused a faith; that this faith has conquered souls is shown by the fact that Fascism can point to its fallen heroes and its martyrs.

Fascism has now acquired throughout the world that universality which belongs to all doctrines which by achieving self-expression represent a moment in the history of human thought.

Fascism: Doctrine and Institutions, Ardita, Rome, 1935, pp. 26, 27, 29, 31

19. *Josef Goebbels led the radical wing of Hitler's National Socialist Party in Germany, and shows here how virulent the rejection of the old order could be. This is part of an open letter to the ex-servicemen of the First World War.*

Dear Veterans,

. . .You have an enviable lack of knowledge of the course of international events since 1918. You have completely missed the development of true German nationalism into German socialism and the resultant radicalization of socialism today. I know that numerically you represent our greatest reservoir of support, but does that prove the correctness of your attitude? There are people in our camp, and there

24

are many worse, who since 1918 and therefore also since 1923 [the year of the unsuccessful Nazi putsch in Munich] have learned their lesson. Today they see not only the falsification of the socialist attitude in Marxism but also and just as clearly the falsification of nationalism in the so-called nationalist parties and organizations of every shade, and are prepared to draw the necessary conclusions from this realization. They attack the bourgeois idea just as sharply as the Marxist–proletarian one and no longer let themselves be waylaid by any apparent unanimity among the national opposition against any particular act. As far as they are concerned, the bourgeoisie in its political organizations has lost the right to criticize the results of the policies of this system just as much as Marxism has, because both must share the guilt for this system, because both have participated in this system and will go on participating in it whenever and wherever there is fodder to be had. Down with the madness of Marxism because it is false socialism! Down with the madness of the so-called nationalist opposition in the Right-wing parties because it is false nationalism! That is the key which makes socialism nationalist and nationalism socialist . . .

. . . What do you know of a national community? You see in one movement the suitable basis on which you can deposit your stale phrases which you can put nowhere else. We have been clear for a long time that the idea of a national community as an attained goal provides a platform on which both the bourgeois and the proletarian can work together towards the final goal—the strengthening of the nation both internally and externally. But this goal will only be reached by one of these two groups, which in the fight for the future will be led by renegades from the other group. If the bourgeoisie of our country lets us down, what else can we do but try and find in the so-called proletariat the fighting force which is necessary to free Germany from her capitalist fetters? . . .

. . . The bourgeois is nationalist as long as the nationalist idea guarantees him prosperity and peace and quiet . . .

. . . Do not think that our present silence means indulgence. We are working ruthlessly and unflinchingly. The day is not far off when we will say all. Then you will have to learn to understand that we are anything but a black-white-and-red riot squad [a reference to the flag of the old Empire] to protect bourgeois selfishness and philistine security.

Then you will be shocked by the radicalism of our demands, by the merciless logic of what must be and what we intend to do, because it must be. Today Germany knows that we allow no one to outdo us in our fanaticism for national freedom.

They will soon have to learn that we are just as committed to fighting in the front rank of socialism.

'The Radicalization of Socialism', in *Nationalsozialistische Briefe* No. 6, 15 December 1925 (translation by Mr and Mrs Jeremy Noakes)

20. *Each year the Soviet communist leadership forecast the imminent collapse of capitalism. In the summer of 1930 with America's economy in ruins Joseph Stalin's predictions could carry more than the usual conviction.*

. . . The crisis has already increased the pressure exerted by the capitalists on the working class. The crisis has already given rise to another wave of capitalist rationalization, to a further deterioration of the conditions of the working class, to increased unemployment, to an enlargement of the permanent army of unemployed, to a reduction of wages. It is not surprising that these circumstances are revolutionizing the situation, intensifying the class struggle and pushing the workers towards new class battles.

As a result of this, Social-Democratic illusions among the masses of workers are being shattered and dispelled. After the experience of Social-Democrats being in power, when they broke strikes, organized lockouts and shot down workers, the false doctrines of 'industrial democracy,' 'peace in industry,' and 'peaceful methods' of struggle sound like cruel mockery to the workers. Will many workers be found today capable of believing the false doctrines of the social-fascists? The well-known workers' demonstrations of August 1, 1929 (against the war danger) and of March 6, 1930 (against unemployment) show that the best members of the working class have already turned away from the social-fascists. The economic crisis will strike a fresh blow at Social-Democratic illusions among the workers. Not many workers will be found now, after the bankruptcies and ruination caused by the crisis, who believe that it is possible for 'every worker' to become rich by holding shares in 'democratized' joint-stock companies. Needless to say, the crisis will strike a crushing blow at all these and similar illusions.

The desertion of the masses of the workers from the Social-Democrats, however, signifies a turn on their part towards communism. That is what is actually taking place. The growth of the trade-union movement that is associated with the Communist Party, the electoral successes of the Communist Parties, the wave of strikes in which the Communists are taking a leading part, the development of economic strikes into political protests organized by the Communists, the mass demonstrations of workers who sympathize with communism, which are meeting a lively response in the working class–all this shows that the masses of the workers regard the Communist Party as the only party capable of fighting capitalism, the only party worthy of the workers' confidence, the only party under whose leadership it is possible to enter, and worth while entering, the struggle for emancipation from capitalism. This means that the masses are turning towards communism.

Works, Foreign Languages Publishing House, Moscow, 1955, vol. xii, April 1929–June 1930, pp. 259–61

Part One
THE NEW DEAL

I

The Depression

Depression hit the United States with catastrophic suddenness in October 1929. A glance at the statistics in Appendix I will help to give some idea of the extent of the damage to the American economy in the years immediately following, but this was infinitely more than just another downturn in the business cycle. Perhaps for the first time a majority of Americans began to call in question the values which their society had so far thrived on. It is not surprising that the Republican government of President Herbert Hoover should suffer from this widespread disillusion, but it compounded its unpopularity, not because it refused to act, but because what it did was both too little and too late. By the time of the presidential election campaign in the summer of 1932 the country was only beginning to climb out of the bottom of the slump and Hoover's fate was sealed.

A Society in Collapse

1. *Little more than a year before the crash Hoover could make this confident forecast in his acceptance speech as Republican candidate.*

We in America today are nearer to the financial triumph over poverty than ever before in the history of our land. The poor man is vanishing from among us. Under these impulses, and the Republican protective system, our industrial output has increased as never before, and our wages have grown steadily in buying power. Our workers with their average weekly wages, can today buy two or even three times more bread and butter than any wage earner in Europe. At one time we demanded for our workers a full dinner pail. We have now gone far beyond that conception. Today we demand a larger comfort and greater participation in life and leisure.

N. HALASZ, *Roosevelt Through Foreign Eyes*, Van Nostrand, New Jersey, 1961, p. 2

2. *The end came suddenly. J. K. Galbraith describes 'Black Thursday', 24 October 1929, on the New York Stock Exchange.*

The panic did not last all day. It was a phenomenon of the morning hours. The market opening itself was unspectacular, and for a while prices were firm. Volume, however, was very large, and soon prices began to sag. Once again the ticker dropped behind. Prices fell further and faster, and the ticker lagged more and more. By eleven o'clock the market had degenerated into a wild, mad scramble to sell. In the crowded boardrooms across the country the ticker told of a frightful collapse. But the selected quotations coming in over the bond ticker also showed that current values were far below the ancient history of the tape. The uncertainty led more and more people to sell. Others, no longer able to respond to margin calls, were sold out. By eleven thirty the market had surrendered to blind, relentless fear. This, indeed, was panic.

The Great Crash 1929, Penguin, Harmondsworth, 1963 edn, p. 121

3. *The American industrial machine ground almost to a standstill. Beulah Amidon, a journalist, described a car factory in Toledo, Ohio.*

When I was taken through some of the eighty-seven buildings that make up the plant I was reminded of the old desert towns left in the wake of a mining rush. There was the same sense of suspended life, as I moved among silent, untended machines or walked through departments where hundreds of half-finished automobile bodies gathered dust while they waited for the next cleaning or finishing process. The effect of a sudden paralysis was intensified by the infrequent groups of workers, almost lost in the vast, dim spaces, going about tasks that seemed very small and futile in the midst of the elaborate equipment for mass production, for an unending stream of assembled, tested, finished cars rolling out of the factory doors.

'Toledo: A City the Auto Ran Over', *Survey*, 1 March 1930, p. 672

4. *In the Tennessee valley the British biologist, Julian Huxley, witnessed a breakdown which had been building up over generations of reckless waste, a powerful symbol of America's plight.*

Much of the rural area of the valley was inhabited by peasant farmers, who, although originally of excellent British stock, had in their mountain isolation too often developed into poverty-stricken poor-whites. Primitive in their reproductive habits as in their farming methods, they multiplied rapidly until they presented a typical Malthusian population, pressing hard upon its means of subsistence. Under the influence of this pressure, the farmers began in many places to encroach upon the wooded mountainside. A steep slope would be burnt off and cleared of its timber, ploughed up, and planted with maize. The climate is moist, with spells of heavy rainfall: more than half of all the rain of over 50 inches a year that occurs in the U.S.A. falls in the Tennessee Valley. With the removal of the forest cover, and with the failure to apply fertilizers, the soil rapidly lost its fertility and large amounts of it were simply washed away. After a few brief years, the slope was no longer worth bothering about, and was abandoned in favour of a fresh cleared area nearby, so that in the heart of the most modern of countries you could find shifting cultivation of the type usually associated with primitive African tribes.

The resultant erosion was appalling. It was brought home to me when, surveying the turbid flow of the Tennessee River, I was told that there were men still living who remembered it as a clear blue stream. Up till that moment I had taken the pea-soup appearance of so many American rivers for a fact of nature; the realization that it was a recent man-made phenomenon was staggering. Here, under my eyes, was the basic productivity being stripped from a vast area and hurried along to sterile waste in the sea. I also saw outcrops of bare rock which three generations back had been covered with rich soil over a yard in depth. For those who like figures, it may be added that the amount of soil annually washed or blown out of the fields of the United States is conservatively estimated at 3,000 million tons.

TVA: Adventure in Planning, Architectural Press, London, 1943, pp. 9–10

5. *The psychological effects of the depression were perhaps the worst, as the sociologists Robert and Helen Lynd discovered in 'Middletown' (Muncie, Indiana).*

The city had been shaken for nearly six years by a catastrophe involving not only people's values but, in the case of many, their very existence. Unlike most socially generated catastrophes, in this case virtually no-body in the community had been cushioned against the blow; the great knife of the depression had cut down impartially through the entire population, cleaving open the lives and hopes of rich as well as poor. The experience had been more nearly universal than any prolonged recent emotional experience in the city's history; it had approached in its elemental shock the primary experiences of birth and death.

Middletown in Transition. A Study in Cultural Conflicts, Constable, London, 1937, pp. 295–6

6. *A report of an unemployment commission for California, published in November 1932, elaborated on this theme.*

This study of the human cost of unemployment reveals that a new class of poor and dependents is rapidly rising among the ranks of young, sturdy, ambitious labourers, artisans, mechanics, and professionals, who until recently maintained a relatively high standard of living and were the stable, self-respecting citizens and taxpayers of this State. Unemployment and loss of income have ravaged numerous homes. It has broken the spirits of their members, undermined their health, robbed them of self-respect, destroyed their efficiency and employability. Loss of income has created standards of living of which the country cannot be proud. Many households have been dissolved; little children parcelled out to friends, relatives, or charitable homes; husbands and wives, parents and children separated, temporarily or permanently. Homes in which life savings were invested and hopes bound up have been lost never to be recovered. Men, young and old, have taken to the road. They sleep each night in a new flophouse. Day after day the country over, they stand in the breadlines for food which carries with it the suggestion 'move-on,' 'We don't want you.' In spite of the unpalatable stew and the comfortless flophouses, the army of homeless grows alarmingly. Existing accommodations fail to shelter the homeless; jails must be opened to lodge honest job-hunters. Destitution reaches the women and children. New itinerant types develop: 'women vagrants' and 'juvenile transients'. There are no satisfactory methods of dealing with these thousands adrift. Precarious ways of existing, questionable methods of 'getting by' rapidly develop. The law must step in and brand as criminals those who have neither desire nor inclination to violate accepted standards of society.

Numerous houses remain physically intact, but morally shattered.

There is no security, no foothold, no future to sustain them. Savings are depleted, and debts mount with no prospect of repayment. Economic make-shifts are adopted. Woman and child labor further undermine the stability of the home. The number of applicants for charitable aid increases seriously. There is not enough money to do the job well and adequately. Food rations are pared down, rents go unpaid, families are evicted. They must uproot their households frequently. Physical privations undermine body and heart. The peace and harmony of the home vanish. The effect upon children differs, but it is invariably detrimental.

Idleness destroys not only purchasing power, lowering the standards of living, but also destroys efficiency and finally breaks the spirit. The once industrious and resourceful worker becomes pauperized, loses faith in himself and society.

Report and Recommendations of the California State Unemployment Commission, State Printing Office, Sacramento, 1932, pp. 145–6

7. *At the end of the depression decade F. L. Allen recalled some of the manifestations.*

The major phenomena of the Depression were mostly negative and did not assail the eye.

But if you knew where to look, some of them would begin to appear. First, the bread lines in the poorer districts. Second, those bleak settlements ironically known as 'Hoovervilles' in the outskirts of the cities and on vacant lots–groups of makeshift shacks constructed out of packing-boxes, scrap iron, anything that could be picked up free in a diligent combing of the city dumps: shacks in which men and sometimes whole families of evicted people were sleeping on automobile seats carried from auto-graveyards, warming themselves before fires of rubbish in grease drums. Third, the homeless people sleeping in doorways or on park benches, and going the rounds of the restaurants for left-over half-eaten biscuits, pie-crusts, anything to keep the fires of life burning. Fourth, the vastly increased numbers of thumbers on the highways, and particularly of freight-car transients on the railroads: a huge army of drifters ever on the move, searching half-aimlessly for a place where there might be a job.

Since Yesterday, Hamish Hamilton, London, 1940, p. 51

8. *One of the transients testified before a Senate committee.*

They do not like you to stay there, especially in New Orleans and a few places where they arrive a couple of hundred a day. The Salvation Army places will feed you for a night, or rather let you sleep there. In the morning they will give you a bowl of beef broth or something. In the other places they give you coffee, soup, and bread. But the soup, as one fellow put it, is just some hot water with a little cabbage dipped in it. . . . Most of the fellows, young fellows that start out, will not pan handle. They have a pride and are sort of scared to go up to a person. But you soon lose that, and there is just a feeling when you are tired and hungry you do not care much what happens to you.

United States. Senate. Committee on Manufactures, *Relief for Unemployed Tenants. Hearings on S.5121*, United States Government Printing Office, Washington, D.C., 1933, pp. 111–12

9. *None of the existing agencies of American society could cope with the burdens of relief.*

The theory was that private charitable organizations and semi-public welfare groups, established to care for the old and the sick and the indigent, were capable of caring for the casuals of a world-wide economic disaster. And the theory in application meant that social agencies manned for the service of a few hundred families, and city shelters set up to house and feed a handful of homeless men, were compelled by the brutal necessities of hunger to care for hundreds of thousands of families and whole armies of the displaced and the jobless. And to depend for their resources upon the contributions of communities no longer able to contribute, and upon the irresolution and vacillation of state Legislatures and municipal assemblies long since in the red on their annual budgets. The result was the picture now presented in city after city . . . heterogeneous groups of official and unofficial relief agencies struggling under the earnest and untrained leadership of the local men of affairs against an inertia of misery and suffering and want they are powerless to overcome.

'No One Has Starved', *Fortune*, September 1932

10. *Violence was not far below the surface, as Irving Bernstein recounts.*

Eleven hundred men standing in a Salvation Army bread line on March 19, 1930, near the Bowery Hotel in Manhattan descended upon two trucks delivering baked goods to the hotel. Jelly rolls, cookies, rolls, and bread were flung into the street, with the hungry jobless chasing after them. Joseph Drusin of Indiana Township, Pennsylvania, in November 1930 stole a loaf of bread from a neighbour for his four starving children. When caught, Drusin went to the cellar and hung himself. Three hundred unemployed men in July 1931 marched on the storekeepers of Henryetta, Oklahoma, to demand food. They insisted that they were not begging; they threatened force if necessary. Violence was avoided only by the unusual tact of several leading citizens. By 1932 organized looting of food was a nation-wide phenomenon. Helen Hall, a Philadelphia social worker, told a Senate committee that many families sent their children out to steal from wholesale markets, to snatch milk for babies, to lift articles from pushcarts to exchange for food.

The Lean Years, Houghton Mifflin, Boston, 1960, p. 422

11. *Even the farmers were roused as they had not been since the days of Populism. In the summer of 1932 militants organized the 'farm strike'.*

In August, 1932, when the strike officially began, farm prices were reported as follows: eggs, 22 cents; oats, 11 cents; butter, 18 cents–all of which were far below the cost-of-production levels named by the Farmers' Union. The farmer's cost of production, according to the Iowa group, had to take into account several items: 5 per cent on his real estate investment, 7 per cent on his personal property and equipment, and $100 per month for the farmer's own labor and management. The average farmer operating a 160-acre farm, in order to obtain these returns, had to receive 92 cents per bushel on corn, 49 cents per bushel on oats, $11.25 per hundred on hogs, 35 cents for eggs, and 62 cents for butterfat.

The earliest attempt to launch the strike was made in the Sioux City area where trouble resulted immediately. Roads were blockaded, fist fights broke out, arrests were made, and gun toting, exhortation, vituperation, picketing, storming of jails and capitol buildings, and stopping of trains and automobiles were among the other events that took place. In some places the old Populist cry of 'Raise less corn and more hell' was heard; in others, Hoover was likened to Louis XIV, and the actions of the strikers were compared to those of the Boston Tea Party and William L. Garrison. A patriotic tone was given when the

Khaki Shirts of America, former members of the Bonus Expeditionary Force that had marched on Washington, took the lead in blockading the Des Moines highways.

T. SALOUTOS AND J. HICKS, *Agricultural Discontent in the Middle West 1900–1939*, Wisconsin U.P., Madison, 1951, pp. 443–4

Agonizing Reappraisals

12. *For some, like the President of the National Association of Manufacturers, Mr John E. Edgerton, the crisis could be shrugged off, in public at least.*

Certainly, nothing has happened to weaken the confidence of understanding minds in the essential parts of our American economic system and in its adaptability to the highest needs of progress, nor in our scheme of government. On the contrary, while the depression has brought into clearer view some egregious abuses of both our economic and political mechanisms, *it has at the same time demonstrated their sufficiency of strength, for as severe a test as yet has been known.* There are, therefore, manifestly sound reasons for not only a continuing but even a greater faith in them as the best vehicles of progress yet devised.

Proceedings of the National Association of Manufacturers, 1930, p. 12 (italics in text)

13. *Others were not so sure. Even a trade union leader as conservative as William Green had qualms.*

Some of us have been wondering whether the present industrial order is to be a success or a failure. No social order is secure where wealth flows at such a rate into the hands of the few away from the many. . . . We will be in favor of having the United States Government take it away through taxation and distribute it to the masses. . . . The right to work is a sacred right that every government, no matter what it's for, must guarantee if it is to endure. What shall we say of a system that relegates men at the prime of life to the human scrap heap and that knows no remedy for the situation other than a reduction in the standard of living? I warn the people who are exploiting the workers that they can only drive them so far before they will turn on them and destroy them! They are taking no account of the history of nations in which governments have been overturned. Revolutions grow out of the depths of hunger.

Time, 19 October 1931, pp. 10–11

14. *Walter Lippmann was one of those who saw the extreme gravity of the situation, in a piece written in September 1931.*

It is now two years since hard times reached this country, and it is no longer open to serious question that we are in the midst, not of an ordinary trade depression, but of one of the great upheavals and re-adjustments of modern history. A dozen governments have been brought down by it. In all the five continents it has upset the normal expectations of men by which they had been planting and making, buying and selling, borrowing and lending. In all the vast confusion which has resulted one thing at least is certain – the world, when the readjustments are made, cannot and will not be organised as it was two years ago. The post-war era of the Nineteen-Twenties is over and done.

Interpretations 1931–1932, Macmillan, New York, 1932, p. 5

15. *Sir Arthur Salter, a British commentator, agreed.*

We have lost many of the benefits of the old economic system without securing the advantages of planned direction. We cannot return to the unregulated competition of the last century; an unwillingness to accept some of its social consequences and the development of modern industrial technique together make that impossible. But we need not therefore aim at a regulated world from which both individual competition and freedom of enterprise are excluded. To take either course is to fail in the specific task of this age. That task is not to find a middle way, but a new way, to fashion a system in which competition and individual enterprise on the one hand, and regulation and general planning on the other, will be so adjusted that the abuses of each will be avoided and the benefits of each retained. We need to construct such a framework of law, custom, institutions and planned guidance and direction, that the thrust of individual effort can only operate to the general advantage.

Recovery: The Second Effort, Bell, London, 1932, p. 21

16. *Marriner Eccles, a banker from Utah who was later to play an important role in the New Deal, pinned his faith on government action in a speech made in June 1932.*

There is only one agency in my opinion that can turn the cycle upward and that is the government. The government, if it is worthy of the support, the loyalty, and the patriotism of its citizens, must so regulate, through its power over the control of money and credit, and hence its volume and use, the economic structure as to give men who are able, worthy and willing to work, the opportunity to work, and to guarantee to them sustenance for their families and protection against want and destitution. If this is not done, the country cannot expect to get the support and loyalty that makes for a good, sound, safe government.

Beckoning Frontiers, Knopf, New York, 1951, pp. 83–4

17. *The chairman of the American Communist Party, William Z. Foster, had other ideas, expressed in his testimony to a House committee on communist activities late in 1930.*

Only an armed struggle succeeded in eliminating the institution of chattel slavery. The same law of history will operate in the transition from capitalism to socialism. The bloody path that capitalism is traveling today over the lives of the workers is conclusive proof that when the workers, who are the majority, will become convinced by their experience of the necessity of changing the capitalist order based upon private property and the enrichment of the few, into a society based upon the common ownership of the means of production and the well-being of the masses, then the capitalists will use their last gun and their last dollar in defense of the only constitutional principle they ever held sacred – that is, the unrestricted right to make profit out of the misery of the masses. . . . The Communist Party is preparing the working class for that day. . . . The Communist Party prepares the working class to carry out in the proletarian revolution that principle announced by the colonial revolutionists in the Declaration of Independence: 'it is the right, it is the duty', of the working masses to throw off such government and to provide new guards for their future security. The only possible guard for the future security of the working class is the dictatorship of the proletariat and the establishment of a Soviet government.

The Republican Reaction

18. *President Hoover did not believe in complete laissez-faire.*

Two schools of thought quickly developed within our administration discussions.

First was the 'leave it alone liquidationists' headed by Secretary of the Treasury Mellon, who felt that government must keep its hands off and let the slump liquidate itself. Mr Mellon had only one formula: 'Liquidate labor, liquidate stocks, liquidate the farmers, liquidate real estate.' He insisted that, when the people get an inflation brainstorm, the only way to get it out of their blood is to let it collapse. He held that even a panic was not altogether a bad thing. He said: 'It will purge the rottenness out of their system. High costs of living and high living will come down. People will work harder, live a more moral life. Values will be adjusted, and enterprising people will pick up the wrecks from less competent people.' . . .

. . . But other members of the Administration, also having economic responsibilities – Under Secretary of the Treasury Mills, Governor Young of the Reserve Board, Secretary of Commerce Lamont and Secretary of Agriculture Hyde – believed with me that we should use the powers of the government to cushion the situation. To our minds, the prime needs were to prevent bank panics such as had marked the earlier slumps, to mitigate the privation among the unemployed and the farmers which would certainly ensue. Panic had always left a trail of unnecessary bankruptcies which injured the productive forces of the country. But, even more important, the damage from a panic would include huge losses by innocent people, in their honestly invested savings, their homes and their farms.

The record will show that we went into action within ten days and were steadily organizing each week and month thereafter to meet the changing tides – mostly for the worse.

The Memoirs of Herbert Hoover. The Great Depression 1929–1941, Hollis and Carter, London, 1953, pp. 30–1

19. *He was certainly enough of a progressive to believe in the regulation of business excesses, as he stated in a letter written in February 1933.*

Democracy cannot survive unless it is master in its own house. The economic system cannot survive unless there are real restraints upon unbridled greed or dishonest reach for power. Greed and dishonesty are not attributes solely of our system – they are human and will infect socialism or any ism. But if our production and distribution systems are to function we must have effective restraints on manipulation, greed, and dishonesty. Our Democracy has proved its ability to put its unruly occupants under control, but never until their conduct has been a public scandal and a stench. For instance, you will recollect my own opposition to government operation of electric power, for that is a violation of the very fundamentals of our system; but parallel with it I asked and preached for regulation of it to protect the public from its financial manipulation.

Ibid., p. 27

20. *On the question of relief he was prepared to use the powers of the government in the last resort; this statement was made in February 1931.*

This is not an issue as to whether people shall go hungry or cold in the United States. It is solely a question of the best methods by which cold and hunger shall be prevented. It is a question as to whether the American people, on one hand, will maintain the spirit of charity and mutual self-help through voluntary giving and the responsibility of local government as distinguished, on the other hand, from appropriations out of the Federal Treasury.

. . . The basis of successful relief in national distress is to mobilize and organize the infinite number of agencies of self-help in the community. That has been the American way of relieving distress among our own people, and the country is successfully meeting its problem in the American way today. . . .

. . . *I am willing to pledge myself* that if the time should ever come that the voluntary agencies of the country together with the local and state governments are unable to find resources with which to prevent hunger and suffering in my country, *I will ask the aid of every resource of the Federal Government because I would no more see starvation amongst our countrymen than would any Senator or Congressman.*

Ibid., pp. 55–6

21. *But he was extremely reluctant to spend Federal money. In a speech in January 1932 he castigated the proposals advanced in Congress.*

The flood of extravagant proposals . . . would imply an increase of government expenditure during the next five years of over forty billions of dollars or more than eight billions per annum. The great majority of these bills have been advanced by some organization or some sectional interest. . . . They . . . represent a spirit of spending in the country which must be abandoned . . . drastic economy requires sacrifice. . . .

Rigid economy is a real road to relief to home owners, farmers, workers, and every element of our population. . . .

Our first duty as a nation is to put our governmental house in order, national, state and local. With the return of prosperity the government can undertake constructive projects both of social character and in public improvement. We cannot squander ourselves into prosperity.

Ibid., pp. 133–4

22. *In short, in spite of his undoubted good intentions, Hoover was unwilling to take the action the critical situation required. His real thinking is perhaps best revealed in this speech of August 1932.*

The function of the Federal government in these times is to use its reserve powers and its strength for the protection of citizens and local governments by supporting our institutions against forces beyond their control. It is not the function of the government to relieve individuals of their responsibilities to their neighbours, or to relieve private institutions of their responsibilities to the public, or of local government to the states, or of state governments to the Federal government. In giving that protection and that aid the Federal government must insist that all of them meet their responsibilities in full. It is vital that the programs of the government shall not compete with or replace any of them but shall add to their initiative and their strength. It is vital that by the use of public revenues and public credit in emergency the Nation shall be strengthened and not weakened.

. . . It does not follow, because our difficulties are stupendous, because there are some souls timorous enough to doubt the validity and effectiveness of our ideals and our system, that we must turn to a state-controlled or state-directed society or economic system in order to cure our troubles. That is not liberalism; it is tyranny. It is the regimentation of men under autocratic bureaucracy with all its extinction of liberty, of hope, and of opportunity. No man of understanding says that our economic system works perfectly. It does not. The human race is not perfect. Nevertheless, the movement of a true civilization is toward freedom rather than regimentation. This is our ideal.

. . . the Federal government should in the presence of great national danger use its powers to give leadership to the initiative, the courage, and the fortitude of the people themselves; but it must insist upon individual, community, and state responsibility . . . to supplement and strengthen the initiative and enterprise of the people. That they must, directly or indirectly, serve all the people. Above all, that they should be set up in such a form that, once the emergency is passed, they can and must be demobilized and withdrawn, leaving our governmental, economic, and social structure strong and wholesome.

Ibid., pp. 36–7

The Verdict on Hoover

23. *Judgments on Hoover reflect the ambiguity of his policies. Walter Lippmann noticed the positive side as early as 1934.*

. . . Mr Hoover tried to do virtually everything that Mr Roosevelt did in his first year. He moved more cautiously; he applied smaller doses of the medicine; he timed the doses differently, and he worked against constantly mounting political opposition. He was less lucky and he was less effective. But on the point which concerns us here, which is that laissez-faire is dead and that the modern state has become responsible for the modern economy as a whole, Mr Hoover is the best of all witnesses. For he acted on a doctrine which he professed to reject. There could be no better evidence of the degree to which the new doctrine is established.

The Method of Freedom, Macmillan, New York, 1934, p. 33

24. *Broadus Mitchell drew the same conclusion.*

. . . Hoover's still waters ran deeper than he has been given credit for. Relative to the period and the party, Hoover was experimental and adaptable. The moratorium on intergovernmental debts was a courageous stroke. The Federal Farm Board plainly pointed to the more effectual curbing of agricultural surpluses. Federal relief to the states was small in amount but big in what it portended. The Reconstruction Finance Corporation was taken over bodily by the New Deal, expanded in function during the remaining depression years, and grew into even greater vigor in the war economy.

Depression Decade, Rinehart, New York, 1947, p. 405

25. *The historian Richard Hofstadter, on the other hand, takes a less charitable view.*

Speaking to his party in 1940, Hoover explained his 1938 trip to Europe by saying that he had gone abroad to find out what causes dictatorships. There were many complex factors involved, he admitted, but he had no difficulty in spotting the main source; it was *economic planning.* 'In every single case before the rise of the totalitarian governments there had been a period dominated by the economic planners.'

Here in all its rigidity was revealed Hoover's religious faith in the planless world of the free market. For a generation managed economics had been developing in all the industrialized nations of the world. Hoover himself said two years earlier that managed economies would 'long continue over a large part of the earth'. Could he have seriously believed that free enterprise might be restored to the postwar world? In all history no more heroic setting-back of the clock had ever been proposed. Since economic planning had become such a universal phenomenon, it might have been natural to ask: 'If planning caused dictatorships, what caused planning? Was it, perhaps, the universal decline of the planless economy under the stewardship of the Hoovers?' That the New Deal might presage an American fascism, as Hoover insisted, was at least a possibility – one that conventional liberals generally refused to admit; but that Hooverism had brought a reaction toward the New Deal was a historical certainty. That there was anything natural, not to say inevitable, about this trend toward managed economies, was a conclusion Hoover could never acknowledge without abandoning the premise upon which his public life had been built – that unmitigated capitalism was an economic system without a major flaw. No, it must be a series of unwise choices based on novel and fallacious thinking; things could easily have happened otherwise; *it was simply a strange coincidence, a curious universal mistake.* Perhaps, then, if we should gird

45

ourselves for a new try, perhaps if we were Spartan enough and wise enough, if we could think a little straighter and work a little harder, we might leap out of the fading world of the twentieth century and land in the one that flourished so brightly in Hoover's mind.

The American Political Tradition (1948), Vintage Books, New York, 1957 edn, pp. 312–13

II
The 1932 Campaign

One of the most extraordinary things about this period is that the mood of despair did not work wonders for the radical political parties in America, above all the Socialists and the Communists. At the presidential election in 1932, however, both failed miserably. The American voter continued to show a remarkable faith in the traditional two-party system of Republican and Democrat, and the 1932 election campaign was fought very much after the usual pattern. The Republican candidate was again Hoover and the Democratic nominee Franklin Delano Roosevelt, Governor of New York since 1929. Yet although as Roosevelt's biographer, Freidel, reminds us, 'the purpose of campaigns is not to blueprint the future but to win elections', this was in a real sense an ideological contest. In November 1932, the United States was asked to choose between a man who had demonstrated his reluctance to govern outside the strict terms of reference set by laissez-faire, and another who appeared willing at least to try. The answer was a decisive victory for the challenger.

The National Mood

1. *To extreme conservatives like General Douglas MacArthur, the country was on the verge of revolution. Here are his comments on the 'Bonus Army' of ex-servicemen which he expelled from Washington in July 1932.*

... That mob ... was a bad looking mob. It was animated by the essence of revolution. The gentleness, the consideration, with which they had been treated had been mistaken for weakness and they had come to the conclusion, beyond the shadow of a doubt, that they were about to take over in some arbitrary way either the direct control of the Government or else to control it by indirect methods. It is my opinion that had the President not acted today, had he permitted this thing to go on for 24 hours more, he would have been faced with a grave situation which would have caused a real battle. Had he let it go on another week I believe that the institutions of our Government would have been very severely threatened.

H. HOOVER, *The Memoirs of Herbert Hoover. The Great Depression 1929-1941*, Hollis and Carter, London, 1953, p. 228

2. *To T. R. Henry, a journalist on the* Washington Star, *however, the position looked somewhat different. What struck him most forcibly about the Bonus marchers was their helplessness.*

. . . nearly all have one thing in common – a curious melancholy, a sense of the futility of individual struggle, a consciousness of being in the grip of cruel, incomprehensible forces . . . .

They are in a struggle which is too severe for them. They have come to the point where they recognize the futility of fighting adverse fate any longer. They are fixating on a symbol – the symbol of the security and plenty of happier days. This symbol happens to be Uncle Sam and the war period with its military relief from responsibility. It is becoming analogous to the infancy period of the psychotic. This bonus march might well be described as a flight from reality – a flight from hunger, from the cries of the starving children, from the humiliation of accepting money from worn, querulous women, from the harsh rebuffs of prospective employers. It is very like the peace of infancy here in the warm June sunshine of the Anacostia field.

Perhaps this may explain the orderliness – the way in which these very diverse elements of the American population have fallen into a semi-military organization, without leaders in authority. Orderliness is a part of the symbol of security to whose protection they have fled from the mysterious, heartless forces that are crushing them in the outside world.

Washington Star, 6 June 1932

3. *The experience of the American Socialist Party in the election seemed to bear out Henry's view.*

Although the party had grown encouragingly during the campaign, although many of the people who mold public opinion in the United States had stated approval of the party's candidates, although there were many indications of further growth, still for the Socialists there was the unpleasant and inescapable truth that the reaction of the American people to the depression had not been revolt against capitalism. Again, for the *n*th time in American history, radicals and reactionaries were mistaken in their predictions as to how the American common people would react to adversity. The Socialists in 1931 hopefully thought that they saw 'seething discontent that may burst into blind fury next winter. . . . Evidences of growing radical sentiment in labor union weeklies indicate that more and more organized workers will turn to political action.' Conservatives fearfully made the same sort of prediction. The officers of the 33rd Division, Illinois National Guard, studied 'Plans for the suppression of radical disorders' that included such police tips as 'Never fire over the heads of rioters' and 'The picking off of a few rioters [in the rear of a mob] will generally cause others to flee.' But, compared to what was expected, relatively little 'blind fury' was manifested, and there were, fortunately, few opportunities for national guardsmen to exercise the brutality of their technical manuals.

D. SHANNON, *The Socialist Party of America*, Macmillan, New York, 1955, pp. 225–6

4. The same held good for the Communists.

Despite momentary successes . . . the Communist program among the unemployed was a failure. Its principal achievement was to raise relief standards in some communities and to hasten the coming of federal relief. This could hardly have been a major objective, if it did not actually defeat the party's purpose.

The real aim – the organization of the jobless for revolution – did not come to pass. In fact, the unemployed had much shorter-term goals: relief and jobs. Their obsession with survival made them bad material for revolution. . . .

The writers who toured the nation in search of revolution confirmed this conclusion. Louis Adamic and Benjamin Stolberg agreed that the American proletariat was physically and spiritually exhausted. 'I have a definite feeling,' Adamic wrote on December 15, 1931, 'that millions of them, now that they are unemployed, are licked.' One reason, he felt, was that the foreign-born feared to expose themselves. Theodore Dreiser, himself an outspoken Communist, admitted in 1932 that 'the workers do not regard Communism as their cause'. Sherwood Anderson was amazed by the absence of bitterness. He discerned a 'breaking down of the moral fiber of the American man.' Anderson picked up hitchhikers on the highway who apologized for being down and out. They accepted the whole responsibility themselves. The only exception he could find was the coalminers. 'There is something distinct and real separating them now from the defeated factory hands of the cities. They are not defeated men.'

Melancholia and defeat had overwhelmed not only the jobless but also those who sought to infuse spirit into them. Workers on the way down were in no mood to improve, far less to reorganize, society. At this time the spirit of revolt was far more evident in agriculture than in labor. American farmers–'the last bastion of individualism'–readily organized to express their grievances by violent means. By contrast, the self-help organizations of the urban jobless were pathetically inadequate and transitory. The Socialists had got nowhere. The Communists, despite the expenditure of considerable energies, had little to show for their efforts beyond yellowing newspaper headlines.

IRVING BERNSTEIN, *The Lean Years*, Houghton Mifflin, Boston, 1960, pp. 434–6

Roosevelt the New

5. *So it was that the United States came to accept Roosevelt and the Demo-crats as the only alternative to Hoover's prescriptions. In some of his speeches during the year Roosevelt threw a novel emphasis on national planning in words quite unlike anything the Republicans had used. Here is part of one such speech made on 18 April.*

...I am not speaking of an economic life completely planned and regimented. I am speaking of the necessity, however, in those imperative interferences with the economic life of the Nation that there be a real community of interest, not only among the sections of this great community, but among its economic units and the various groups in these units; that there be common participation in the work of remedial figures, planned on the basis of a shared common life, the low as well as the high. In much of our present plans there is too much disposition to mistake the part for the whole, the head for the body, the captain for the company, the general for the army. I plead not for a class control but for a true concert of interests.

The plans we may make for this emergency, if we plan wisely and rest our structure upon a base sufficiently broad, may show the way to a more permanent safeguarding of our social and economic life to the end that we may in a large number avoid the terrible cycle of prosperity crumbling into depression. In this sense I favor economic planning, not for this period alone but for our needs for a long time to come.

The Public Papers and Addresses of Franklin D. Roosevelt, ed. S. Rosenman, Random House, New York, 1938, vol. i, p. 632

6. *He elaborated on this theme in a further speech at Oglethorpe University on 22 May.*

. . . we cannot review carefully the history of our industrial advance without being struck with its haphazardness, the gigantic waste with which it has been accomplished, the superfluous duplication of productive facilities, the continued scrapping of still useful equipment, the tremendous mortality in industrial and commercial undertakings, the thousands of dead-end trails into which enterprise has been lured, the profligate waste of natural resources. Much of this waste is the inevitable by-product of progress in a society which values individual endeavor and which is susceptible to the changing tastes and customs of the people of which it is composed. But much of it, I believe, could have been prevented by greater foresight and by a larger measure of social planning. Such controlling and directing forces as have been developed in recent years reside to a dangerous degree in groups having special interests in our economic order, interests which do not coincide with the interests of the Nation as a whole. I believe that the recent course of our history has demonstrated that, while we may utilize their expert knowledge of certain problems and the special facilities with which they are familiar, we cannot allow our economic life to be controlled by that small group of men whose chief outlook upon the social welfare is tinctured by the fact that they can make huge profits from the lending of money and the marketing of securities – an outlook which deserves the adjectives 'selfish' and 'opportunist' . . .

. . . [what] seems most important to me in the long run is the problem of controlling by adequate planning the creation and distribution of those products which our vast economic machine is capable of yielding . . .

. . . Too many of the so-called leaders of the Nation fail to see the forest because of the trees. Too many of them fail to recognize the vital necessity of planning for definite objectives. True leadership calls for the setting forth of these objectives and the rallying of public opinion in support of these objectives . . .

. . . The country needs and, unless I mistake its temper, the country demands bold, persistent experimentation. It is common sense to take a method and try it: If it fails, admit it frankly and try another. But above all, try something. The millions who are in want will not stand by silently for long while the things to satisfy their needs are in easy reach.

Ibid., vol. i, pp. 642, 644, 646

Roosevelt the Old

7. There was another Roosevelt, however. Like Hoover, Roosevelt carried much of the intellectual furniture of past generations around with him, and he had to take care not to advance too far ahead of voting opinion. Lippmann describes the Democratic platform on which he fought.

. . . The basic philosophy of the platform was supplied by a group of elder statesmen who have survived from the Wilson administration. The main themes of the platform are those of the Cleveland and Wilson Democracy; they represent a revival of what can with fair accuracy be described as old-fashioned American liberalism. There are exceptions here and there, but in its central inspiration the platform conforms more closely to the kind of individualism which Woodrow Wilson called the 'New Freedom' than it does to the kind of collectivism which progressives like Senator La Follette believe in, and, in certain of his moods, Governor Roosevelt himself.

Thus the platform starts with a declaration for drastic economy and for a balanced budget to maintain the nation credit and a sound currency. It does not contemplate a currency inflation in the spirit of Bryanism or an expansion of governmental activity to create a new social order, as progressives with a collectivist philosophy advocate. The general attitude is favourable to retrenchment and laissez-faire, to competition among small producers rather than to planned and centralized establishments. The intention is to repeal government favors rather than to increase positive government activity. The power of the government is involved to protect the small depositors, the small tradesmen, so that they may work out their own salvation. A Communist would say that the ideal of the platform is not conservative, but in the exact sense of the word reactionary; that what the platform looks to is a return to the simpler, freer capitalism of a generation ago.

It is a truly Jeffersonian platform, not merely as to liquor but in its economic philosophy. It is a platform which Gladstone and the Victorian liberals in England would have understood: its ideals are the peace, retrenchment and reform of the pre-war world, of that simpler world for which, though it may be irrevocably gone, most Americans instinctively yearn. Therefore, the platform should prove to be very popular with the voters and rather difficult to live up to.

Interpretations 1931–1932, Macmillan, New York, 1932, p. 309

8. *Like Hoover, Roosevelt believed in balancing the national budget.*

People suggest that a huge expenditure of public funds by the Federal Government and by State and local government will completely solve the unemployment problem. But it is clear that even if we could raise many billions of dollars and find definitely useful public works to spend these billions on, even all that money would not give employment to the seven million or ten million people who are out of work. Let us admit frankly that it would be only a stop-gap. A real economic cure must go to the killing of the bacteria in the system rather than to the treatment of external symptoms.

The Public Papers and Addresses of Franklin D. Roosevelt, ed. S. Rosenman, Random House, New York, 1938, vol. i, p. 625

9. *And he appeared to reject the very agricultural planning his own administration was to attempt in 1933.*

When the futility of maintaining prices of wheat and cotton, through so-called stabilization, became apparent, the President's Farm Board . . . invented the cruel joke of advising farmers to allow twenty per cent of their wheat lands to lie idle, to plow up every third row of cotton and to shoot every tenth dairy cow. Surely they knew that this advice would not–indeed, could not–be taken.

Ibid., vol. i, p. 709

The Clash of Ideologies

10. *Yet there was, in spite of the similarities, a deep difference of belief between the two candidates, and it was best summed up in two speeches made towards the end of the campaign. Here is Roosevelt talking at the Commonwealth Club, San Francisco. Two assumptions are dominant, namely, that the country can at best hope only to recover the position lost in 1929, and also, that within these reduced perspectives the government must have ultimate powers of direction. How right Roosevelt was to make the second, how wrong to make the first. Conversely, how justified Hoover was in continuing to believe in expansion, how misguided in thinking that government still had only a marginal rôle to play in bringing it about. It was the tragedy of the thirties for America that the unions of restrictionism and intervention, on the one hand, and of expansionism and laissez-faire, on the other, should have to be considered indissoluble. Not until the very end of the decade did the true partners begin to discover each other.*

... A glance at the situation today clearly indicates that equality of opportunity as we have known it no longer exists. Our industrial plant is built; the problem just now is whether under existing conditions it is not overbuilt. Our last frontier has long since been reached, and there is practically no more free land. More than half of our people do not live on the farms and on lands and cannot derive a living by cultivating their own property. There is no safety valve in the form of a Western Prairie to which those thrown out of work by the Eastern economic machines can go for a new start. We are not able to invite the immigration from Europe to share our endless plenty. We are now providing a drab living for our own people ...

... Just as freedom to farm has ceased, so also the opportunity in business has narrowed ... The unfeeling statistics of the past three decades show that the independent business man is running a losing race ... Recently a careful study was made of the concentration of business in the United States. It showed that our economic life was dominated by some six hundred odd corporations who controlled two-thirds of American industry. Ten million small business men divided the other third . . . Put plainly, we are steering a steady course toward economic oligarchy, if we are not there already.

Clearly all this calls for a re-appraisal of values . . . The day of the great promoter or the financial Titan, to whom we granted anything if only he would build, or develop, is over. Our task now is not discovery or exploitation of natural resources, or necessarily producing more goods. It is the soberer, less dramatic business of administering resources and plants already in hand, of seeking to reestablish foreign markets for our surplus production, of meeting the problem of under-consumption, of adjusting production to consumption, of distributing wealth and products more equitably, of adapting existing economic organizations to the service of the people. The day of enlightened administration has come . . .

. . . As I see it, the task of Government in its relation to business is to assist the development of an economic declaration of rights, an economic constitutional order. This is the common task of statesman and business man. It is the minimum requirement of a more permanently safe order of things . . .

. . . I feel that we are coming to a view through the drift of our legislation and our public thinking in the past quarter century that private economic power is, to enlarge an old phrase, a public trust as well. I hold that continued enjoyment of that power by any individual or group must depend on the fulfilement of that trust . . .

. . . Every man has a right to life; and this means that he has also a right to make a comfortable living . . . Our Government . . . owes to everyone an avenue to possess himself of a portion of that plenty sufficient for his needs, through his own work.

Every man has a right to his own property; which means a right to be assured, to the fullest extent attainable, in the safety of his savings. By no other means can men carry the burdens of those parts of life which in the nature of things, afford no chance of labor; childhood, sickness, old age. In all thought of prosperity, this right is paramount; all other property rights must yield to it. If, in accord with this principle, we must restrict the operations of the speculator, the manipulator, even the financier, I believe we must accept the restriction as needful, not to hamper individualism but to protect it.

These two requirements must be satisfied, in the main, by the individuals who claim and hold control of the great industrial and financial combinations which dominate so large a part of our industrial life. They have undertaken to be, not business men but princes of property. I am not prepared to say that the system which produces them is wrong. I am very clear that they must fearlessly and competently assume the responsibility which goes with the power . . .

. . . The Government should assume the function of economic regulation only as a last resort, to be tried only when private initiative, inspired by high responsibility, with such assistance and balance as Government can give, has finally failed . . .

. . . We know that the old 'rights of personal competency', the right to read, to think, to speak, to choose and live a mode of life, must be respected at all hazards. We know that liberty to do anything which deprives others of those elemental rights is outside the protection of any compact; and that Government in this regard is the maintenance of a balance, within which every individual may attain such power as his ability permits, consistent with his assuming the accompanying responsibilities.

Ibid., vol. i, pp. 750–5

11. *Hoover's riposte, made in New York, clung passionately to the faith which Roosevelt seemed to be abandoning.*

This campaign is more than a contest between two men. It is more than a contest between two parties. It is a contest between two philosophies of government.

We are told by the opposition that we must have a change, that we must have a new deal. It is not the change that comes from the normal development of national life to which I object, but the proposal to alter the whole foundations of our national life, which have been builded through generations of testing and struggle, and the principles upon which we have builded the nation. The expressions our opponents use must refer to important changes in our economic and social system and our system of government; otherwise they are nothing but vacuous words. And I realize that in this time of distress many of our people are asking whether our social and economic system is incapable of that great primary function of providing security and comfort of life to all of the firesides of our 25,000,000 homes in America, whether our social system provides for the fundamental development and progress of our people, whether our form of government is capable of originating and sustaining that security and progress.

This question is the basis upon which our opponents are appealing to the people in their fears and distress. They are proposing changes and so-called new deals which would destroy the very foundations of our American system.

. . . Our system is the product of our race and of our experience in building a nation to heights unparalleled in the whole history of the world. It is a system peculiar to the American people. It differs essentially from all the others in the world. It is an American system.

It is founded on the conception that only through ordered liberty, through freedom to the individual and equal opportunity to the individual will his initiative and enterprise be summoned to spur the march of progress . . .

. . . I contend that this American system has demonstrated its validity and superiority over any system yet invented by human mind . . .

. . . *This thirty years of incomparable improvement in the scale of living, the advance of comfort and intellectual life, inspiration, and ideals did not arise without right principles animating the American system which produced them. Shall that system be discarded because vote-seeking men appeal to distress and say that the machinery is all wrong and that it must be abandoned or tampered with? Is it not more sensible to realize the simple fact that some extraordinary force has been thrown into the mechanism, temporarily deranging its operation? Is it not wiser to believe that the difficulty is not with the principles upon which our American system is founded and designed through all these generations of inheritance? Should not our purpose be to restore the normal working of that system which has brought to us such immeasurable benefits, and not destroy it?*

. . . I do challenge the whole idea that we have ended the advance of America, that this country has reached the zenith of its power, the height of its development. That is the counsel of despair for the future of America. That is not the spirit by which we shall emerge from this depression. That is not the spirit that made this country. If it is true, every American must abandon the road of countless progress and unlimited opportunity. I deny that the promise of American life has been fulfilled, for that means we have begun the decline and fall. No nation can cease to move forward without degeneration of spirit. . . .

. . . *the spirit of liberalism is to create free men; it is not the regimentation of men. It is not the extension of bureaucracy. I have said in this city before now that you cannot extend the mastery of government over the daily life of a people without somewhere making it the master of people's souls and thoughts. Expansion of government in business means that the government, in order to protect itself from the political consequences of its errors, is driven irresistibly without peace to greater and greater control of the nation's press and platform. Free speech does not live many hours after free industry and free commerce die. It is a false liberalism that interprets itself into government operation of business. Every step in that direction poisons the very roots of liberalism. It poisons equality, free speech, free press, and equality of opportunity. It is the road not to liberty but to less liberty. True liberalism is found not in striving to spread bureaucracy, but in striving to set bounds to it. True liberalism seeks all legitimate freedom first in the confident belief that without such freedom the pursuit of other blessings is in vain. Liberalism is a force truly of the spirit proceeding from the deep realization that economic freedom cannot be sacrificed if political freedom is to be preserved.*

Even if the government conduct of business could give us the maximum of efficiency, it would be purchased at the cost of freedom. It would increase rather than decrease abuse and corruption, stifle initiative and invention, undermine development of leadership, cripple mental and spiritual energies of our people, extinguish equality of opportunity, and dry up the spirit of liberty and progress. Men who are going about this country announcing that they are liberals because of their promises to extend the government in business are not liberals, they are reactionaries of the United States. And I do not wish to be misquoted or misunderstood. I do not mean that our government is to part with one iota of its national resources without complete protection to the public interest. I have already stated that democracy must remain master in its own house. I have stated that abuse and wrong-doing must be punished and controlled. Nor do I wish to be misinterpreted as saying that the United States is a free-for-all and devil-take-the-hindmost society.

The very essence of equality of opportunity of our American system is that there shall be no monopoly or domination by any group or section in this country, whether it be business, sectional, or a group interest. On the contrary, our American system demands economic justice as well as political and social justice; it is not a system of *laissez-faire.*

I am not setting up the contention that our American system is perfect. No human ideal has ever been perfectly attained, since humanity itself is not perfect. But the wisdom of our forefathers and the wisdom of the thirty men who have preceded me in this office hold to the conception that progress can be attained only as the sum of accomplishments of free individuals, and they have held unalterably to these principles. . . .

... *My countrymen, the proposals of our opponents represent a profound change in American life—less in concrete proposal, bad as that may be, than by implication and by evasion. Dominantly in their spirit they represent a radical departure from the foundations of 150 years which have made this the greatest nation in the world. This election is not a mere shift from the ins to the outs. It means deciding the direction our nation will take over a century to come.*

The Memoirs of Herbert Hoover. The Great Depression 1929–1941, Hollis and Carter, London, 1953, pp. 336, 338, 339–43

III

First New Deal

Roosevelt's first task, on assuming office on 4 March 1933, was to restore national confidence after one of the most shocking blows yet, the collapse of the American banking system. The celebrated 'Hundred Days', from March to June, succeeded in doing this, but there were more long-term objectives behind what has become known as the First New Deal. Many of the lawyers and academics who formed Roosevelt's 'Brain Trust' in the election campaign believed that the surest way out of the crisis was Federal planning. There were two divergent interpretations of 'planning', however, and the distinction between them was important. Men like Moley and General Johnson laid the emphasis on co-operation between government and business, trusting in business to execute policy with government playing a relatively minor role. Others like the economist Tugwell, on the other hand, believed that government must hold the whip hand if the experiment were to succeed. As it turned out, events followed the Moley–Johnson line. In both the principal agencies of the First New Deal, the National Recovery Administration (NRA) and the Agricultural Adjustment Administration (AAA), big business interests predominated, abetted by the administrators. Yet if the policy failed to realize the aspirations of advocates like Tugwell and laid itself open to the charge of being a poor imitation of Fascist corporatism, all the indices of business activity showed marked gains and the AAA could certainly claim the credit for halting the catastrophic fall in farm prices. Moreover, various other New Deal authorities were doing an enormous amount to relieve the distress brought on by mass unemployment. By 1935, mid-way through Roosevelt's first term, the economy as a whole was making a slow but steady recovery.

The First Inauguration

1. *We open with the comments of Arnold Toynbee, then editor of the Chatham House* Survey of International Affairs.

In A.D. 1933 the state of the World already afforded a crushing refutation of the creed of Humanism which had inspired the march of Western

Civilization for more than four hundred years and which had received its definitive formulation, in nineteenth-century England, in the apotheosis of 'Enlightened Self-Interest' . . . it could already be seen in retrospect that the confutation of the modern Western version of the cult of Humanism had been self-inflicted, and that this self-confutation was a consequence of the very success, up to a point, of the enterprises that had been undertaken in the idol's name. The demoniac Western effort to wrest into Man's hands the mastery of his material environment had had the effect of putting an unprecedently powerful material 'drive' into the human relationships of men with one another, without introducing any simultaneous change into these relations in respect of their intrinsic moral content and character. . . . By the end of the year 1933 the Great Society which the modern Western cult of Humanism had 'assembled' was inescapably confronted with a choice between persisting in its special errors, at the price of committing suicide, and saving its soul alive on condition of making a far-reaching and widely extended spiritual advance in the spirit of the very religion which the votaries of Enlightened Self-Interest had tacitly repudiated. . . .

. . . The internal history of the United States during the year 1933 was a matter of world-wide importance and interest, not only because of the violence and range of the repercussions produced abroad by the American people's domestic experiences and actions, but also because the recent world-wide transition from brilliant successes in mastering Physical Nature to humiliating failures in fumbling with human problems had occurred in North America more abruptly, and therefore with a more disturbing pyschological effect, than in any other region.

In the United States the outward manifestation of this transition may be dated from the break on Wall Street in the autumn of 1929. Till then the American people's nineteenth-century faith in the omnipotence of human technique had remained virtually unshaken; for the General War of 1914–18, which had re-demonstrated Man's impotence, unenlightened, to order his own affairs, had not had in North America that shattering psychological effect which it had produced in Europe. In American minds the frustration and suffering and destruction which were the essence of the War were inevitably overshadowed by the demonstration which the War had given of America's economic strength and by the wealth which the War had placed in American pockets. In the American version of modern Western history the war and post-war years, so far from representing a disastrous break with the prosperous pre-war century, were the years of this century's culmination and apogee. In the twentieth-century life of the United States the year 1914 was not more epoch-making than the years 1861 or 1870 (so fateful for America and France and Germany) had been in the nineteenth-century life of the British Empire. And the feelings and ideas that were associated in European minds with the month of August 1914 were rather associated in American minds with the month of October 1929 . . .

. . . Down to 1929 the economic expansion of the United States – an expansion which had continued for a whole generation after the technical 'closing of the frontier' – had provided *Homo Economicus Americanus*, as an individual, with a physically growing community in which he could be practically certain of remaking his private fortune after he had lost it. But in 1933 there was a general feeling that the break on Wall Street in the autumn of 1929 had differed from its many predecessors in marking the end of an epoch – in the same sense that, this time, the old lavishness of individual economic opportunity had gone for good. Those who had lost their fortunes in this slump were not displaying the traditional confidence in their ability to make them again . . .

. . . a generation which had been bent on rifling the cornucopia of a virgin continent . . . had had little patience with any call that threatened to divert or detain the 'go-getters' on their way. But in 1933, when the automatically self-replenishing American cornucopia was unexpectedly and inexplicably 'jamming', a free hand for each and all to plunder Nature was becoming of less importance to the individual than a fair deal between man and man. And 'the new deal' which was to turn the old mining camp into a new commonwealth was now looked for wistfully, by millions, from the President's hand. Franklin Roosevelt was hailed as the *deus ex machinâ* who had made his epiphany at Washington, at the crucial moment, in order to save American society by bringing this miraculous moral change about.

In thus pinning their faith to the hem of the garments of a superman, the American people in 1933 were reacting to the world crisis in somewhat the same fashion as their German and Italian and Russian contemporaries. In externals, no doubt, President Roosevelt's bearing was as different from that of an Old World dictator as a Boston policeman's uniform was different from General Göring's. The reigning President was the peacefully and lawfully elected incumbent of an ancient constitutional office, and not the child of revolution. Nor could the state of American feeling which preceded or followed his election and in-auguration be described as revolutionary in any ordinary sense. The fading vision of the nineteenth-century eldorado was still so deeply imprinted upon the American people's imagination that it endued this temperamentally impatient nation with an immense and magnifi-cent patience in enduring unaccustomed and unparalleled hardships. How long this habitual patience might survive the disappearance of the social conditions from which it had sprung was a question which could not be answered in 1933. The foreign observer of the American state of mind in that year could merely take note of its likeness to the war-time state of mind in the European belligerent countries during the General War of 1914–18. During these four years of extreme tribula-tion, the European belligerent peoples had sought relief from their psychological tension by perpetually demanding of their war-time rulers that they should do some new thing—and what thing mattered little so long as it was something drastic and sensational and ostensibly directed towards 'winning the War'. In the United States of 1933, which was a country psychologically at war with the Economic Depression, a similar demand was perpetually being made upon the President by the public, and was perpetually being satisfied by the President in the war-time manner. The successive 'new things' which President Roosevelt launched in that year were fateful for the future, not only of the United States, but of the World at large, in whose destinies the policy of the United States was at this time one of the decisive factors.

Survey of International Affairs for 1933, O.U.P., London, 1934, pp. 4, 6, 7, 9, 10, 13, 15–16

2. Robert Sherwood noted the undertones of dictatorship at the inauguration ceremony on 4 March.

No cosmic dramatist could possibly devise a better entrance for a new President—or a new Dictator, or a new Messiah—than that accorded to Franklin Delano Roosevelt. The eternally ironic fact is that the stage was so gloriously set for him not only by his friends and supporters, who were then relatively obscure people, but by those who were to become his bitterest enemies. Herbert Hoover was, in the parlance of vaudeville, 'a good act to follow'. Roosevelt rode on a wheel chair in-stead of a white horse, but the roll of drums and the thunderclaps which attended him were positively Wagnerian as emotional stimuli and also as ugly warnings of what might happen to American democracy if the new President should turn out to possess any of the qualities of a Hitler or even of a Huey Long.

The White House Papers of Harry L. Hopkins, Eyre and Spottiswoode, London, 1948, vol. i, p. 39

3. *The Inaugural Address itself, however, was reassuringly old-fashioned in its semi-Biblical rhetoric and gave little indication of drastic new departures.*

. . . Values have shrunk to fantastic levels; taxes have risen; our ability to pay has fallen; government of all kinds is faced by serious curtailment of income; the means of exchange are frozen in the currents of trade; the withered leaves of industrial enterprise lie on every side; farmers find no market for their produce; the savings of many years in thousands of families are gone.

More important, a host of unemployed citizens face the grim problem of existence, and an equally great number toil with little return. Only a foolish optimist can deny the dark realities of the moment.

Yet our distress comes from no failure of substance. We are stricken by no plague of locusts. Compared with the perils which our forefathers conquered because they believed and were not afraid, we still have much to be thankful for. Nature still offers her bounty and human efforts have multiplied it. Plenty is at our doorstep, but a generous use of it languishes in the very sight of the supply. Primarily this is because rulers of the exchange of mankind's goods have failed through their own stubbornness and their own incompetence, have admitted their failure and have abdicated. Practices of the unscrupulous money changers stand indicted in the court of public opinion, rejected by the hearts and minds of men.

True they have tried, but their efforts have been cast in the pattern of an outworn tradition. Faced by failure of credit they have proposed only the lending of more money. Stripped of the lure of profit by which to induce our people to follow their false leadership, they have resorted to exhortations, pleading tearfully for restored confidence. They know only the rules of a generation of self-seekers. They have no vision, and where there is no vision the people perish.

The money changers have fled from their high seats in the temple of our civilization. We may now restore that temple to the ancient truths.

The measure of the restoration lies in the extent to which we apply social values more noble than mere monetary profit. . . .

. . . Restoration calls, however, not for changes in ethics alone. This Nation asks for action, and action now.

Our greatest primary task is to put people to work. This is no unsolvable problem if we face it wisely and courageously. It can be accomplished in part by direct recruiting by the Government itself, treating the task as we would treat the emergency of a war, but at the same time, through this employment, accomplishing greatly needed projects to stimulate and reorganize the use of our natural resources.

Hand in hand with this we must frankly recognize the overbalance of population in our industrial centers and, by engaging on a national scale in a redistribution, endeavor to provide a better use of the land for those best fitted for the land. The task can be helped by definite efforts to raise the values of agricultural products and with this the power to purchase the output of our cities. It can be helped by preventing realistically the tragedy of the growing loss through foreclosure of our small homes and our farms. It can be helped by insistence that the Federal, State and local governments act forthwith on the demand that their cost be drastically reduced. It can be helped by the unifying of relief activities which today are often scattered, uneconomical, and unequal. It can be helped by national planning for and supervision of all forms of transportation and of communications and other utilities which have a definitely public character. There are many ways in which it can be helped, but it can never be helped merely by talking about it. We must act and act quickly.

Finally, in our progress toward a resumption of work we require two safeguards against a return of the evils of the old order: there must be strict supervision of all banking and credits and investments, so that there will be an end to speculation with other people's money; and there must be provision for an adequate but sound currency. . . .

The basic thought that guides these specific means of national recovery is not narrowly nationalistic. It is the insistence, as a first consideration, upon the interdependence of the various elements in and parts of the United States—a recognition of the old and permanently important manifestation of the American spirit of the pioneer. It is the way to recovery. It is the immediate way. It is the strongest assurance that the recovery will endure. . . .

If I read the temper of our people correctly, we now realize as we have never realized before our interdependence on each other; that we cannot merely take but we must give as well: that if we are to go forward, we must move as a trained and loyal army willing to sacrifice for the good of a common discipline, because without such discipline no progress is made, no leadership becomes effective. We are, I know, ready and willing to submit our lives and property to such discipline, because it makes possible a leadership which aims at a larger good. This I propose to offer, pledging that the larger purposes will bind upon us all as a sacred obligation with a unity of duty hitherto evoked only in time of armed strife.

With this pledge taken, I assume unhesitatingly the leadership of this great army of our people dedicated to a disciplined attack upon our common problems. . . .

For the trust reposed in me I will return the courage and the devotion that befit the time. I can do no less.

We face the arduous days that lie before us in the warm courage of national unity; with the clear consciousness of seeking old and precious moral values; with the clean satisfaction that comes from the stern performance of duty by old and young alike. We aim at the assurance of a rounded and permanent national life.

We do not distrust the future of essential democracy. The people of the United States have not failed. In their need they have registered a mandate that they want direct, vigorous action. They have asked me for discipline and direction under leadership. They have made me the present instrument of their wishes. In the spirit of the gift I take it.

The Public Papers and Addresses of Franklin D. Roosevelt, ed. S. Rosenman, Random House, New York, 1938, vol. ii, pp. 11–16

The First Hundred Days

4. *Within weeks of taking office Roosevelt had carried off his first triumph, the restoration of national confidence. The British Chancellor of the Exchequer, Neville Chamberlain, said this in the House of Commons on 22 March.*

. . . Only a few weeks ago anybody looking at the United States could only have done so with feelings of the gravest anxiety. Today, thanks to the initiative, courage and wisdom of the new President, a change has taken place which we might almost call miraculous. Confidence has largely been restored, people who had withdrawn their deposits from the banks are bringing their hoardings back, and a new sense of hope and anticipation is coming back to the American people. That confidence is being reflected over here in the City of London, in the stock markets and financial markets on this side of the Atlantic.

House of Commons Debates, fifth series, vol. 276, column 389

5. *On 6 April Walter Lippmann wrote the following.*

. . . At the beginning of the month [March] the country was in such a state of confused despair that it would have followed almost any leader anywhere he chose to go. It was a moment when an intoxicated demagogue could have aroused section against section and class against class, when a dull politician would have been bewildered and would not have known what to do. By the greatest good fortune which has befallen this country in many a day a kindly and intelligent man had the wit to realize that a great crisis is a great opportunity. He has taken advantage of it. Without preachment or rhetoric, merely by a series of simple, crisp and orderly measures, he has convinced the country that it need not wait dumbly and miserably for 'the turn', but that it can deal positively and promptly with the difficulties before it.

Interpretations 1933–1935, Macmillan, New York, 1936, p. 44

6. *Edmund Wilson noticed the changed atmosphere in Washington with pleasure and anticipation.*

Just now [Washington] is more entertaining than I have ever known it before, and more lively than at any time since the war. The last administration weighed on Washington, as it did on the entire country, like a darkness, like an oppressive bad dream, in which one could neither speak nor act; and the talk and animation in Washington today are a relief like waking up from a dream. The social life has been much enlivened by the arrival of young college graduates. The bright boys of the Eastern universities, instead of being obliged to choose, as they were twenty years ago, between business, the bond-selling game and the field of foreign missions, can come on and get jobs in Washington –with the result that, as one lady said to me, the place is like a Yale–Harvard–Princeton reunion. Then there are the New York 'intelligentzia'. It is equally true that, for a graduate of the school of New

York liberalism, it is Old Home Week today in Washington. Everywhere in the streets and offices you run into old acquaintances: the editors and writers of the liberal press, the 'progressive' young instructors from the colleges, the intelligent foundation workers, the practical idealists of settlement houses, the radicals who are not too radical not to conceive that there may be just a chance of turning the old order inside out and the Marxists who enjoy looking on and seeing how the half-baked liberals are falling victims to their inherent bourgeois contradictions.

The American Earthquake, Allen, London, 1958, p. 536

7. *Professor Moley saw it rather differently.*

... As the weeks ran on in March, the city of Washington became a mecca for the old Socialists, single-taxers, utility reformers, Civil Service reformers, and goo-goos of all types who at last perceived that a new political era was at hand and who took it to be a kind of crusade which the discontented of every variety were invited to join. Their eagerness to enlist was accentuated, in many cases, by their simple need for a job. That a government composed of men who could agree on neither the nature of our economic disease nor the character of the treatment would be the last blow for the stricken country never occurred to them. Each wanted to put on his surgical mask and rubber gloves and go to work.

After Seven Years, Harper, New York, 1939, p. 128

The New Legislation

8. *The pillars of the First New Deal were the Agricultural Adjustment Administration (AAA) and the National Recovery Administration (NRA). The key sections of the Agricultural Adjustment Act of 12 May read as follows.*

DECLARATION OF EMERGENCY

That the present acute economic emergency being in part the consequence of a severe and increasing disparity between the prices of agricultural and other commodities, which disparity has largely destroyed the purchasing power of farmers for industrial products, has broken down the orderly exchange of commodities, and has seriously impaired the agricultural assets supporting the national credit structure, it is hereby declared that these conditions have affected transactions in agricultural commodities with a national public interest, have burdened and obstructed the normal currents of commerce in such commodities, and render imperative the immediate enactment of title I of this Act. . . .

. . . Sec. 8. In order to effectuate the declared policy, the Secretary of Agriculture shall have power –

(1) To provide for reduction in the acreage or reduction in the production for market, or both, of any basic agricultural commodity, through agreements with producers or by other voluntary methods, and to provide for rental or benefit payments in connection therewith or upon that part of the production of any basic agricultural commodity required for domestic consumption, in such amounts as the Secretary deems fair and reasonable, to be paid out of any moneys available for such payments. . . .

(2) To enter into marketing agreements with processors, associations of producers, and others engaged in the handling, in the current of interstate or foreign commerce of any agricultural commodity or project thereof, after due notice and opportunity for hearing to interested parties. The making of any such agreement shall not be held to be in violation of any of the antitrust laws of the United States, and any such agreement shall be deemed to be lawful. . . .

Documents of American History, ed. H. S. Commager, 7th edn, Apple-ton-Century-Crofts, New York, 1963, vol. ii, pp. 243–4

9. *Section 1 of the National Industrial Recovery Act of 16 June set out its purposes.*

A national emergency productive of widespread unemployment and disorganization of industry, which burdens interstate and foreign commerce, affects the public welfare, and undermines the standards of living of the American people, is hereby declared to exist. It is hereby declared to be the policy of Congress to remove obstructions to the free flow of interstate and foreign commerce which tend to diminish the amount thereof; and to provide for the general welfare by promoting the organization of industry for the purpose of cooperative action among trade groups, to induce and maintain united action of labor and management under adequate governmental sanctions and supervision, to eliminate unfair competitive practices, to promote the fullest possible utilization of the present productive capacity of industries, to avoid undue restriction of production (except as may be temporarily required), to increase the consumption of industrial and agricultural products by increasing purchasing power, to reduce and relieve unemployment, to improve standards of labor, and otherwise to rehabilitate industry and to conserve natural resources.

Ibid., vol. ii, p. 272

10. *A third great innovation was the creation of the Tennessee Valley Authority (TVA) to plan the rehabilitation of the area Huxley had seen so devastated (I, 4). Broadus Mitchell gives what would now be regarded as an overoptimistic assessment of its achievements; however, they were undoubtedly considerable in the context of the 1930s.*

Of all the works of the New Deal, that undertaken and wrought by the Tennessee Valley Authority may live longest for bold simplicity of conception and honesty of execution. Here hurtful tradition was not deferred to, but was displaced. Here patching did not substitute for planning. Here greedy private claims were set aside for the common good. Here people came before politics. Here abundance was not expected somehow to profit from induced scarcity, but 'the fuller life' was translated from a hopeful phrase into more food, clothing, shelter, conveniences, and recreation. The TVA addressed itself to the greatest public works project in history, with the engineer, the architect, the chemist and men of a score of other sciences commanded to lead the way. It was and is literally a down-to-earth experiment, with all that we know from test tube and logarithmic table called on to help. It was a union of heart and mind to restore what had been wasted. It was a social resurrection. . . . It was, in large little, what Soviet Russia undertook in a vaster fashion.

Depression Decade, Rinehart, New York, 1947, p. 340

11. *Then there was the curbing of the 'money changers'. Ferdinand Pecora, chairman of a Senate committee investigating the activities of Wall Street, describes what he found.*

The investigation was not completed until June 1934. But long before that date the defects it had laid bare in our financial structure had already led to the institution of a sweeping program of reforms. The old regime of unlimited license may be said to have definitely come to an end. The testimony had brought to light a shocking corruption in our banking system, a widespread repudiation of old fashioned standards of honesty and fair dealing in the creation and sale of securities, and a merciless exploitation of the vicious possibilities of intricate corporate chicanery. The public had been deeply aroused by the spectacle of cynical disregard of fiduciary duty on the part of many of its most respected leaders; of directors, who conveniently subordinated their official obligations to an avid pursuit of personal gain; of great banks, which combined the functions of a bank with those of a stock jobber; of supposedly impartial public markets for the sale of securities, actually operated as private clubs for the individual benefit of their members.

Wall Street Under Oath, Cresset Press, London, 1939, pp. 283–4

12. *Meanwhile, the various relief agencies, notably the Federal Emergency Relief Administration (FERA) and the Civil Works Administration (CWA), both operated by Harry Hopkins, and the Public Works Administration (PWA), run by the Secretary of the Interior, Harold Ickes, were keeping the unemployed from despair. By the end of 1934 the government had spent over two thousand million dollars on relief. The President of the National Emergency Council, Frank Walker, saw some of the results of CWA for himself.*

... He said that in his own home state of Montana, 'I saw old friends of mine–men I had been to school with–digging ditches and laying sewer pipe. They were wearing their regular business suits as they worked, because they couldn't afford overalls and rubber boots. If I ever thought, "There, but for the grace of God–" it was right then.' The sight of these old friends made him feel sick at heart, but when he talked to individuals he felt very differently, for they were happy to be working and proud of what they doing. One of them pulled some silver coins out of his pocket and showed them to Walker. 'Do you know, Frank,' he said, 'this is the first money I've had in my pockets in a year and a half? Up to now I've had nothing but tickets that you exchange for groceries.' Another said: 'I hate to think what would have happened if this work hadn't come along. The last of my savings had run out. I'd sold or hocked everything I could. And my kids were hungry. I stood in front of the window of the bake-shop down the street and I wondered just how long it would be before I got desperate enough to pick up a rock and heave it through that window and grab some bread to take home.'

ROBERT SHERWOOD, *The White House Papers of Harry L. Hopkins*, Eyre and Spottiswoode, London, 1948, vol. i, p. 54

13. *Roosevelt himself noticed changes after a tour of several states in the summer of 1934, as he reported to the National Emergency Council in August.*

The important thing, in the last analysis, is the psychology of the people themselves. This is the first time I have been west of the Mississippi since 1932. The difference was perfectly apparent in the faces of the people. You could tell what that difference was by standing on the end of the car and looking at the crowd. They were a hopeful people. They had courage written all over their faces. They looked cheerful. They knew they were 'up against it' but they were going to see the thing through; whereas, in 1932 there was a look of despair, not only through that section, but practically throughout the South. That was best illustrated when one day I went through a town in the agricultural section of Tennessee, and Senator Barkley said it was perfectly obvious that the women had only one garment because they could not afford more than one, and that was a very cheap one; and the men had a sweater and pair of trousers which could possibly hold together for another 24 hours. Of course, as far as the South is concerned, they are richer now than they have been at any time since the war. Of course, they claim they were rich in 1860, but they were not quite as rich as some of the elderly people claim at this time. In other words, they are richer now than they have been at any time in the history of the country.

New Deal Mosaic, eds. L. G. Seligman and E. E. Cornwell Jr., Oregon University Press, 1965, pp. 281–2

What was the First New Deal?

14. *Roosevelt from the outset stressed the elements of planning and co-operation.*

. . . The legislation which has been passed or is in the process of enactment can properly be considered as part of a well-grounded plan. . . .

... It is wholly wrong to call the measures that we have taken Government control of farming, industry, and transportation. It is rather a partnership between Government and farming and industry and transportation, not partnership in profits, for the profits still go to the citizens, but rather a partnership in planning, and a partnership to see that the plans are carried out.

The Public Papers and Addresses of Franklin D. Roosevelt, ed. S. Rosenman, Random House, New York, 1938, vol. ii, pp. 161, 164

15. *To Samuel Rosenman, most of the things Roosevelt had done had been foreshadowed during his Governorship in New York.*

After Roosevelt became President, writers and commentators expressed surprise at the rapid succession of legislative proposals urged by him during the 'first hundred days' of his Presidency in 1933. Many have spoken and written of these proposals as though they suddenly sprang from Roosevelt in 1933 as a new kind of political philosophy. Many have wondered where they all came from in such a short time. The fact is that the basic philosophy and social objectives of the New Deal proposals can all be found in Governor Roosevelt's speeches and messages during the four years *before* he became President. The details are different, because the proposals in 1933 were framed for national rather than state action. But, as an examination of the earlier documents will show, the concepts are basically the same.

In those messages and speeches from 1929 through 1932 you will find proposals for appropriate action in the same fields in which he later urged action by the Congress: minimum wages and maximum hours, old age insurance, unemployment relief through public works and other means, unemployment insurance, regulation of public utilities, stricter regulation of banks and of the use of other people's money, improved housing through the use of public subsidies, farm relief, public development of water, cheaper electricity, especially in rural areas, greater use of state funds for education, crippled persons and the mentally and physically handicapped, repeal of prohibition laws, reforms in the administration of justice, re-afforestation and proper land use.

You will also find extended discussion of many of the themes that he was later to use so frequently that they came to be well known as a part of the Roosevelt philosophy: the interdependence of all groups of the population—city and farm; subsistence homesteads and the resettlement of population; regional planning; bringing industry into rural areas; conservation of natural resources; separation of legislative from executive functions.

Working With Roosevelt, Hart-Davis, London, 1952, p. 43

16. *To Frances Perkins, the Secretary of Labour, the impulse behind the New Deal was simple but powerful.*

When Franklin Roosevelt and his administration began their work in Washington in March 1933, the New Deal was not a plan with form and content. It was a happy phrase which he had coined during the campaign, and its value was psychological. It made people feel better, and in that terrible period of depression they needed to feel better.

As Roosevelt described it, the 'new deal' meant that the forgotten man, the little man, the man nobody knew much about, was going to be dealt better cards to play with.

The idea was not specific; it was general, but it was potent. On Roosevelt's part it was truly and profoundly felt. He understood that the suffering of the depression had fallen with terrific impact upon the people least able to bear it. He knew that the rich had been hit hard too, but at least they had something left. But the little merchant, the small householder and home owner, the farmer who worked the soil by himself, the man who worked for wages–these people were desperate. And Roosevelt saw them as principal citizens of the United States, numerically and in their importance to the maintenance of the ideals of American democracy. . . .

. . . The idea was that all the political and practical forces of the community should and could be directed to making life better for ordinary people. This was accepted by most of the dominant elements in the Democratic party in 1933.

The Roosevelt I Knew, Hammond, London, 1947, p. 135

17. *To the members of the Brain Trust, however, this was above all, the golden opportunity to bring planning to the United States for the first time. Here is Raymond Moley, then a devout New Nationalist.*

. . . Third was the rejection of the traditional Wilson–Brandeis philosophy that if America could once more become a nation of small proprietors, of corner grocers and smithies under spreading chestnut trees, we should have solved the problems of American life. We agreed that the heart of our difficulty was the anarchy of concentrated economic power which, like a cannon loose on a frigate's deck, tore from one side to another, crushing those in its path. But we felt that the remedy for this was not to substitute muskets for cannon or to throw the cannon overboard. We believed that any attempt to atomize big business must destroy America's greatest contribution to a higher standard of living for the body of its citizenry—the development of mass production. We agreed that equality of opportunity must be preserved. But we recognized that competition, as such, was not inherently virtuous; that competition (when it was embodied in an employer who survived only by sweating his labor, for example) created as many abuses as it prevented. So we turned from the nostalgic philosophy of the 'trust busters' toward the solution first broached in modern times by Charles Richard Van Hise's *Concentration and Control.*

After Seven Years, Harper, New York, 1939, p. 24

18. *General Hugh Johnson looked for inspiration to the First World War in which he had helped to operate the American war machine.*

The old honeycomb machine of the United States couldn't produce things fast enough in this race to destroy everything. We had to scrap it. And in the short period between April, 1917, and November, 1918, we literally tore it apart and put it together again. On the call of government and under the pressure of patriotism the old individualist battlers royal became an organized squad—all marching toward the sound of the guns.

We did not repeal the Anti-Trust Acts. *We simply ignored them.* Competitors pooled their resources, their trade secrets, their facilities. Industries organized themselves into groups and figures with the speed and almost the precision of a highly drilled chorus on a musical comedy stage and government took charge of both production and consumption and to a large extent, prices. It worked. It poured forth such a flood of production for the uses of war as the world has never seen in one country. It won the war.

The Blue Eagle From Egg to Earth, Doubleday, New York, 1935, p. 172

19. *The answer to the depression as he saw it was a controlled balance of interests.*

The apostles of Plenty must temper their doctrine. The answer is not to produce as much as you can at the lowest cost you can get, especially if that low cost comes out of wages or too abruptly out of employment. That simply starts the descent into the economic Avernus –cut employment, cut consuming power, cut production and so cut employment again. We simply must supervise these trends. Always the answer is *'balance'*–balance of supply to demand, balance of prices at fair exchange parity throughout the whole economic structure, and balance of benefits among great economic areas. You cannot even move toward this balance in this modern muddle without *some* direction. NRA offers one way to get that supervision in industry just as AAA offers it in agriculture and the various securities and fiscal acts in investment and banking. These statutory makeshifts are not the final answer. Everybody knows that. They are hasty and imperfect. *But* the very heart of the New Deal is the principle of concerted action in industry and agriculture under government supervision looking to a balanced economy as opposed to the murderous doctrine of savage and wolfish competition and rugged individualism, looking to dog-eat-dog and devil take the hindmost. This Utopian balance will never be achieved–there will never be perfection. But every plan should try to achieve it instead of trying to prevent it.

Ibid., p. 168

20. *The Columbia economist Rexford Tugwell shared the same premisses as Moley and Johnson, but he stood well to their left. Here he talks about laissez-faire and his alternative.*

. . . Behind that system (so it was said and thoroughly believed) was an invisible hand which beneficently guided warring business men to the promotion of the general welfare.

The jig is up. The cat is out of the bag. There is no invisible hand. There never was. If the depression has not taught us that, we are incapable of education. Time was when the anarchy of the competitive struggle was not too costly. Today it is tragically wasteful. It leads to disaster. We must now supply a real and visible guiding hand to do the task which that mythical non-existent, invisible agency was supposed to perform, but never did. . . .

... The various recovery acts proceeded from a theory which ... recognized the changes which had occurred in industrial society and it sought to secure the benefits of industry as it actually existed for the public good. It said, 'Industry has developed out of the face-to-face stage; huge factories exist; central-office organizations control many even of these organizations, great as they are in themselves; financial controls are superimposed on this; scientific management has come to stay–therefore, the Government must legalize all these heretofore horrid developments so that it may shape them into social instruments.'

The Battle for Democracy, Columbia U.P., New York, 1935, pp. 14, 259

21. *The United States, Walter Lippman believed, was at last on the way to discovering a new pattern of society.*

... For generations it has been supposed that an exclusive choice had to be made between collectivism and the freedom of private initiative, that the management of affairs had either to be left to individuals or assumed by the state. Whichever way one looked at these alternatives, the prospect was unsatisfactory. To concentrate initiative in officials was a certain way to kill initiative and liberty and to establish a state which in the ordinary course of events was bound to be despotic and inefficient. On the other hand, to let individualism run loose in a complex social order was to let it run wild and thus to produce disorder and injustice.

This dilemma is being resolved not by the arguments of collectivists and individualists but by the gradual uncovering of a new social principle. It provides both for individual initiative and collective initiative. The one is not the substitute for the other. The two are complementary. It is the method of freedom. The authority of the government is used to assist men in maintaining the security of an ordered life. The state, though it is powerful, is not the master of the people, but remains, as it must be where they have liberty, their servant.

The Method of Freedom, Macmillan, New York, 1934, pp. 59–60

22. *Liberal democrats everywhere, as Keynes declared at the end of 1933, were looking to Roosevelt and the New Deal for guidance in a troubled world.*

You have made yourself the trustee for those in every country who seek to mend the evils of our condition by reasoned experiment within the framework of the existing social system. If you fail, rational change will be gravely prejudiced throughout the world, leaving orthodoxy and revolution to fight it out. But, if you succeed, new and bolder methods will be tried everywhere, and we may date the first chapter of a new economic era from your accession to office.

R. F. HARROD, *The Life of John Maynard Keynes*, Macmillan, London, 1951, p. 447

IV

Second New Deal

In May 1935 the highest court in the United States, the Supreme Court, unanimously declared the act setting up the NRA to be unconstitutional and the death of the NRA symbolized the close of the First New Deal. It now seems clear that the action of the Court gave Roosevelt the opportunity he needed to change direction and push through the so-called Second New Deal in a 'Second Hundred Days' between June and August 1935. The ideological differences between the two were considerable. Whereas the First New Deal had accepted the fact of the large-scale business corporation, the Second New Deal was permeated with an intense hostility to big business. Its disciples, Ickes, Jackson, Cohen and Corcoran – and above, all, Justice Brandeis of the Supreme Court – believed not only in close government regulation of the corporations but in breaking up their monopolies and restoring competitive conditions in favour of the small businessman. For men like Tugwell this was a futile retrogression but to the supporters of the Second New Deal it marked a return to the true principles of reformist liberalism in America betrayed by the policies of 1933–35. Roosevelt's adoption of the new course was almost certainly decided on for important political reasons, because of the need to undercut the growing radical movements across the continent, led by Dr Francis Townsend, Father Charles Coughlin and Senator Huey Long of Louisiana. It paid large dividends. The combination of provisions for social security and a full-blooded attack on the business interests won Roosevelt the 1936 election by what till then was the largest popular margin in American history.

Thunder on the Right

BUSINESS

1. On 23 April 1935, Walter Lippmann, now moving into a more conservative stance, remarked on the growing disaffection of business from the New Deal.

At no time since Mr Roosevelt took office has it been truer than it is to-day that the progress of recovery is better than the sentiment in business. Partisan Democrats have a number of explanations for this paradox which they find rather reassuring. But the wiser heads in the Administration would do well not to be satisfied with them.

For underneath the obvious partisan attack on the New Deal and underneath the propaganda from vested interests which the President has challenged, there are solid causes for the lack of confidence which can and should be met. They come down, it seems to me, to two fundamental things: first, to the fact that the program of reforms which affect the mainsprings of enterprise has been dealt out item by item, with no clear view of the whole program and therefore with no definite assurance as to how far the program extends; second, to the fact that the Administration has decided to incur the largest *voluntary* deficit in our history without any statement of what it proposes to do after this deficit is spent.

The result is that a very large number of the ablest business men are in the grip of a nightmare in which they see before them an endless series of drastic reforms and an interminable series of budgetary deficits.

Interpretations 1933–1935, Macmillan, New York, 1936, p. 207

2. *Already in August 1934 the businessmen had formed the American Liberty League to defend their privileges against the New Deal's alleged encroachments. Here is a sample of one of its pamphlets, dated 31 May 1935.*

The New Deal is nothing more or less than an effort sponsored by inexperienced sentimentalists and demagogues to take away from the thrifty what the thrifty and their ancestors have accumulated, or may accumulate, and give it to others who have not earned it, or whose ancestors haven't earned it for them, and who never would have earned it and never will earn it, and thus indirectly to destroy the incentive for all future accumulation. Such a purpose is in defiance of all the tenets upon which our civilization has been founded.

RALPH SHAW, *The New Deal: Its Unsound Theories and Irreconcilable Policies*, p. 13 (quoted in G. Wolfskill *The Revolt of the Conservatives*, Houghton Mifflin, Boston, 1962, p. 124)

3. In another, dated 20 January 1936, the President of Colgate University was to say this of social security.

Nothing could threaten the race as seriously as this. It is begging the unfit to be more unfit. Even such a measure as old-age insurance, which I am sure must touch the sympathies of every one, especially if he has the intelligence to think things through, removes one of the points of pressure which has kept many persons up to the strife and struggle of life.

GEORGE B. CUTTEN, *Professors and the New Deal*, p. 15 (quoted in *ibid.*, pp. 124–5)

4. In a third pamphlet dated 21 May 1935 the President of the Detroit Steel Casting Company, Mr S. Wells Utley, denounced the New Dealers in forthright terms.

They contend that there is a tremendous disparity in the distribution of the 'good things of life' due to greed, corruption, and crookedness in the economic system; I contend that the maladjustment is not nearly so great as they claim; that the distribution of wealth under our system is infinitely more widespread than ever attained by any other; that what maladjustment there is, is due largely to the difference in human capacity and human capability; that the amassing of wealth honestly made is but a badge of service performed to the community, and that the remedy of the defects of the present system lies not in the destruction but in the improvement of the character of the race, through Christian education. They claim that the present depression is quite different from those of the past, and was brought about by the criminal errors of a few of the bankers and business men; I claim that it is world-wide, brought about by the errors of the race, of yourself and myself as much as anyone else; that it is not essentially different from other depressions; that after all these periodic slumps are only nature's brakes to keep us from dashing to our own destruction.

The Duty of the Church to the Social Order, pp. 2–3 (quoted in *ibid.*, pp. 123–4)

THE DEMAGOGUES

5. A more serious challenge in political terms sprang from the various radical movements springing up across the country. Alistair Cooke sets the scene.

. . . America was still the land of the middle class, the largest middle class in the world. And it was left to them, to the wage-earners with their savings gone, the fore-closed farmers, not least the business men and small broken bankers, to all who had prospered in the twenties and still had the energy to feel the outrage of betrayal; it was left to them to berate 'the system', the bankers, and capitalism itself; it was they who spawned demagogues who proposed radical surgery on an America which, they said, had been poisoned by 'the bankers, the brokers, the politicians.' Huey Long in Louisiana, Father Coughlin in Michigan, Dr Townsend and Upton Sinclair in California offered between them everything from a poor man's dictator and a capital levy to an old-age pension. For a short dreadful time these men were the real possible alternatives to a social-security act. There was abroad for at least three more years what Raymond Daniell called 'a national yearning for an easy way out, a general desire to reap the benefits of collective action without swallowing the prescription of Dr Marx'.

A Generation on Trial, Hart-Davis, London, 1951, p. 14

6. *The Townsend movement drew its strength from the elderly of California and other western states, a group particularly badly hit by the depression, as might be expected. The Townsendites placed their faith in the Townsend Plan, which envisaged a pension of $200 a month for every retired person over the age of sixty, on condition that it was spent within the month. Here is a convert talking about the movement.*

. . . It is the New Dealers and these people working on the Social Security Act who are fighting the Townsend Plan. It's not the capitalists and manufacturers. *They* know what the Plan would do for them, and they understand it is designed for them as well as old people. . . .

. . . I went to the Cleveland Convention as a delegate, and I received the deepest impression there of the value of the Plan. You could see it in the faces of those 2,000 people that they believed in it so thoroughly as a godsend to this country that they'd stake their lives on it. In helping old people today, and posterity, by bettering national economic conditions, buying power is everything and that is what the Townsend Plan would supply. I believe so strongly in all that I've told you that I wish I didn't have to earn my living. I'd like to spend my time, all my time, just working for the movement, talking about it to people and selling them our literature.

HADLEY CANTRIL, *The Psychology of Social Movements*, Wiley, New York, 1941, p. 198

7. *Much uglier was the influence wielded by Father Coughlin, a Roman Catholic priest whose radio broadcasts captured vast audiences all over the country and who soon became one of America's leading Fascists and anti-Semites. A letter from one of his followers, a woman in Toledo, Ohio, to Monsignor John Ryan, a priest highly critical of Coughlin, gives a hint of the depth of feeling which Coughlin exploited.*

Don't it stand to reason that you, nor I, nor anybody else can live decently and pay rent, Gas, lights, Insurance, Dr. bills, buy cloths, food, and numerous other things on the few measly dollars they will get [from Social Security]. Rosvelt should have to try it out first for about 3 years. Give him . . . just what us poor devels would have and let him as any ordinary person would have to live on what they get from the Old Age pension . . . and see how quick he would change his mind. You, nor he couldent do it but he expects us poor devils to do it and like it.

J. P. SHENTON, 'The Coughlin Movement and the New Deal', *The Political Science Quarterly*, 1958, pp. 369–70

8. *Wallace Stegner later discussed the meaning of Coughlinism.*

. . . Father Coughlin was lucky in that he didn't have a real and enduring desperation to play with; the depression was brutal and hard and long, but it did not go deep enough to give a demagogue real anguish to manipulate. Discomfort, want, hunger, but not quite anguish, not quite hopelessness or despair. And Father Coughlin was fortunate, too, that Franklin D. Roosevelt was his contemporary. The presence of a leader with all the personal magnetism of the führers, but without their venality or their vanity or their incurable lust for a white horse, robbed Coughlin of his chance to hang himself and possibly ruin the nation in the process.

But it would be well to ponder the enormous following he had at his peak. It would be well to consider how vague, misty, unformed, contradictory, and insincere his program was, and yet how it won the unstinting belief of hundreds of thousands, even millions. It would be well to remember that even a people like the Americans, supposedly politically mature and with a long tradition of very great personal liberty, can be brought to the point where millions of them will beg to be led, and will blindly follow when a leader steps forward.

'The Radio Priest and his Flock', in *The Aspirin Age 1919–1941*, ed. I. Leighton, Bodley Head, London, 1950, p. 256

9. *The worst threat to Roosevelt, however, came from a member of his own party, Huey Long, Senator for Louisiana, where he was virtually dictator. From this base Long exerted considerable influence in the country at large. If he had chosen, he could have damaged Roosevelt seriously in the 1936 election. Harnett Kane describes his hold over his home state.*

He possessed the state government, the Governor, the university, all commissions and departments, the Legislature, the public schools, the treasury, the buildings, and the Louisianans inside them. The courts were his, except in isolated instances, and he had the highest judges. He had a secret police which did anything he asked: kidnapped men, held them incommunicado, inquired without check into private matters of opponents. He ran the elections. He counted the votes. He disqualified any man or woman whom he wanted disqualified. He could order the addition to the rolls of any number of voters that his judgment dictated. He was becoming local government in Louisiana. The officials of no town or city were secure. Let a brother or an uncle offend, and Huey would have a mayor or an alderman out of a job and his own man appointed in his place. He was reaching into local police affairs; he was controlling municipal finances by new boards. He could ruin a community by cutting off its taxes, preventing it from adopting substitutes, and then forcing new obligations to break its back. He was moving in upon the parish district attorneys, using his attorney-general as a club.

Louisiana Hayride, Morrow, New York, 1941, p. 128

10. *James Farley, controller of the Democratic party machine, the man who forecast exactly how many states would vote for Roosevelt in the 1936 election, had a confidential poll made of Long's prospects.*

It indicated that, running on a third-party ticket, Long would be able to poll between 3,000,000 and 4,000,000 votes for the Presidency. The poll demonstrated also that Huey was doing fairly well at making himself a national figure. His probable support was not confined to

Louisiana and near-by states. On the contrary, he had about as much following in the North as in the South, and he had as strong an appeal in the industrial centers as he did in the rural areas. Even the rock-ribbed Republican state of Maine, where the voters are steeped in conservatism, was ready to contribute to Long's total vote in about the same percentage as other states.

While we realized that polls are often inaccurate and that conditions could change perceptibly before the election actually took place, the size of the Long vote made him a formidable factor. He was head and shoulders stronger than any of the other 'Messiahs' who were gazing wistfully at the White House and wondering what chance they would have to arrive there as the result of a popular uprising. It was easy to conceive a situation whereby Long, by polling more than 3,000,000 votes, might have the balance of power in the 1936 election. For example, the poll indicated that he would command upward of 100,000 votes in New York State, a pivotal state in any national election; and a vote of that size could easily mean the difference between victory or defeat for the Democratic or Republican candidate. Take that number of votes away from either major candidate, and they would come mostly from our side, and the result might spell disaster.

Behind the Ballots, Harcourt, Brace, New York, 1938, pp. 249–50

11. *The administration certainly took the threat seriously, as this transcript of the National Emergency Council meeting of 5 February 1935 indicates.*

SECRETARY WALLACE:	In a delicate situation like Louisiana we may have to ask your advice.
PRESIDENT ROOSEVELT:	You don't have to do that. Don't put anybody in and don't keep anybody that is working for Huey Long or his crowd! That is a hundred per cent!
VICE-PRESIDENT GARNER:	That goes for everybody!
PRESIDENT ROOSEVELT:	Everybody and every agency. Anybody working for Huey Long is not working for us.

New Deal Mosaic, eds. L. G. Seligman and E. E. Cornwell Jr., Oregon University Press, 1965, p. 437

In September 1935, however, Long was assassinated and since there was no comparable successor, Roosevelt was relieved of his most dangerous rival.

The New Deal Response

12. *In the mid-term Congressional elections of 1934 the Democrats, instead of suffering the usual losses, actually consolidated their hold on both the Senate and the House of Representatives. For New Dealers like Harry Hopkins, this was the signal for action, as he remarked to his entourage.*

Boys–this is our hour. We've got to get everything we want–a works programme, social security, wages and hours, everything–now or never. Get your minds to work on developing a complete ticket to provide security for all the folks of this country up and down and across the board.

ROBERT SHERWOOD, *The White House Papers of Harry L. Hopkins*, Eyre and Spottiswoode, London, 1948, vol. i, p. 65

13. *Roosevelt, however, was not ready to take the plunge. He was waiting as indecisively as he was to wait in the autumn and winter of 1937–38. H. G. Wells noticed this on his visit to the United States.*

. . . The rôle of the President in a free-thinking democracy is to sublimate, clarify and express the advancing thought of the community. And the President this time seemed to me to be *listening* and talking interestedly rather than decisively, of what he was hearing. He has not been heard upon the air for some time. For the very good reason that upon many issues he is plainly in a state of suspense. . . . But I think he would be glad if something more definite and constructive began to come in from other quarters. He has rather an air of waiting for that.

The New America: The New World, Cresset Press, London, 1935, p. 50

14. *Roosevelt himself explained it in these terms, in a letter of 20 March.*

I know . . . you will be sympathetic to the point of view that the public psychology and, for that matter, individual psychology, cannot, because of human weakness, be attuned for long periods of time to a constant repetition of the highest note in the scale. . . . Whereas in this country there is a free and sensational press, people tire of seeing the same name, day after day, in the important headlines of the papers, and the same voice, night after night, over the radio . . . if I had tried to keep up the pace of 1933 and 1934, the inevitable histrionics of the new actors, Long and Coughlin and Johnson, would have turned the eyes of the audience away from the main drama itself.

R. E. NEUSTADT, *Presidential Power*, Wiley, New York, 1960, p. 103

THE END OF NRA

15. *On 27 May the Supreme Court destroyed the constitutional basis of the NRA. But the NRA had been under fire for some time. In the spring of 1934 a review board headed by the celebrated criminal lawyer Clarence Darrow condemned the Administration in a series of wildly contradictory but damaging reports. Here is an extract from the third.*

[In] virtually all the codes we have examined, one condition has been persistent, undeniable and apparent to any impartial observation. . . . The code has offered an opportunity for the more powerful and more profitable interests to seize control of an industry or to augment and extend a control already obtained. In Industry after Industry, the larger units, sometimes through the agency of what is called an Institute, sometimes by other means, have for their own advantage written the codes, and then, in effect and for their own advantage, assumed the administration of the code they have framed. Thus privilege has exerted itself to gather more privilege. . . . To deliver industry into the hands of its greatest and most ruthless units when the protection of the anti-trust laws had been withdrawn was a grave error. It may safely be said that not in many years have monopolistic tendencies in industry been so forwarded and strengthened.

National Recovery Review Board, *Third Report to the President*, pp. 35, 39 (mimeographed copy only, held in Princeton University Library)

16. *President Hoover had said much the same when the plan which fathered the NRA had first been put forward in September 1931.*

This plan provides for the mobilization of each variety of industry and business into trade associations, to be legalized by the government and authorized to 'stabilize prices and control distribution'. There is no stabilization of prices without price fixing and control of distribution. This feature at once becomes the organization of gigantic trusts such as have never been dreamed of in the history of the world. This is the creation of a series of complete monopolies over the American people.

It means the repeal of the entire Sherman and Clayton Acts, and all other restrictions on combinations and monopoly. In fact, if such a thing were ever done, it means the decay of American industry from the day this scheme is born, because one cannot stabilize prices without restricting production and protecting obsolete plants and inferior managements. It is the most gigantic proposal of monopoly ever made in history.

The Memoirs of Herbert Hoover. The Great Depression 1929–1941, Hollis and Carter, London, 1953, p. 334

17. *When the Supreme Court delivered its blow, Walter Lippmann could not have agreed more. Two days after the Court had handed down its decision he wrote this.*

. . . What midsummer madness possessed the New Dealers in July, 1933, will never be completely understood. But madness it was and ever since they have been paying the price for it. The N.R.A. was their supreme folly. *As they decided to administer the law in July, 1933,* they violated the essential principles of the American constitutional system; they imposed upon industry an economic policy which virtually every economist in the world has denounced as a brake upon recovery–a policy which ran counter to and has neutralized in greater or lesser degree their agricultural policy, their public works program, and their monetary policy. Finally, as politicians, they made the most irreparable mistake of identifying an extremely dubious experiment in one field with the whole national recovery effort.

Interpretations 1933–1935, Macmillan, New York, 1936, p. 113

18. *Few thought, as Broadus Mitchell later did, that the trouble lay in the government's reluctance to plan.*

. . . NRA proved, if anything, that the country had reached a stage in economic development in which old methods would not serve. Private property in the great means of production, and their operation under the profit motive and by reliance on the price system–however overlaid with a spirit of cooperation–could not give full use of materials, machines and men. Frictions and contradictions inhibited on every hand. Exhortation of government was at first promising, then disappointing, and finally irritating. Instead of forthright planning for a plain social objective, there was circumspect strategy, and that mostly of the moment.

Depression Decade, Rinehart, New York, 1947, p. 259

19. *In short, the public mood was overwhelmingly against planning and pre-sumably ready for a return to the ancient verities of progressivism. Roosevelt himself was only too anxious to wash his hands of NRA, as he confided to Frances Perkins, his Secretary of Labour.*

'You know the whole thing is a mess,' Roosevelt told me. 'It has been an awful headache. Some of the things they have done in NRA are pretty wrong, though I think it is going better now. We have got the best out of it anyhow. Industry got a shot in the arm. Everything has started up. I don't believe they will go back to their old wage-levels. I think the forty-hour week will stick, except in a few instances. I think perhaps NRA has done all it can do. I don't want to impose a system on this country that will set aside the anti-trust laws on any permanent basis.

'I have been talking to other lawyers besides Homer Cummings, and they are pretty certain that the whole process is unconstitutional and that we have to restudy and revise our whole programme. Perhaps we had better do it now. So let's give the NRA a certain amount of time to liquidate. Have a history of it written, and then it will be over.'

The Roosevelt I Knew, Hammond, London, 1947, p. 204

THE SECOND HUNDRED DAYS

20. *The burden of the Second Hundred Days was an onslaught on big busi-ness in the true Wilsonian tradition. Most of the important legislation – social security, the holding companies bill and the labour relations bill – had been before Congress for some months, but it was not until after the NRA decision that Roosevelt began to throw his weight decisively behind it. Here is part of his recommendation for the regulation of public utility holding companies, made on 12 March.*

It is time to make an effort to reverse that process of the concentration of power which has made most American citizens, once traditionally independent owners of their own businesses, helplessly dependent for their daily bread upon the favor of a very few, who, by devices such as holding companies, have taken for themselves unwarranted economic power. I am against private socialism of concentrated private power as thoroughly as I am against governmental socialism. The one is equally as dangerous as the other; and destruction of private socialism is utterly essential to avoid governmental socialism.

The Public Papers and Addresses of Franklin D. Roosevelt, ed. S. Rosenman, Random House, New York, 1938, vol. iv, p. 101

21. *The same anti-big business theme ran through the message to Congress urging heavy taxation of the rich and of business corporations, sent on 19 June.*

... the drain of a depression upon the reserves of business puts a disproportionate strain upon the modestly capitalized small enterprise. Without such small enterprises our competitive economic society would cease. Size begets monopoly. . . .

. . . It seems only equitable, therefore, to adjust our tax system in accordance with economic capacity, advantage and fact. The smaller corporations should not carry burdens beyond their powers; the vast concentrations of capital should be ready to carry burdens commensurate with their powers and their advantages.

Ibid., vol. iv, p. 275

22. *The President's belated espousal of the National Labour Relations Bill of Senator Robert Wagner was likewise a slap in the face for business. Here is part of the statement Roosevelt made on signing the act on 5 July.*

A better relationship between labor and management is the high purpose of this Act. By assuring the employees the right of collective bargaining it fosters the development of the employment contract on a sound and equitable basis. By providing an orderly procedure for determining who is entitled to represent the employees, it aims to remove one of the chief causes of wasteful economic strife. By preventing practises which tend to destroy the independence of labor, it seeks for every worker within its scope, that freedom of choice and action which is justly his.

Ibid., vol. iv, p. 294

23. *At the same time, Roosevelt was intent on providing relief for the continuing millions of unemployed and a measure of social security for themselves*

and their dependants. In the spring of 1935 the unprecedented sum of $4,800 million was authorized by Congress for relief, almost one-third of it for Hopkins's new agency the Works Progress Administration. Then in August, at the close of the long congressional session, the President signed the Social Security Act which, for all its many faults, represented a firm rejection of the assumptions of a laissez-faire society. Here is part of Roosevelt's statement on signing the act; notice the emphasis on public thrift.

This law . . . represents a cornerstone in a structure which is being built but is by no means complete. It is a structure intended to lessen the force of future possible depressions. It will act as a protection to future Administrations against the necessity of going deeply into debt to furnish relief to the needy. The law will flatten out the peaks and valleys of deflation and of inflation. It is, in short, a law that will take care of human needs and at the same time provide for the United States an economic structure of vastly greater soundness.

Ibid., vol. iv, p. 324

What was the Second New Deal?

24. In any consideration of the Second New Deal, it should not be forgotten that 1935 was the year of the Popular Front, the summons by the Soviet Union to an anti-Nazi, anti-Fascist alliance of communists, socialists and liberal democrats. Now the New Deal could claim something in common with progressive movements the world over. Joseph Freeman wrote this to Daniel Aaron in the summer of 1958.

. . . now you could be for every kind of social reform here, for the Soviet Union, for the Communist Party, for Proletarian Literature– for everything and anything that was at one time radical, rebellious, subversive, revolutionary and downright quixotic–and in doing so you were on the side of all the political angels of the day; you were on the side of the Roosevelt administration, on the side of Labor, the Negroes, the middle classes; on the side of Hitler's victims, on the side of all the oppressed colonial peoples in the world. In short, this is the only period in all the world's history when you could be at one and the same time an *ardent revolutionary* and an *arch-conservative* backed by the government of the United States *and* the Soviet Union.

D. AARON, *Writers on the Left*, Harcourt, Brace, New York, 1961, pp. 270–1

25. *Tugwell believed that the change of course at home was intimately bound up with international events, and Roosevelt's speech of 27 June 1936 [IV, 32] does lend a certain colour to this view.*

The influence of the Brandeis philosophy and its purveyors was enhanced by the way things were going in the world. The collectivism they hated and feared had, for their purposes, an ideal embodiment in the totalitarians, Hitler and Mussolini. The ruthlessness of dictatorship could be represented as inseparable from collectivism. This, to the Brandeis group, was very useful and they made the most of it. When Franklin turned from the collectivistic First to the atomistic Second New Deal and Corcoran became a White House favorite, the association had given Franklin the feeling of being approved by those whose opinion he valued. He liked that. Besides, as we have seen, the atomism of Brandeis was congruous with the progressive liberalism Franklin believed politically acceptable.

That there was something much deeper involved, no one apparently understood. But there is no doubt in my mind, as I review the subsequent years, that Franklin's turn to atomism was a deliberate long-range political choice. Collectivism would be represented by Hitler. His own position must stand in the clearest contrast with that of the man who was to be his rival for the regard of a generation.

The Democratic Roosevelt, Doubleday, New York, 1957, pp. 545–6

26. *The move from a First to a Second New Deal is usually explained in domestic terms, however. The first influential history to suggest that there was a definite change of policy after 1934 and that the Second New Deal marked the real period of reform was published by Basil Rauch in 1944.*

A fundamental change in the political philosophy and policies of the Roosevelt administration did occur during 1934. It divides the six years covered in this book into two distinct periods, and its importance justifies the designations First New Deal and Second New Deal. The reorientation was undertaken deliberately, and it fulfilled the President's campaign promise that his method would be experimental. Only two policies were pursued consistently through both periods: political foreign policy, and the extension of government regulation of the kind first imposed on railroads by the Interstate Commerce Act of 1887 to further selected fields, such as aircraft and motor carriers, public utilities, securities, and banks. In the broad fields of agricultural, industrial, labor, tariff, money, and unemployment relief legislation the policies of the First New Deal were fundamentally altered and in some cases reversed to create a Second New Deal.

These changes may be described in general terms of purpose and political philosophy. The primary aim of the First New Deal was recovery, while that of the Second was reform. Higher prices for industry and agriculture were the immediate objective during the first period; increased purchasing power and social security for the population as a whole were the immediate objectives during the second period. The policies of the first period were expressions of the philosophy of economic nationalism and scarcity, while those of the second illustrated the philosophy of international coöperation and economic abundance. The First New Deal was chiefly beneficial to big business and large farmers. The Second New Deal was chiefly beneficial to labor and smaller farmers. . . .

. . . By 1936, the transition to the Second New Deal was complete. The President appealed to the country for re-election as the leader of a liberal reform administration carrying out the program of farmers and laborers. His victory was the most overwhelming in party-election history, and it was a victory for the Second New Deal. In 1937, the administration undertook to complete the structure of the Second New Deal with measures designed to benefit particularly the less well-organized groups of farmers and workers. By the end of 1938, this process had stopped, and the creative period of the New Deal ended: no important new reform law has been passed since that year.

The History of the New Deal 1933–1938, Creative Age Press Inc., New York, 1944, p.v

27. *In 1957, however, the appearance of a biography of Roosevelt by a convinced First New Dealer, Tugwell, offered an entirely different point of view.*

The developments of 1934 led to the position Franklin had begun to assume during the campaign [of 1932] under the pressures of politics. It may be best to put it another way: he was returning to an accepted version of the progressive position in all these matters. This was the result, I think, of a number of combined estimates on his part. One of these was that the weight of the movement still lay with the older orthodox progressives. They believed in bearing down on big business and encouraging little business; in the development of foreign trade outlets by reducing barriers and even by subsidizing exports; in the favoring of farmers in their perennial contest with processors; and in the development of extensive welfare measures. Going along with this was probably a judgment that, if these policies were developed in all their ramifications, the likely defection of reactionaries in the South and their linking up with the Republicans in the Congress would be offset by strength among urban workers and the city machines, which he had not hitherto been able to rely on.

The progressive orthodoxy was simple. It was regarded as having been reinforced by the occurrence of the depression. Big business and big finance had been responsible. The admission of these very persons and interests to governmental partnership in the NRA had set up a kind of unnatural union. General Johnson became with the progressives a kind of *bête noire*, and their disapproval was made known in emphatic terms. Then, too, the many representatives around him of the Brandeis philosophy were annoyed, and in Franklin's Valhalla no figure loomed larger than the old justice. His disciples, beginning with Frankfurter, had infiltrated the administrative organization to an almost incredible extent, and this was a movement that tended to enlarge. The partnership theory was one they refused to accept.

This year is spoken of by one New Deal historian – Professor Rauch – as a year of transition, and this is a just comment. Franklin was in process of making a complete turn-around. It is no exaggeration to speak of the situation after the legislation of 1934 as a Second New Deal. It not only had new objectives, it had a new personnel. This is not evident at the higher levels. There were no cabinet changes except at the Treasury. But the first group of secondary helpers, beginning with Moley, were by year's end almost wholly replaced with Frankfurter nominees. This was achieved through two of his energetic lieutenants – Corcoran and Cohen – who personify this Second New Deal as the Brains Trust personifies the First.

General Johnson departed from the scene in October and was replaced by a board whose policies were obviously going to be very different from his. This change was carried out in a storm of publicity which, in his subsequent years as a pungent newspaper columnist, turned him into a sharp critic of Franklin and all his helpers. Franklin seldom succeeded in getting rid of people gracefully. But the going of Peek and Johnson, the Baruch twins, was particularly embarrassing. However, it was finally done, and the Brandeis influence came uppermost. From this time on, collectivism and planning would have no place in Franklin's policy. Whatever he secretly believed, he had now publicly placed himself squarely in the older progressive tradition, and there he would stay.

The Democratic Roosevelt, Doubleday, New York, 1957, pp. 326–7

28. *Tugwell's colleague on the Brain Trust, Raymond Moley, reached similar conclusions. His New Deal, like Tugwell's, was dead.*

It was easy to see that the early New Deal, with its emphasis on agricultural and industrial planning, was dominated by the theory of Concentration and Control . . .

But with the invalidation of the N.I.R.A., there was a shift in emphasis. And this shift took not the form of a complete repudiation of Concentration and Control, but of an endless wavering between it and the philosophy advocated by those Brandeis adherents, like Corcoran, who preached the 'curse of bigness', the need for breaking up great corporations on the ground that their growth was the result of the desire for financial control rather than increased efficiency, the desirability of 'atomizing' business in order to achieve a completely flexible competitive system which would work without much intervention by government.

After Seven Years, Harper, New York, 1939, p. 372

29. *Less partisan commentators have been able to view the transition with greater detachment. Thus A. M. Schlesinger Jr.*

The year 1935 marked a watershed. In this year the strategy and tactics of the New Deal experienced a subtle but pervasive change. The broad human objectives remained the same. But the manner in which these objectives were pursued—the techniques employed, the economic presuppositions, the political style, the vision of the American future itself—underwent a significant transformation.

The early New Deal had accepted the concentration of economic power as the central and irreversible trend of the American economy and had proposed the concentration of political power as the answer. The effort of 1933 had been to reshape American institutions according to the philosophy of an organic economy and a co-ordinated society. The new effort was to restore a competitive society within a framework of strict social ground rules and on the foundation of basic economic standards–accompanied, as time went on, by a readiness to use the fiscal pulmotor to keep the economy lively and expansive. . . .

In the end, the basic change in 1935 was in atmosphere–a certain lowering of ideals, waning of hopes, narrowing of possibilities, a sense that things were, not opening out, but closing in. The Hundred Days had been a golden spring, like Versailles in 1919, when for a moment a passionate national response to leadership which asked great things made anything–everything–seem possible. The First New Dealers had a utopian and optimistic and moral cast of mind; the Second New Dealers prided themselves on their realism. The First New Dealers thought well of human rationality and responsibility. It was their faith that man was capable of managing the great instrumentalities he had invented. The Second New Dealers accepted Brandeis's maxim, 'Man is weak and his judgment is fallible'; they said with Frankfurter, 'We know how slender a reed is reason–how recent its emergence in man, how deep the countervailing instincts and passions, how treacherous the whole rational process.' If man could not be relied on to assume responsibility for his own creations, he could be saved from his weakness only as these creations were cut down to his own size.

The shift from the First to the Second New Deal was not a whimsical change of direction so much as it was an almost inevitable response to the new necessities of the American situation. The problem had changed between 1933 and 1935, so policies changed, too, and men with them. The next wave of New Dealers, more skeptical, more hard-boiled, more tough-minded, ostensibly more radical but essentially more conservative, were prepared to work within the existing moral attitudes and the existing institutional framework and to generate by sheer vigor and combativeness the energy to fuel their more limited purposes. As children of light, the First New Dealers had believed in the capacity for justice which, in Niebuhr's phrase, makes democracy possible. As children of darkness, the Second New Dealers believed in the inclination to injustice which makes democracy necessary.

The Politics of Upheaval, Houghton Mifflin, Boston, 1960, pp. 385, 397–8

30. *The author of the most recent single-volume history of the New Deal has emphasized the element of compromise provided by Roosevelt.*

Both views [Rauch and Tugwell] contain helpful insights, as well as some questionable assumptions, but both share the handicap of exaggerating the shift from 1933 to 1935. Many of the 1935 measures—social security, utility regulation, progressive taxation—had long been in the works, and it was only a question of time when they would be adopted. Nor can the Second Hundred Days be viewed simply as a triumph of the Brandeis faction. It had won little of substance save the Holding Company Act, and many of the NRA emphases persisted. If Roosevelt found more use for Brandeisian lieutenants in 1935, in part because his earlier advisers were now politically vulnerable, he never wholly adopted the viewpoint either of the Brandeisians or the spenders. As late as 1937, newsmen identified Donald Richberg [Johnson's successor as head of NRA] as the 'number-one boy of the White House,' and as late as 1938 Roosevelt contemplated reviving, in a revised form, the NRA.

The President had scant patience with the theological discussions that revolved around him. When someone reported to him a conversation in which Tugwell had once remarked to a Brandeisian, 'I do not see why your crowd and ours cannot work together,' Roosevelt replied: 'I always hate the frame of mind which talks about "your group" and "my group" among Liberals. . . . Brandeis is one thousand per cent right in principle,' the President added, 'but in certain fields there must be a guiding or restraining hand of Government because of the very nature of the specific field.' Roosevelt no longer had the same hope of converting businessmen, but he still held the wistful belief that he might, perhaps by showing them he could balance his books, yet win their favor. If the atomizers like Brandeis had not won as much as appeared, the planners like Tugwell could claim still less. At no time had Roosevelt seriously considered the creation of a planned economy, and to represent the events of 1935 as the defeat of the planners is to confuse shadow with substance. A planned economy had never been in the cards. Of the President's close advisers, only Tugwell had collectivist ideas; he had little chance to express them, still less to carry them out, and in 1936 he gracefully resigned.

W. E. LEUCHTENBURG, *Franklin D. Roosevelt and the New Deal 1932–1940*, Harper and Row, New York, 1963; Torchbook edn, pp. 163–4

The Election

31. *Yet whatever else it was, there is little doubt that the Second New Deal was the first salvo in Roosevelt's campaign for re-election in 1936. Most importantly, an enemy of the people had been identified and Roosevelt could pose convincingly as the people's champion. The next fifteen months were an extended amplification of this theme. In his annual message to Congress on 3 January 1936, the President said this.*

Our resplendent economic autocracy does not want to return to that individualism of which they prate, even though the advantages under that system went to the ruthless and the strong. They realize that in thirty-four months we have built up new instruments of public power. In the hands of a people's Government this power is wholesome and proper. But in the hands of political puppets of an economic autocracy such power would provide shackles for the liberties of the people. Give them their way and they will take the course of every autocracy of the past—power for themselves, enslavement for the public.

The Public Papers and Addresses of Franklin D. Roosevelt, ed. S. Rosenman, Random House, New York, 1938 vol. v, p. 16

32. *In his speech accepting the renomination for the Democratic candidacy at Philadelphia on 27 June, he repeated his challenge, and looked to the future.*

The royalists of the economic order have conceded that political freedom was the business of the Government, but they have maintained that economic slavery was nobody's business. They granted that the Government could protect the citizen in his right to vote, but they denied that the Government could do anything to protect the citizen in his right to work and his right to live.

Today we stand committed to the proposition that freedom is no half-and-half affair. If the average citizen is guaranteed equal opportunity in the polling place, he must have equal opportunity in the market place.

These economic royalists complain that we seek to overthrow the institutions of America. What they really complain of is that we seek to take away their power. Our allegiance to American institutions requires the overthrow of this kind of power. . . .

. . . There is a mysterious cycle in human events. To some generations much is given. Of other generations much is expected. This generation of Americans has a rendezvous with destiny.

In this world of ours in other lands, there are some people, who, in times past, have lived and fought for freedom, and seem to have grown too weary to carry on the fight. They have sold their heritage of freedom for she illusion of a living. They have yielded their democracy.

I believe in my heart that only our success can stir their ancient hope. They begin to know that here in America we are waging a great and successful war. It is not alone a war against want and destitution and economic demoralization. It is more than that; it is a war for the survival of democracy. We are fighting to save a great and precious form of government for ourselves and for the world.

Ibid., vol. v, pp. 233, 235–6

33. *For Roosevelt, the battle of words reached its climax at Madison Square Garden, New York City, on 31 October.*

We have not come this far without a struggle and I assure you that we cannot go further without a struggle.

For twelve years this Nation was afflicted with hear-nothing, see-nothing, do-nothing Government. The Nation looked to Government but the Government looked away. Nine mocking years with the golden calf and three long years of the scourge! Nine crazy years at the ticker and three long years in the breadlines! Nine mad years of mirage and three long years of despair! Powerful influences strive today to restore that kind of government with its doctrine that that Government is best which is most indifferent. . . .

. . . We had to struggle with the old enemies of peace–business and financial monopoly, speculation, reckless banking, class antagonism, sectionalism, war profiteering.

They had begun to consider the Government of the United States as a mere appendage to their own affairs. We know now that Government by organized money is just as dangerous as Government by organized mob.

Never before in all our history have these forces been so united against one candidate as they stand today. They are unanimous in their hate for me–and I welcome their hatred.

I should like to have it said of my first Administration that in it the forces of selfishness and of lust for power met their match. I should like to have it said of my second Administration that in it these forces met their master.

Ibid., vol. v, pp. 568–9

34. *The rich returned the taunts with venom, as Marquis Childs reported.*

A resident of Park Avenue in New York City was sentenced not long ago to a term of imprisonment for threatening violence to the person of President Roosevelt. This episode, with the conclusions as to the man's probable sanity, was recorded at length on the front pages of the newspapers of the land. In itself it was unimportant. Cranks with wild ideas are always to be found here and there in any large community. Yet it was significant as a dramatically extreme manifestation of one of the most extraordinary phenomena of our day, a phenomenon which social historians in the future will very likely record with perplexity if not with astonishment: the fanatical hatred of the President which to-day obsesses thousands of men and women among the American upper class.

No other word than hatred will do. It is a passion, a fury, that is wholly unreasoning. Here is no mere political opposition, no mere violent disagreement over financial policies, no mere distrust of a national leader who to these men and women appears to be a demagogue. Opposition, disagreement, distrust, however strong are quite legitimate and defensible, whether or not one agrees that they are warranted. But the phenomenon to which I refer goes far beyond objection to policies or programs. It is a consuming personal hatred of President Roosevelt and, to an almost equal degree, of Mrs Roosevelt.

It permeates, in greater or less degree, the whole upper stratum of American society. It has become with many persons an *idée fixe*. One encounters it over and over again in clubs, even in purely social clubs, in locker and card rooms. At luncheon parties, over dinner tables, it is an incessant theme. And frequently in conversation it takes a violent and unlawful form, the expression of desires and wishes that can be explained only, it would seem, in terms of abnormal psychology.

In history this hatred may well go down as the major irony of our time. For the extraordinary fact is that whereas the fanatic who went to prison had lost his fortune and, therefore, had a direct grievance, the majority of those who rail against the President have to a large extent had their incomes restored and their bank balances replenished since the low point of March 1933.

'They Hate Roosevelt', *Harper's*, May 1936, p. 634

35. *After Roosevelt's victory, one of the spokesmen for this rabid opposition gave characteristic reasons for it.*

The President's victory was due to one thing and one thing only, to that one great rabbit–the spending rabbit–he had so reluctantly pulled out of his hat in 1933. This put into his hands a fund amounting to nearly 20 billion dollars with which he has been able to gratify the appetites of vast groups of people in every county in America–not merely the poor and disconsolate victims of the depression, but the long deferred ambitions of every town, county, city and state for expensive and even grandiose projects otherwise hopelessly out of their reach. It enabled him to engage in that succession of grandiose and reckless adventures which had the appearance of great daring and captivated the imagination of so many young men and women who understood little or nothing about the great laws of both nature and economics which he flouted. The meager campaign funds spent on Presidential elections in the past were so much chicken-feed compared with that stupendous barrel of billions which the President had to dispense twelve months a year. Of all those fictitious rabbits the President pulled out of his hat this was the one and only one which survived and was any good for the great job ahead. It became a snorting steed of incredible vigor. It had become a little wild. But it was this monstrous rabbit with Roosevelt on its back that carried him on that wild ride through the polling places of 46 states and shot him breathlessly back into the White House for another four years.

JOHN T. FLYNN, *The Roosevelt Myth*, rev. edn, Devin-Adair, New York, 1956, p. 93

36. *So 1936 had seen a devastating triumph for the New Deal. At this point mid-way between Roosevelt's first and second terms a British journal summed up its achievements and its prospects.*

If the criterion be Utopian, the achievements of the New Deal appear to be small. Relief there has been, but little more than enough to keep the population fed, clothed and warmed. Recovery there has also been, but only to a point still well below the pre-depression level. Reform there has also been, but it is slight in comparison with the reformers' blueprints. The great problems of the country are still hardly touched. There has been no permanent adjustment of agriculture to meet its changed environment. Very little has been done to iron out the fluctuations of industrial production for the future. The monetary structure of the country, on balance, is less under control than formerly. All these problems have barely been touched. Moreover, the great overriding political problem of how America is to construct a socially responsible and socially regulated economy with her present Constitution has been shirked. . . .

. . . If the New Deal be compared, not with the absolute standards of Utopia, but with the achievements of other Governments the former adverse judgment must be modified. If it be compared with either the performance or the promise of its rivals, it comes out well. If its achievements be compared with the situation which confronted it in March, 1933, it is a striking success. Mr Roosevelt may have given the wrong answers to many of his problems. But he is at least the first President of modern America who has asked the right questions.

The Economist, 3 October 1936, p. 7

V

The Supreme Court
Battle

*Roosevelt's first act after his reinauguration in January 1937 was to try con-
clusions with the Supreme Court. During 1935 and 1936 the Court had declared no less than four major items of Federal legislation unconstitutional,
including both the National Industrial Recovery Act and the Agricultural
Adjustment Act. By so using its powers of judicial review, Roosevelt argued,
the Court was threatening the entire basis of the New Deal and making it impossible for his government to carry through its programme. The President
had a point: the Court was undoubtedly being obstructive and four of the
nine Justices–Butler, McReynolds, Sutherland and Van Devanter–were
inflexible devotees of laissez-faire. But bringing the fight out into the open as
he did, was an irretrievable mistake. Instead of waiting for the Court to 'follow
the election returns', as it might well have done if left to itself, Roosevelt flung
down his challenge and alienated many even of his most enthusiastic supporters.
Politically the outcome was disastrous. The President was henceforth branded
as a would-be dictator, the unity of his party was destroyed, and a powerful
coalition of conservative Republicans and Democrats had been forged, determined to seize every opportunity to hamstring further New Deal measures in
Congress. The constitutional results were mixed; the attempted lunge for
additional presidential power was beaten off and the Court remained as it was,
but since 1937 social and economic legislation on New Deal lines has passed
the bench unscathed and this almost certainly represents a permanent retreat
on the part of the judiciary.*

Anti-New Deal

1. *The judicial opponents of the New Deal were men imbued with the principles of laissez-faire. Here is part of the dissenting opinion of Justices Butler,
McReynolds, Sutherland and Van Devanter in the case of Home Building*

and Loan Association v. *Blaisdell, heard in January 1934. In this case the right of the state of Minnesota to pass a law aiding householders unable to pay their mortgages was upheld by the Court. The four justices did not agree.*

The present exigency is nothing new. From the beginning of our existence as a nation, periods of depression, of industrial failure, of financial distress, of unpaid and unpayable indebtedness, have alternated with years of plenty. The vital lesson that expenditure beyond income begets poverty, that public or private extravagance, financed by promises to pay, either must end in complete or partial repudiation or the promises be fulfilled by self-denial and painful effort, though constantly taught by bitter experience, seems never to be learned; and the attempt by legislative devices to shift the misfortune of the debtor to the shoulders of the creditor without coming into conflict with the contract impairment clause has been persistent and oft-repeated.

R. H. JACKSON, *The Struggle for Judicial Supremacy*, Knopf, New York, 1941, p. 79

2. The New York State Bar Association was likewise convinced that interference by the government was subverting traditional values.

. . . There is nothing more unfortunate in governmental administration than a policy of playing fast and loose with great economic and political principles which have stood the strain of changing circumstance and the stress of time and have become part of our fundamental wisdom. . . . Conditions which such a principle governs may change–indeed, in this forward moving world of ours, they must change–but the principle itself is immutable; once righteous, it is always righteous. . . . There are certain fundamental social and economic laws which are beyond the power, and certain underlying governmental principles, which are beyond the right of official control, and any attempt to interfere with their operation inevitably ends in confusion, if not disaster.

E. S. CORWIN, *The Twilight of the Supreme Court*, Yale University Press, 1934, p. 213

3. The most spectacular blow against the New Deal was, of course, the invalidation of the National Industrial Recovery Act. These are extracts from Chief Justice Hughes's opinion, given on 27 May 1935.

... We are told that the provision of the statute authorizing the adoption of codes must be viewed in the light of the grave national crisis with which Congress was confronted. Undoubtedly, the conditions to which power is addressed are always to be considered when the exercise of power is challenged. Extraordinary conditions may call for extraordinary remedies. But the argument necessarily stops short of an attempt to justify action which lies outside the sphere of constitutional authority. Extraordinary conditions do not create or enlarge constitutional power. The Constitution established a national government with powers deemed adequate, as they have proved to be both in war and peace, but these powers of the national government are limited by the constitutional grants. Those who act under these grants are not at liberty to transcend the imposed limits because they believe that more or different power is necessary. Such assertions of extra-constitutional authority were anticipated and precluded by the explicit terms of the Tenth Amendment, – 'The powers not delegated to the United States by the constitution, nor prohibited by it to the States, are reserved to the States respectively, or to the people.'

... The power of Congress extends not only to the regulation of transactions which are part of interstate commerce, but to the protection of that commerce from injury.

... But where the effect of intrastate transactions upon interstate commerce is merely indirect, such transactions remain within the domain of state power. If the commerce clause were construed to reach all enterprises and transactions which could be said to have an indirect effect upon interstate commerce, the federal authority would embrace practically all the activities of the people and the authority of the State over its domestic concerns would exist only by sufferance of the federal government. ...

It is not the province of the Court to consider the economic advantages or disadvantages of such a centralized system. It is sufficient to say that the Federal Constitution does not provide for it ... the recuperative efforts of the federal government must be made in a manner consistent with the authority granted by the Constitution.

Documents of American History, ed. H. S. Commager, 7th edn, Appleton-Century-Crofts, New York, 1963, vol. ii, pp. 279–80, 282, 283

4. *The following year, on 6 January 1936, it was the turn of the AAA. This time sentence was pronounced by Justice Roberts.*

. . . There should be no misunderstanding as to the function of this court in such a case. It is sometimes said that the court assumes a power to overrule or control the action of the people's representatives. This is a misconception. The Constitution is the supreme law of the land ordained and established by the people. All legislation must conform to the principles it lays down. When an act of Congress is appropriately challenged in the courts as not conforming to the constitutional mandate the judicial branch of the government has only one duty,—to lay the article of the Constitution which is invoked beside the statute which is challenged and to decide whether the latter squares with the former. All the court does, or can do, is to announce its considered judgment upon the question. The only power it has, if such it may be called, is the power of judgment. This court neither approves nor condemns any legislative policy. Its delicate and difficult office is to ascertain and declare whether the legislation is in accordance with, or in contravention of, the provisions of the Constitution; and, having done that, its duty ends. . . .

Congress has no power to enforce its commands on the farmer to the ends sought by the Agricultural Adjustment Act. It must follow that it may not indirectly accomplish those ends by taxing and spending to purchase compliance. The Constitution and the entire plan of our government negative any such use of the power to tax and to spend as the act undertakes to authorize. It does not help to declare that local conditions have created a situation of national concern; for that is but to say that wherever there is a widespread similarity of local conditions, Congress may ignore constitutional limitations on its own powers and usurp those reserved to the states. If in lieu of compulsory regulation of subjects within the states' reserved jurisdiction, which is prohibited, the Congress could invoke the taxing and spending power as a means to accomplish the same end, clause 1 of Section 8 of Article I would become the instrument for total subversion of the governmental powers reserved to the individual states. . . .

. . . Until recently no suggestion of the existence of any such power in the federal government has been advanced. The expression of the framers of the Constitution, the decisions of this court interpreting that instrument and the writings of great commentators will be searched in vain for any suggestion that there exists in the clause under discussion or elsewhere in the Constitution, the authority whereby every provision and every fair implication from that instrument may be subverted, the independence of the individual states obliterated, and the United

States converted into a central government exercising uncontrolled police power in every state of the Union, superseding all local control or regulation of the affairs or concerns of the states.

Ibid., vol. ii, pp. 249, 251, 252

Pro-New Deal

5. *Several Justices on the Court—Brandeis, Stone and Cardozo consistently, Hughes and Roberts intermittently—believed that both the Federal administration and the state governments had a positive obligation to act to minimize the consequences of the depression. Here is part of the dissenting opinion of Brandeis in the case of New State Ice Company v. Liebmann, heard in 1932.*

. . . The people of the United States are now confronted with an emergency more serious than war. Misery is widespread, in a time, not of scarcity, but of overabundance. The long-continued depression has brought unprecedented unemployment, a catastrophic fall in commodity prices, and a volume of economic losses which threatens our financial institutions. . . . But rightly or wrongly, many persons think that one of the major contributing causes has been unbridled competition. Increasingly, doubt is expressed whether it is economically wise, or morally right, that men should be permitted to add to the producing facilities of an industry which is already suffering from overcapacity. . . . Many insist there must be some form of economic control. There are plans for pro-ration. There are many proposals for stabilization.

Some people assert that our present plight is due, in part, to the limitations set by courts upon experimentation in the fields of social and economic science; and to the discouragement to which proposals for betterment there have been subjected otherwise. There must be power in the states and the nation to remould, through experimentation, our economic practices and institutions to meet changing social and economic needs. I cannot believe that the framers of the Fourteenth Amendment, or the states which ratified it, intended to deprive us of the power to correct the evils of technological unemployment and excess productive capacity which have attended progress in the useful arts.

To stay experimentation in things social and economic is a grave responsibility. Denial of the right to experiment may be fraught with serious consequences to the nation. It is one of the happy incidents of the federal system that a single courageous state may, if its citizens choose, serve as a laboratory, and try novel social and economic experiments without risk to the rest of the country. This Court has the power to prevent an experiment. We may strike down the statute which embodies it on the ground that, in our opinion, the measure is arbitrary, capricious or unreasonable. We have power to do this, because the due process clause has been held by the Court applicable to matters of substantive law as well as to matters of procedure. But, in the exercise of this high power, we must be ever on our guard, lest we erect our prejudices into legal principles. If we would guide by the light of reason, we must let our minds be bold.

Ibid., vol. ii, pp. 231–2

6. *Justice Roberts could be interventionist on occasion. Here is part of his opinion upholding the right of New York State to fix the price of milk.*

Under our form of government the use of property and the making of contracts are normally matters of private and not of public concern. The general rule is that both shall be free of governmental interference. But neither property rights nor contract rights are absolute; for government cannot exist if the citizen may at will use his property to the detriment of his fellows, or exercise his freedom of contract to work them harm. Equally fundamental with the private right is that of the public to regulate it in the common interest.

The Fifth Amendment, in the field of federal activity, and the Fourteenth, as respects state action, do not prohibit governmental regulation for the public welfare. They merely condition the exertion of the admitted power, by securing that the end shall be accomplished by methods consistent with due process. And the guaranty of due process, as has often been held, demands only that the law shall not be unreasonable, arbitrary or capricious, and that the means selected shall have a real and substantial relation to the object sought to be attained. . . .

. . . So far as the requirement of due process is concerned, and in the absence of other constitutional restriction, a state is free to adopt whatever economic policy may reasonably be deemed to promote public welfare, and to enforce that policy by legislation adapted to its purpose. . . . With the wisdom of the policy adopted, with the adequacy or practicability of the law enacted to forward it, the courts are both incompetent and unauthorized to deal. . . .

. . . If the law-making body within its sphere of government concludes that the conditions or practices in an industry make unrestricted competition an inadequate safeguard of the consumer's interests, produce waste harmful to the public, threaten ultimately to cut off the supply of a commodity needed by the public, or portend the destruction of the industry itself, appropriate statutes passed in an honest effort to correct the threatened consequences may not be set aside because the regulation adopted prices reasonably deemed by the legislature to be fair to those engaged in the industry and to the consuming public. And this is especially so where, as here, the economic maladjustment is one of price, which threatens harm to the producer at one end of the series and the consumer at the other. The Constitution does not secure to anyone liberty to conduct his business in such fashion as to inflict injury upon the public at large, or upon any substantial group of the people.

Ibid., vol. ii, pp. 299–300, 301

7. *In his opinion on the AAA case, Justice Roberts appeared to have contradicted this view, as Justice Stone pointed out by his dissent.*

. . . It is a contradiction in terms to say that there is power to spend for the national welfare, while rejecting any power to impose conditions reasonably adapted to the attainment of the end which alone would justify the expenditure. . . .

. . . If appropriation in aid of a program of curtailment of agricultural production is constitutional, and it is not denied that it is, payment to farmers on condition that they reduce their crop acreage is constitutional. It is not any the less so because the farmer at his own option promises to fulfill the condition.

. . . A tortured construction of the Constitution is not to be justified by recourse to extreme examples of congressional spending which might occur if courts could not prevent expenditures which, even if they could be thought to effect any national purpose, would be possible only by action of a legislature lost to any sense of public responsibility. Such suppositions are addressed to the mind accustomed to believe that it is the business of the courts to sit in judgment on the wisdom of legislative action. Courts are not the only agency of government that must be assumed to have the capacity to govern. Congress and the courts both unhappily may falter or be mistaken in the performance of their constitutional duty. But interpretation of our great charter of government which proceeds on any assumption that the responsibility for the preservation of our institutions is the exclusive concern of any one of the three branches of government, or that it alone can save them from destruction is far more likely, in the long run, 'to obliterate the constituent members' of 'an indestructible union of indestructible states' than the frank recognition that language, even of a constitution, may mean what it says: that the power to tax and to spend includes the power to relieve a nationwide maladjustment by conditional gifts of money.

Ibid., vol. ii, pp. 253, 254–5

8. *Soon after Roosevelt introduced his bill for the reorganization of the judiciary, the Chief Justice reversed his previous narrow interpretation of the powers of the Federal government. Here is an extract from his opinion upholding the National Labour Relations Act on 12 April 1937.*

. . . we are not at liberty to deny effect to specific provisions, which Congress has constitutional power to enact, by superimposing upon them inferences from general legislative declarations of an ambiguous character, even if found in the same statute. The cardinal principle of statutory construction is to save and not to destroy. We have repeatedly held that as between two possible interpretations of a statute, by one of which it would be unconstitutional and by the other valid, our plain duty is to adopt that which will save the act. . . .

When industries organize themselves on a national scale, making their relation to interstate commerce the dominant factor in their activities, how can it be maintained that their industrial labor relations constitute a forbidden field into which Congress may not enter when it is necessary to protect interstate commerce from the paralyzing consequences of industrial war? We have often said that interstate commerce itself is a practical conception. It is equally true that interferences with that commerce must be appraised by a judgment that does not ignore actual experience.

Experience has abundantly demonstrated that the recognition of the right of employees to self-organization and to have representatives of their own choosing for the purpose of collective bargaining is often an essential condition of industrial peace. Refusal to confer and negotiate has been one of the most prolific causes of strife. . . .

. . . It is not necessary again to detail the facts as to respondent's enterprise. Instead of being beyond the pale, we think that it presents in a most striking way the close and intimate relation which a manufacturing industry may have to interstate commerce and we have no doubt that Congress had constitutional authority to safeguard the right of respondent's employees to self-organization and freedom in the choice of representatives for collective bargaining.

Ibid., vol. ii, pp. 320, 322–3

9. *Six weeks later the Court went on to support the Social Security Act. After nearly fifty years it had finally turned its back on laissez-faire. This is part of Justice Cardozo's opinion.*

. . . The purge of nation-wide calamity that began in 1929 has taught us many lessons. Not the least is the solidarity of interests that may once have seemed to be divided. Unemployment spreads from state to state, the hinterland now settled that in pioneer days gave an avenue of escape. Spreading from state to state, unemployment is an ill not particular but general, which may be checked, if Congress so determines, by the resources of the nation. . . .

. . . The problem is plainly national in area and dimensions. Moreover, laws of the separate states cannot deal with it effectively. Congress, at least, had a basis for that belief. States and local governments are often lacking in the resources that are necessary to finance an adequate program of security for the aged. This is brought out in a wealth of studies of the problem. Apart from the failure of resources, states and local governments are at times reluctant to increase so heavily the burden of taxation to be borne by their residents for fear of placing themselves in a position of economic disadvantage as compared with neighbors or competitors. . . . Only a power that is national can serve the interests of all.

Whether wisdom or unwisdom resides in the scheme of benefits set forth in Title II, it is not for us to say. The answer to such inquiries must come from Congress, not the courts. Our concern here as often is with power, not with wisdom. Counsel for respondent has recalled to us the virtues of self-reliance and frugality. There is a possibility, he says, that aid from a paternal government may sap those sturdy virtues and breed a race of weaklings. If Massachusetts so believes and shapes her laws in that conviction, must her breed of sons be changed, he asks, because some other philosophy of government finds favor in the halls of Congress? But the answer is not doubtful. One might ask with equal reason whether the system of protective tariffs is to be set aside at will in one state or another whenever local policy prefers the rule of *laissez-faire*. The issue is a closed one. It was fought out long ago. When money is spent to promote the general welfare, the concept of welfare is shaped by Congress, not the states. So the concept be not arbitrary, the locality must yield.

Ibid., vol. ii, pp. 339, 340–1

The Presidential Reaction

10. *Roosevelt's first public reaction to the inroads the Court was making on the New Deal came after the NRA decision at a press conference on 31 May 1935. Compare this with his remarks to Perkins [IV, 19].*

. . . The whole tendency over these years has been to view the interstate commerce clause in the light of present-day civilization. The country was in the horse-and-buggy age when that clause was written . . . the whole picture was a different one when the interstate commerce clause was put into the Constitution from what it is now. . . . We are interdependent—we are tied in together. And the hope has been that we could, through a period of years, interpret the interstate commerce clause of the Constitution in the light of these new things that have come to the country. . . .

. . . the issue is this: Is the United States going to decide, are the people of this country going to decide that their Federal Government shall in the future have no right under any implied power or any court-approved power to enter into the solution of the national economic problem, but that the national economic crisis must be decided only by the states?

The other part of it is this: Shall we view our social problems—and in that I include employment of all kinds—shall we view them from the same point of view or not; that the Federal Government has no right under this or following opinions to take any part in trying to better national social conditions? . . .

. . . Can it be done by voluntary action on the part of business? Can we go ahead as a Nation with the beautiful theory, let us say, of some of the press: 'At last the rule of Christ is restored. Business can do anything it wants and business is going to live up to the golden rule so marvelously that all our troubles are ended.' It is a school of thought that is so delightful in its naïveté.

And so we are facing a very, very great non-partisan issue. We have got to decide one way or the other. . . . Don't call it left or right. . . . It is not left or right. We are the only Nation in the world that has not solved that problem. We thought we were doing it and now it has been thrown straight in our faces. We have been relegated to the horse-and-buggy definition of the interstate commerce clause.

The Public Papers and Addresses of Franklin D. Roosevelt, ed. S. Rosenman, Random House, New York, 1938, vol. iv, pp. 209–21

11. *After the AAA decision the Secretary of the Interior, Harold Ickes, wrote this in his diary after a cabinet meeting.*

The President made the point, based upon some statement by Harold J. Laski, that the Supreme Court in its decisions on New Deal legislation, was dictating what it believed should be the social philosophy of the nation. Miss Perkins is fearful that the general run of citizens will be against the Administration on this issue and that they will feel that the New Deal has proved a failure, as the result of the opinions of the Supreme Court on New Deal legislation. It is plain to see from what the President said today and has said on other occasions, that he is not at all averse to the Supreme Court declaring one New Deal statute after another unconstitutional. I think he believes that the Court will find itself pretty far out on a limb before it is through with it and that a real issue will be joined on which we can go to the country.

For my part, I hope so. Here is an issue that must be faced by the country sooner or later, unless we are prepared to submit to the arbitrary and final dictates of a group of men who are not elected by the people and who are not responsible to the people; in short, a judicial tyranny imposed by men appointed for life and who cannot be reached except by the slow and cumbersome process of impeachment.

The Secret Diary of Harold L. Ickes, Weidenfeld and Nicolson, London, 1955, vol. i, p. 524

12. *Roosevelt waited until after the 1936 election before unfolding his plan, on 5 February 1937. By the terms of the plan the President could turn the*

flank of the Court by appointing up to six more Justices, one for each Justice
who failed to retire within six months of reaching the age of seventy. He de-
clared his aims in a radio broadcast on 9 March.

. . . The American people have learned from the depression. For in the
last three national elections an overwhelming majority of them voted a
mandate that the Congress and the President begin the task of providing
. . . protection–not after long years of debate, but now.

. . . The Courts . . . have cast doubts on the ability of the elected
Congress to protect us against catastrophe by meeting squarely our
modern social and economic conditions. . . .

We are at a crisis in our ability to proceed with that protection. It
is a quiet crisis. There are no lines of depositors outside closed
banks. But to the far-sighted it is far-reaching in its possibilities of
injury to America. . . . In the last four years the sound rule of giving
statutes the benefit of all reasonable doubt has been cast aside. The
Court has been acting not as a judicial body, but as a policy-making
body. . . .

. . . We must have men worthy and equipped to carry out impartial
justice. But, at the same time, we must have Judges who will bring to
the Courts the judicial functions of a court, and reject the legislative
powers which the courts have today assumed. . . .

. . . This plan of mine is no attack on the Court; it seeks to restore
the Court to its rightful and historic place in our system of Constitutional Government and to have it resume its high task of building anew
on the Constitution 'a system of living law'. The Court itself can best
undo what the Court has done.

. . . This proposal of mine will not infringe in the slightest upon the
civil or religious liberties so dear to every American. . . . The present
attempt by those opposed to progress to play upon the fears of danger
to personal liberty brings to mind that crude and cruel strategy tried
by the same opposition to frighten the workers of America in a pay-
envelope progaganda against the Social Security Law. The workers
were not fooled by that propaganda then. The people of America will
not be fooled by such propaganda now. . . .

. . . During the past half century the balance of power between the
three great branches of the Federal Government has been tipped out
of balance by the Courts in direct contradiction of the high purposes of
the framers of the Constitution. It is my purpose to restore that balance.
You who know me will accept my solemn assurance that in a world in

which democracy is under attack, I seek to make American democracy succeed. You and I will do our part.

The Public Papers and Addresses of Franklin D. Roosevelt, ed. S. Rosenman, Macmillan, New York, 1941, vol. vi, pp. 123–33

The Debate

13. *In the days of Hoover Walter Lippmann had written this.*

The awful paradox of our time, that there should be want in the midst of abundance, is self-evident proof that the prevailing political and economic arrangements and policies and methods of administering affairs are deeply and seriously at fault. A period of great changes is not merely indicated. It is certain.

In such a period it is crucial whether or not change is continuous with the past, whether there is a sudden break with established wisdom or the use of that wisdom to season new enterprise. Of all the Western peoples the English-speaking have been the most successful in finding ways to preserve and yet to change. Their secret is their sense of the law, which in their great periods they have looked upon not as an iron frame, but as a garment which can be cut and altered so that it always covers them and yet allows them to move freely.

It is the business of the Court in our political system to oversee this cutting and alteration of the garment that it may always fit comfortably a nd endure.

Interpretations 1931–1932, Macmillan, New York, 1932, p. 323

14. *This was essentially what Roosevelt's supporters believed the Court should do. What it did in fact, they argued, was something quite different.*

. . . Today the stronghold of conservatism and wealth lies in the industrial North and East. That area has profited by a high protective tariff as the South once prospered through the protection of slavery.

And today the Supreme Court has become the protector of the industrial overlords. Its staunchest supporters are the Du Ponts, the Morgans, the Mellons, the Rockefellers, Alfred E. Smith, John W. Davis, Herbert Hoover, the United States Chamber of Commerce, the

National Manufacturers' Association, all representatives of an industrial oligarchy, all laboring to deify the judiciary, the doctrine of judicial autocracy; all striving to block legislation to redistribute the wealth of the nation, to remedy the forces which catapulted the country into the last depression.

DREW PEARSON and ROBERT S. ALLEN, *The Nine Old Men*, Doubleday, New York, 1937, pp. 72–3

15. *Robert Jackson, later Roosevelt's Attorney-General, and a zealous Brandeisian, wrote this.*

. . . by 1933, by the efficacy of its words, the Court had not only established its ascendancy over the entire government as a source of constitutional doctrine, but it had also taken control of a large and rapidly expanding sphere of policy. It sat almost as a continuous constitutional convention which, without submitting its proposals to any ratification or rejection, could amend the basic law. And it had used that supremacy to cripple departments of government and to disable the nation from adopting social or economic policies which were deemed inconsistent with the Justices' philosophy of property rights.

. . . The peculiar character of judicial tenure had enabled a past that was dead and repudiated in the intellectual and political world to keep a firm grip on the judicial world. What we demanded for our generation was the right consciously to influence the evolutionary process of constitutional law, as other generations had done.

The Struggle for Judicial Supremacy, Knopf, New York, 1941, pp. x, xiv

16. *Max Lerner provided the New Dealers' arguments with a Marxist gloss.*

From Coke to Marshall, Story, and Chancellor Kent, to Cooley on 'Constitutional Limitations', to the New Deal cases, is a series of legal steps, but the continuity in them is the appeal to a higher law in the interests of the mercantile and industrial class. There is one paradox worth noting: in England, Coke's doctrine has been maintained only so far as it called for a legal check upon the monarch, but not so far as it applied to a legal check upon the Parliament; in America the check was placed on both the executive and the legislature. From having such a check it was only a step to identify it with the Constitution, and from that point only another step to identify it with the guardians and interpreters of the Constitution, and thus to establish judicial supremacy. The paradox, however, resolves itself when ideas are referred back to the interests they serve. It was no accident that the idea of the rule of law was among the reigning forces at our nativity as a nation. It is historically, as well as psychologically, linked with the development and power of the middle class in the Western world. It is part of the body of liberal doctrine that the middle class forged in the centuries during which it was clearing its way to power, and that the same class used as a rationalization and as an instrument for achieving power. Just as it was useful originally to the rising capitalist class in removing the obstruction of monarchical and aristocratic interference, so it is useful now to the entrenched capitalist class in fighting off the threat of democratic and labor groups.

Ideas for the Ice Age, Viking Press, New York, 1941, p. 253

17. *At the Senate Judiciary Committee's hearings on the Roosevelt bill, Professor E. S. Corwin put the case for the administration.*

I think the realities of the situation are these: In the first place, the doctrines of constitutional law of the majority of the Court involve the entire program of the administration in a fog of doubt as to constitutionality; and second, that cloud or doubt can be dispelled within a reasonable time only by reestablishing that mode of reading the Constitution which adapts it to present needs in harmony with its intent as announced by its earliest expounders, that it should 'endure for ages to come, and consequently be adapted to various crises in human affairs.' Those are the words of Chief Justice Marshall. And also in harmony with the idea that the Constitution was intended for an 'indefinite and expanding future'.

The controlling majority of the Court has turned its back upon this point of view. Also it has forgotten the principal maxim to which the Court adhered for nearly 100 years, that all reasonable doubts are to be resolved in favor of challenged legislation. . . . It has repeatedly, when it had a free choice, chosen the alternative which set it against the other branches of the Government. And why? There is only one explanation that fits the situation. It has been endeavoring to elevate into constitutional law a particular bias of its own; the theory of political economy that government must keep its hands off of business and, particularly, must not interfere with the relations of employer and employee. The latter, it would have us believe, was placed by the Constitution beyond the reach of Government in this country, either State or National.

United States. Senate. Committee on the Judiciary, *Hearings on the Reorganization of the Federal Judiciary*, United States Government Printing Office, Washington, D.C., 1937, pp. 167–8

18. *The opponents of the plan founded their case on the ideal of the rule of law, and their appeal to patriotism and tradition found a wide response at a time when totalitarianism still appeared to be gaining ground throughout the world. Lippmann expressed their faith in the higher authority of law in a piece written soon after the invalidation of the NIRA.*

. . . The authority of the Court is one of the most extraordinary things in the history of government. Here are nine men who, without physical power of any kind, can, under certain conditions, override the will of Congress and the President. Their verdicts are obeyed absolutely. On what does the power of the Court rest? It rests on the conviction of the people that the Court interprets the disinterested and considered and permanent judgement of the people as against the momentary, impulsive, expedient, and short-sighted opinions of temporary majorities. In the annals of democracy the Court stands forth as a unique institution. For the first time in the history of popular government the people themselves have imposed upon themselves conditions of comprehensive restraint to which they willingly submit. This is a very great thing. The Court represents the people's own moral conviction that they must not act hastily or arbitrarily, that the voice of reason must in the end prevail over the prompting of appetite and of impulse.

Interpretations 1933–1935, Macmillan, New York, 1936, p. 278

19. *Hoover was not slow to take up the challenge, in a speech of 20 February.*

. . . no one can conclude other than that the President seeks not to secure a Supreme Court that will find in accordance with the Constitution as it stands. He wants one that will revise the Constitution so that it will mean what he wishes it to mean. . . .

. . . If a troop of 'President's judges' can be sent into the halls of justice to capture political power, then his successor with the same device can also send a troop of new 'President's judges' to capture some other power. That is not judicial process. That is force.

The Court and the Constitution thus become the tool of the Executive and not the sword of the people. . . .

In all the centuries of struggle for human freedom the independence of the judiciary from political domination has been the first battle against autocratic power.

In America we have builded over these two centuries certain sacred rights which are the very fibers of human freedom. . . . Upon them depends security from individual oppression. . . .

But these securities and these rights are no stronger than their safeguards. And of these safeguards none is so final and so imperative as the independence of the courts. It is here alone where the humblest citizen and the weakest minority have their only sanctuary. . . .

Self-government never dies from direct attack. No matter what his real intentions may be, no man will arise and say that he intends to suspend one atom of the rights guaranteed by the Constitution. Liberty dies from the encroachments and disregard of the safeguards of those rights. . . .

. . . Liberty is crumbling over two-thirds of the world. In less than a score of years the courts in a dozen nations have been made subjective to political power, and with this subjection the people's securities in those countries have gone out of the window. And, mark you this—in every instance the persuaders have professed to be acting for the people and in the name of progress. As we watch the parade of nations down that suicide road every American has cause to be anxious for our republic.

. . . We have already gone far on the road of personal government. The American people must halt when it is proposed to lay hands on the independence of the Supreme Court. That is the ultimate security of every cottage. It is the last safeguard of free men.

The Memoirs of Herbert Hoover. The Great Depression 1929–1941, Hollis and Carter, London, 1953, pp. 374–5

20. *Moley, by now completely estranged from Roosevelt, also appeared before the Senate Judiciary Committee.*

. . . What, after all, is the distinguishing feature of a democratic government? Is it not the objectives of such a government alone? Justice for all in economic life, a fair division of the good things of life, education, health, better housing and security – these were the objectives in the German Empire of Bismarck. They are the objectives in nearly all of the western world today. But it is the glory of the democracies of the world that the means to these ends involve that spiritual education of citizens gained only when the citizens participate in the attainment of those ends. It is the glory of democracies that they educate the citizen in the practice of self-government while they protect his political, religious and economic freedom.

Democracy continues to exist only insofar as objectives are attained in terms of its own institutions. We cannot hold democracy as a basic ideal and ignore the method of democracy in the attainment of that ideal. There may be coercion of a minority by a majority in a democracy, but that coercion must always be exercised within the terms of our own institutions, safeguarded, as they are by the Constitution and its custom. The majority does rule; but it rules in terms of a covenant deliberately adopted and scrupulously maintained. Government by the consent of the people means not the unrestrained exercise of the will of the majority; it means that the agents of the people act only in the light of public consent secured by customary means.

And this does not imply that such consent may be secured by inference, as from the last election, say. As the Federalist points out:

Until the people have, by some solemn and authoritative act, annulled or changed the established form, it is binding upon themselves collectively as well as individually; and no presumption, or even knowledge, of their sentiments can warrant their representatives in a departure from it.

This fundamental stricture of democratic government applies not only to infractions of the Constitution, but to impairment of the established tradition of an independent judiciary.

United States. Senate. Committee on the Judiciary, *Hearings on the Reorganization of the Federal Judiciary*, United States Government Printing Office, Washington, D.C., 1937, pp. 546–7

21. *On 14 June the Committee presented its hostile report on the bill. Roosevelt had suffered a humiliating defeat.*

. . . We recommend the rejection of this bill as a needless, futile and utterly dangerous abandonment of constitutional principle.

It was presented to Congress in a most intricate form and for reasons that obscured its real purpose.

It would not banish age from the bench nor abolish divided decisions.

It would not affect the power of any court to hold laws unconstitutional nor withdraw from any judge the authority to issue injunctions.

It would not reduce the expense of litigation nor speed the decision of cases.

It is a proposal without precedent and without justification.

It would subjugate the courts to the will of Congress and the President and thereby destroy the independence of the judiciary, the only certain shield of individual rights.

It contains the germ of a system of centralized administration of law that would enable an executive so minded to send his judges into every judicial district in the land to sit in judgment on controversies between the Government and the citizen.

It points the way to the evasion of the Constitution and establishes the method whereby the people may be deprived of their right to pass upon all amendments of the fundamental law.

It stands now before the country, acknowledged by its proponents as a plan to force judicial interpretation of the Constitution, a proposal that violates every sacred tradition of American democracy.

Under the form of the Constitution it seeks to do that which is unconstitutional.

Its ultimate operation would be to make this Government one of men rather than one of law, and its practical operation would be to make the Constitution what the executive or legislative branches of the Government choose to say it is—an interpretation to be changed with each change of administration.

It is a measure which should be so emphatically rejected that its parallel will never again be presented to the free representatives of the free people of America.

Documents of American History, ed. H. S. Commager, 7th edn, Appleton-Century-Crofts, New York, 1963, p. 391

VI

The Emergence of Labour

When the depression hit the United States, the American trade unions were in an extremely weak position. For one thing, their development was severely hampered by the privileged legal status of their employers the business corporations, the rights of which were invariably supported in the courts by an ingenious construction of the fourteenth amendment to the Constitution (originally framed to guarantee the civil rights of Negro freedmen). But faults also lay in the union leadership which represented the skilled craftsmen of the country in the American Federation of Labour (AFL) and virtually ignored the interests of the great mass of unskilled industrial workers. The situation was changed first by the action of the Roosevelt government, then by a revolution within unionism itself. The celebrated Section 7(a) of the National Industrial Recovery Act of 1933 and then, more decisively, the National Labour Relations Act of 1935 paved the way for an upsurge and helped to make possible what followed. Late in 1935 the industrial unionists broke away from the AFL to form their own grouping the Committee for Industrial Organization (CIO), which led a wave of unionization in the hitherto impregnable steel and automobile industries in 1937. So emerged a new political constituency in America, and one more or less totally committed to Roosevelt and the Democratic party.

Growth

1. *In the very worst areas of industrial America, employees were literally wage slaves. Here is the letter of a miner from the notorious Harlan County, Kentucky, where depression conditions were cruelly aggravated by the hopeless bargaining position of the workers.*

We are half fed because we can't feed ourselves and family's with what we make. And we can't go to a Cut rate Store and buy food because most all the company forbids such tradeing. If you got the cash. But now we have no cash. And the companies keeps their food stuffs at high prices at all time. So you can not clear enough to go anywhere. And if you do go some where and buy food you are subjects to be canned. . . .

We have been eating wild green . . . such as Polk salad. Violet tops, wild onions. forget me not wild lettuce and such weeds as cows eat as a cow wont eat a poison weeds. . . . Our family are in bad shake child-rens need milk women need nourishments food shoes and dresses—that we cannot get. and there at least 10,000 hungry people in Harlan County daily. I know because I am one off them. . . . I would leave Harlan County if I had only $6 to send my wife and boy to Bristol, Va. and I could walk away—But I can't clear a dollar per month that why I am here. that why hundreds are here.

Nation, 8 June 1932 (quoted in I. BERNSTEIN, *The Lean Years*, Hough-ton Mifflin, Boston, 1960, p. 377)

2. *The Roosevelt administration's first response to the situation of the unions was the reluctant, last-minute insertion into the National Industrial Recovery Act of June 1933 of the famous Section 7(a), which read as follows.*

Every code of fair competition, agreement, and license approved, pre-scribed or issued under this title shall contain the following conditions: (1) That employees shall have the right to organize and bargain col-lectively through representatives of their own choosing, and shall be free from the interference, restraint, or coercion of employers of labor, or their agents, in the designation of such representatives or in self-organization or in other concerted activities for the purpose of collec-tive bargaining or other mutual aid and protection; (2) that no em-ployee and no one seeking employment shall be required as a condition of employment to join any company union or to refrain from joining, organizing, or assisting a labor organization of his own choosing; and (3) that employers shall comply with the maximum hours of labor, minimum rates of pay, and other conditions of employment, approved or prescribed by the President.

Documents of American History, ed. H. S. Commager, 7th edn, Appleton-Century-Crofts, New York, 1963, vol. ii, p. 273

3. *Unfortunately for the unions, the head of the NRA, General Johnson, and his entourage, were much too kindly disposed to the employers and soon the workers were describing the NRA as 'the national run-around'.*

The position of organized labor is more uncertain and stands in greater jeopardy than at any time since the Recovery Act became law. Labor may be forced to accept compulsory arbitration within the NRA code machinery. Compulsory arbitration means the abrogation of the right to strike for any purpose. . . . How could it come to pass that a policy admittedly favorable to labor and the rights of collective bargaining could result in leaving those rights without effective safeguards? The trouble is, of course, that the Administration has had no firm labor policy. It has vacillated constantly and has abandoned one principle after another. . . . Early in his term of office, President Roosevelt declared that 'there should be no discord or dispute–the workers of this country have rights under this law–no aggression is now necessary to obtain those rights.' It is now clear not only that strikes are frequently necessary if labor is to gain its rights, but that the government cannot be expected to bargain for labor. . . . The indecision has already given reactionary industrialists too much support. They, too, want labor disputes brought under the jurisdiction of the NRA code machinery. Undoubtedly this will be the beginning of a concerted assault on organized labor unless the administration immediately asserts itself and backs up the rights of collective bargaining promised labor.

New Republic, 9 May 1934, pp. 351–2

4. *Part of the trouble was in Roosevelt's own attitude, in the opinion of Frances Perkins.*

There were many things about trade unions that Roosevelt never fully understood. I doubt that he understood what solidarity really means in the trade union movement. He tended to think of trade unions as voluntary associations of citizens to promote their own interests in the field of wages, hours, and working conditions. He did not altogether grasp that sense of their being a solid bloc of people united to one another by unbreakable bonds which gave them power and status to deal with their employers on equal terms.

The Roosevelt I Knew, Hammond, London, 1947, p. 263

5. *To change this situation Senator Wagner of New York, in 1934 and again in 1935, introduced a bill providing for a new Federal agency, the National Labour Relations Board, with powers to compel employers to accept unions*

which were not of their own choosing. Even as conservative a unionist as William Green, head of the American Federation of Labour, was for it.

I do not mind telling you that the spirit of the workers in America has been aroused. They are going to find a way to bargain collectively. The day of individualism is past, and they are tired of it, because they have been exploited. If they are denied the right to bargain collectively in an orderly way and through orderly processes, they are going to use their economic strength, and the American Federation of Labor will encourage them to use it, support them in using it. . . . The establishment of labor in our whole economic and political system in a place where it belongs must be recognized. Labor must have its place in the sun.

United States. House of Representatives. Committee on Labor, *Hearings on the National Labor Relations Bill*, United States Government Printing Office, Washington, D.C., 1935, vol. v, p. 203

6. Shortly before the demise of the NRA a resolution of a conference of unionists made their feelings clear.

The right of Labor to organization, to majority representation, and to collective action and collective bargaining, can no longer be dependent upon the provisions of any code of fair competition. Our experience during the last two years has made it imperative that Labor's right to organize, to apply the principle of majority representation, to collective action and collective bargaining, must be definitely declared by Congress instead of being left as it has been to the constructions, interpretations, and evasions which we have experienced under the administration of NRA.

Resolution adopted by a conference of representatives of national and international, state and city central bodies, 29 April 1935 (quoted in P. TAFT, *The A.F. of L. from the Death of Gompers to the Merger*, Harper, New York, 1959 p. 126)

7. The employers naturally felt differently and they protested by telegram to the President. The Wagner bill, they believed, was

. . . unfair to both worker and employer. It takes from the worker certain essential rights [of which] he is now assured. It is bound to increase industrial strife. . . . It will put into the hands of agitators a new weapon with which to coerce men into joining outside labor unions. It will encourage coercive methods on the part of labor. It condemns coercive action by employers, but says nothing about coercion of employees by labor organizations. Gives immunity to organized labor. It gives labor a monopoly of labor representation in all American industry. Rights of minority groups would be practically destroyed.

Part of a telegram from the National Automobile Chamber of Commerce, 7 July 1934 (quoted in *ibid.*, p. 124)

8. *On 21 March 1935, Walter Lippmann put the business point of view.*

. . . Where labor is in fact well organized, bargaining takes place, not because the law compels it, but because the unions are strong. But when the unions are weak or virtually non-existent, it is the employers who determine what kind of collective bargaining, if any, there is to be, and government compulsion cannot create a different situation. The government cannot with any power it possesses or could conceivably obtain under the Constitution produce by fiat a collective bargain between employers and labor unions that do not exist. The attempt to enforce simultaneously the right to organize and collective bargaining was absurd. It is only when organization has taken place that collective bargaining is possible. And when organization has taken place, it is not necessary to make bargaining compulsory.

Interpretations 1933–1935, Macmillan, New York, 1936, p. 146

9. *During their investigation of 'Middletown', Robert and Helen Lynd found considerable evidence of anti-union sentiment as business revived.*

. . . Middletown businessmen are coming out of the depression with their asset of being an 'open-shop town' nailed to the city's masthead – and they mean to keep it there. At the great public welcoming dinner to General Motors at the Chamber of Commerce in June, 1935, the mayor stated that 'Our people are in no mood for outsiders to come into [Middletown] to agitate,' and he assured the company that such agitators would not be tolerated. A leading businessman remarked to a member of the research staff in a tone of quiet determination: 'We're not going to have any labor trouble here. We're not going to let it happen. Our mayor was pretty radical back years ago in his first term, but he is more co-operative now. During the Toledo automobile strike this spring the mayor had policemen stationed on roads leading into town, and they'd stop cars, look men over, and those that didn't look desirable they'd tell to keep right on going through town and not stop.'

Middletown in Transition, Constable, London, 1937, pp. 36–7

10. *After well over a year of evasion, Roosevelt adopted the Wagner proposals and the signing of the National Labour Relations Act on 5 July 1935 marked a turning point in American labour history. Its most important provisions read as follows.*

Sec. 7. Employees shall have the right of self-organization, to form, join, or assist labor organizations, to bargain collectively through representatives of their own choosing, and to engage in concerted activities, for the purpose of collective bargaining or other mutual aid or protection.

Sec. 8. It shall be an unfair labor practice for an employer–

(1) To interfere with, restrain, or coerce employees in the exercise of the rights guaranteed in section 7.

(2) To dominate or interfere with the formation or administration of any labor organization or contribute financial or other support to it: *Provided*, That subject to rules and regulations made and published by the Board pursuant to section 6(a), an employer shall not be prohibited from permitting employees to confer with him during working hours without loss of time or pay.

(3) By discrimination in regard to hire or tenure of employment or any term or condition of employment to encourage or discourage membership in any labor organization: *Provided*, That nothing in this Act or in the National Industrial Recovery Act (U.S.C., Supp. VII, title 15, secs. 701–712), as amended from time to time, or in any code or agreement approved or prescribed thereunder, or in any other statute of the United States, shall preclude an employer from making an agreement with a labor organization (not established, maintained, or assisted by any action defined in this Act as an unfair labor practice) to require as a condition of employment membership therein, if such labor organization is the representative of the employees as provided in section 9(a), in the appropriate collective bargaining unit covered by such agreement when made.

(4) To discharge or otherwise discriminate against an employee because he has filed charges or given testimony under this Act.

(5) To refuse to bargain collectively with the representatives of his employees, subject to the provisions of section 9(a).

Sec. 9. (a) Representatives designated or selected for the purposes of collective bargaining by the majority of the employees in a unit appropriate for such purposes, shall be the exclusive representatives of all the employees in such unit for the purposes of collective bargaining in respect to rates of pay, wages, hours of employment, or other conditions of employment: *Provided*, That any individual employee or a group of employees shall have the right at any time to present grievances to their employer.

Documents of American History, ed. H. S. Commager, 7th edn, Appleton-Century-Crofts, New York, 1963, vol. ii, pp. 315–16

11. *The Wagner Act, as it came to be called, gave the signal for the activists within the American Federation of Labour to press their case for immediate unionization of the heavy industries. At the Atlantic City convention of the AFL in October 1935 they urged the Federation to adopt this policy.*

The time has arrived when common sense demands [that] the organization policies of the American Federation of Labor must be molded to meet present-day needs. In the great mass-production industries and those in which the workers are composite mechanics, specialized and engaged upon classes of work which do not fully qualify them for craft union membership, industrial organization is the only solution. Continuous employment, economic security and the ability to protect the individual worker depends upon organization upon industrial lines. . . .

The Executive Council of the American Federation of Labor is expressly directed and instructed to issue charters to organizations formed in accordance with the policy herein enunciated. The Executive Council is also instructed to enter upon an aggressive campaign in those industries in which the great mass of workers are not now organized, issue unrestricted charters to workers organized into independent unions, company-dominated unions and those organizations now affiliated with associations not recognized by the American Federation of Labor as bona fide unions.

Report of Proceedings of the Fifty-fifth Annual Convention of the American Federation of Labor, 1935, pp. 523-4

12. *The president of the AFL, William Green, believed in the principle of industrial unionism, as he stated in a letter of 18 July 1933.*

You know enough about these mass production plants to know and understand that no success can attend any organizing effort unless these workers are organized into Federal Unions. The craft lines have practically been wiped out because the workers employed specialize and thus the services of the rounded-out skilled machinists and other skilled workers are not required. We can only succeed in organizing these workers employed in mass production plants by forming Federal Unions, embracing within them, all the workers employed in the different industries.

J. O. MORRIS, *Conflict Within the AFL*, Cornell University Press, 1958, p. 153

13. *But the craft unions were adamantly opposed to mass unionization. As one of their leaders, John Frey, later put it:*

In many of the industries these skilled workers are in a minority, perhaps a small one. The outnumbering majority [are] so-called mass production or semi-skilled workers. It is obvious that if a vote of all employees were taken on the question of establishing one organization as the sole body to represent all of the employees, that the semi-skilled or production workers could easily prove a majority in favor of the organization they desired. A vote taken on such a basis and under such circumstances would be a denial of the rights of a minority, the very minority who had first established trade union organization, a minority having a prior right to consideration.

P. TAFT, *The A.F. of L. from the Death of Gompers to the Merger*, Harper, New York, 1959, pp. 130-1

14. *None the less, the industrial unionists went ahead with their plans and in November 1935 hived off from the AFL to form their own Committee for Industrial Organization. Samuel Lubell comments on its significance.*

The formation of the CIO marked the fusing of the interests of the immigrant and native-stock workers. That, I believe, is perhaps the most telling accomplishment of the CIO. Its political importance can hardly be exaggerated. The mass production industries had been the ones in which racial and religious antagonisms among the workers were most divisive. Carnegie–Illinois, for example, had sprinkled clusters of different nationalities in each of its mines, reasoning correctly that a Balkanized working force would be more difficult to unionize. In some industries immigrants and Negroes had first been introduced as strike-breakers or because they would work for lower wages than native-born workers. The failure of the Knights of Labor in the 1880s was largely a failure to unite the immigrant working groups. Much of the A.F. of L.'s reluctance to embark on a real organizing drive in the mass production industries reflected the dislike of the 'aristocrats of labor' in the skilled crafts for the immigrant 'rubbish'.

The Future of American Politics, Hamish Hamilton, London, 1952, p. 46

15. *In December Green repeated a warning to the CIO.*

I deem it my duty to emphasize the note of warning sounded in my letter dated November 23rd and as I repeat it now, against the formation of an organization within the American Federation of Labor. I am confident that it will lead to serious consequences. It is bound to invite counter-action and reprisals from those who are uncompromising in their opposition to the purpose for which the organization with which you are associated is formed. We may attempt to reason otherwise or we may try to convince ourselves that cleavage and division will not occur, but experience, which after all is the best teacher, has shown that unity, solidarity and cooperation cannot be maintained where an organization, within an organization, is formed for the declared purpose of promoting a policy which is in conflict with the one adopted by a majority vote in a legally convened convention representative of the entire membership of the organization itself.

Report of the Proceedings of the Fifty-sixth Convention of the American Federation of Labor, 1936, p. 74

16. *The head of the CIO, John L. Lewis, replied as follows:*

... I am not concerned with history. Rather I am concerned with the problems of today and tomorrow. You do not deny that the American Federation of Labor has frittered away two years of valuable time without effectuating the organization of a single worker in the steel industry. You do not deny that your Executive is even now scheming to eject your union from the house of labor. You do not deny that the crime for which such ejection will be punishment is the crime of lending aid to the unorganized workers and seeking an expansion of the numerical strength of the American Federation of Labor. Your lament is that I will not join you in a policy of anxious inertia. Candidly, I am temperamentally incapable of sitting with you in sackcloth and ashes, endlessly intoning 'O tempora! O mores!'

It is of course needless to discuss further the points of honor involved. You will make your own decisions. For myself, I prefer to err on the side of America's underprivileged and exploited millions, if erring it be.

J. O. MORRIS, *Conflict Within the AFL*, Cornell University Press, 1958, p. 232

Breakthrough

17. *The campaign for industrial unionization began soon after the 1936 election and concentrated on the automobile and steel industries. As early as 11 February 1937, the Committee scored a remarkable victory when General Motors agreed to bargain with the United Automobile Workers after weeks of bitter struggle in which the workers had resorted to the controversial tactic of the sit-down strike. The Secretary of the Michigan District of the American Communist Party here describes its advantages.*

Sit-down strikes give to the workers a greater feeling of strength and security because the strikes are inside the plants, in the solid confines of the factory, at the machines which are the sources of their livelihood, instead of away from the plant, moving around in 'empty space,' on the sidewalks surrounding the factories.

Sit-down strikes give to the workers greater sureness that there are no scabs within the plants and no production is being carried on and makes it difficult to run in scabs. . . .

The sit-down strike furthermore makes it difficult to resume operations even partially where scabs have gotten in because by holding down one section of the plant it is hard to begin operations.

The sit-down strike affords strikers greater possibility of defending themselves against the violence of the police and the company men. . . .

The sit-down strike makes for a greater discipline, group conscious-ness and comradeship among the workers because of the very position in which they find themselves and thereby enhances the militancy and fighting spirit of the workers.

Finally, the sit-down strike arouses the widest sympathy and support among the working population because of the courage of the workers in taking 'possession' of the factory and because of the self-sacrifice and hardship which such action entails.

w. WEINSTONE, *The Great Sit-Down Strike*, New York, 1937, pp. 29–32

18. *Wagner himself supported the sit-down in a letter to the* New York Times.

The sit-down has been used only in protest against repeated violations of industrial liberties which Congress has recognized. The sit-down, even in the few cases where labor has used it effectively, has succeeded in winning for labor only such industrial liberties as both law and morals have long sanctioned. The sit-down has been provoked by the long-standing ruthless tactics of a few corporations who have hamstrung the National Labor Relations Board by invoking court actions . . .; who have openly banded together to defy this law of Congress quite inde-pendently of any Court action . . .; and who have systematically used spies and discharges and violence and terrorism to shatter the workers' liberties as defined by Congress.

New York Times, 1 April 1937

19. *Business, however, saw the sit-down as only the latest of the many in-vasions of their property rights promoted by the New Deal. The law depart-ment of the National Association of Manufacturers described it as follows:*

There can be no legal justification for the sitdown strike because, in addition to all other factors, it begins with a physical seizure of the property of others, which, in a country established on the basis of the private ownership of property, can never be sanctioned. The sitdown strikers are trespassers from the beginning of the strike; they maintain their position by means of a conspiracy among themselves and their confederates on the outside; and the holding of another's property against his will, under threat of permanent occupancy unless he will accede to their demands, is itself a species of extortion.

A. W. JONES, *Life, Liberty and Property*, Lippincott, New York, 1941, p. 131

20. *One business spokesman was so alarmed by the sit-down at the rubber factories at Akron, Ohio, that he could ascribe it to a high-level conspiracy.*

To an observer Akron presents a disturbing train of thought. A large number of people outside Akron have savings, perhaps major life-time nest-eggs, invested in rubber company securities. They are uneasy about this Akron situation. They object instinctively to unauthorized seizure of 'their' property.

Disregard for property ownership cannot but result in a swing of public opinion. People who shudder at the thought of dictatorship today, may welcome it as the means of controlling unlawful seizure. Willingness of officialdom to close its eyes to property rights and laws they are sworn to enforce is not lost upon the 'man in the street' whether in Akron or elsewhere.

Is it possible that, entirely outside labor's ranks, individuals in high places are using labor as a tool slowly to sluice public opinion into channels right for their own purposes?

DEAC MARTIN in *Nation's Business*, June 1937 (quoted in *ibid.*, pp. 131–2)

21. *At the same time, the CIO turned its attention to the steel industry. Edmund Wilson reminds us of the formidable task they were taking on.*

. . . Labor leaders for forty years have been breaking their backs against steel. The government tried vainly for seven years to win a suit against the Steel Corporation. Woodrow Wilson exerted in vain all his moral force and all his eloquence to induce the Steel Corporation to arbitrate the 1919 strike. And the Roosevelt administration, from the beginning of the NRA, has had no co-operation from the steel people: they walked out last summer from a conference at which William Green was to be present and so flustered General Johnson that he declared – what was not the case–that Green had not been invited; and they did their best to prevent Frances Perkins, the Secretary of Labor, from speaking to the steel workers at Homestead, driving her out of a hall into a park, and out of the park into a post office, where she made a stand on federal property as yet uncontrolled by the Steel Corporation.

The American Earthquake, Allen, London, 1958, p. 559

22. *Yet in the event, United States Steel gave way without a fight and on 2 March it too reached agreement with the CIO. Then in May at Aliquippa, the headquarters of the Jones and Laughlin Steel Corporation (no doubt under-mined by losing its action against the National Labour Relations Board the previous month), the union leaders gained another surprising success, as an eyewitness relates.*

No one, not even the union, believed it possible. It was fantastic. They expected to get the men out, certainly. But not all of them, and not without some opposition from 'loyal groups' or from city or company police. The walk-out was complete. For the first time in years the valley is not brilliant red at night with smoke and fire from the Besse-mers. . . .

. . . Remember that Jefferson once said something about a revolu-tion every twenty years or so being a blessing? The same is true of a strike. There is real solidarity now. And certainly no fear. In fact workers go out of their way to thumb their noses at company police by whom they have been cowed for years. Thousands of men have joined the union during the last few days–especially after the strike was called. The union ran out of receipt books, membership cards and dues buttons. One fellow who signed up just before the strike paid two dollars in dues, for May and June. He said, 'Here is two dollars. Call the strike. If you don't, I'll never pay any more.' . . .

. . . Sure all successful strikes are the 'greatest victory labor ever had.' But this is certainly the most remarkable. Think of it, the toughest Corporation in America brought to its knees in exactly forty hours.

R. R. R. BROOKS, *As Steel Goes . . .*, Yale University Press, 1940, pp. 123–5

23. *The strikers were not so successful with the Republic Steel Corporation in Chicago. On Memorial Day (30 May) 1937, in a clash outside the works,*

ten marchers were shot dead and at least eighty-three were wounded; thirty-five policemen were injured. The Senate Committee on Education and Labour, headed by the Progressive Senator Robert La Follette, reported as follows:

To break the strikes of 1937, 'Little Steel' resorted to the traditional practices of espionage, the 'rough shadowing' of union organizers and men, the arming and deputizing of private persons, and coercion of law-enforcement officers. In pursuit of these practices, the 'Little Steel' strike of 1937 was no less brutal and violent than previous strikes in the industry which have been the subject of other congressional investigations.

The strike of 1937, however, was more ominous than the others since in it the companies sought to incite a spirit of vigilantism in the citizens and to subvert the community to strikebreaking activities. . . .

The bloodshed, bitterness, and economic disorganization of communities resulting from the 'Little Steel' strike might easily have been avoided had the companies conformed to the laws of the United States, instead of ranging their combined economic strength and the prestige and influence of their employer associations in opposition to collective bargaining. Their determination to flout the law, and their efforts, through a careful campaign of propaganda, to enlist local communities to assist them, must be condemned as dangerous to lawful government.

United States. Senate. Committee on Education and Labor, *Report No. 151*, United States Government Printing Office, Washington, D.C., pp. 330-1

24. *The head of Republic Steel, Tom Girdler, stated his case as follows:*

An employer or a manager of a business can hire or fire, justly or un-justly. All of us would welcome the invention of an arrangement that would eliminate injustice from the relationship. However, even a tyrannical businessman's tyranny is limited to the enterprise he runs. But if the C.I.O. embraces all workers—and John L. Lewis was striving openly for that goal—then no American could work except by permission of this pompous ruler. Republic's workers knew that in 1937. We who run the company never fooled ourselves that these people on our payrolls were fighting chiefly for Republic Steel Corporation when they resisted Lewis and his mobs. They were fighting for themselves.

Tolerance for socialistic propaganda has increased in this country because Americans who know better have not sufficiently resisted the idea that a man with payroll responsibilities is necessarily less of a humanitarian than people of prominence without such responsibilities. . . . The mere fact that Eugene Grace, Frank Purnell and I were heads of big corporations put a tag on us. We were 'bosses'. It is impossible to be a boss and be popular with everybody. If Grace, Purnell and Girdler had been other than resolute men we would not have been running big industrial organizations. Because we were resolute men who understood not only our duty to our stockholders, but our duty to our workers and likewise to our country, we did not surrender. We did not sign.

A terribly *disorganizing* influence is at work at the base of all industry in America. The boss is no longer the boss. . . . Not greed but some perception of this must have been the thing that made so many employers the bitter opponents of the labor union movement in the old days. They foresaw what now eats at us.

Boot Straps, Scribner's, New York, 1943, pp. 317, 358–9, 449–50

25. *Another citadel remained inviolate. In the Ford Company a reign of terror persisted which had perhaps its closest contemporary parallel in Nazi Germany. Even the chroniclers of Ford, Nevins and Hill, call this description of the secret police and its chief, Harry Bennett, 'essentially accurate'.*

There are about eight hundred underworld characters in the Ford Service organization. They are the Storm Troops. They make no pretense of working, but are merely 'keeping order' in the plant community through terror. Around this nucleus of eight hundred yeggs there are, however, between 8000 and 9000 authentic workers in the organization, a great many of them spies and stool-pigeons and a great many others who have been browbeaten into joining this industrial mafia. There are almost 90,000 workers in River Rouge, and because of this highly organized terror and spy system the fear in the plant is something indescribable. During the lunch hour men shout at the top of their voices about the baseball scores lest they be suspected of talking unionism. Workers seen talking together are taken off the assembly line and fired. Every man suspected of union sympathies is immediately discharged, usually under the framed-up charge of 'starting a fight', in which he often gets terribly beaten up.

Harry Bennett's power extends beyond Dearborn to Detroit. In certain localities in Michigan judges and other State officials cannot run for office without a petition with a specified number of signatures. Bennett simply puts such petitions on the conveyor belt, and in one afternoon the prospective candidate has all the signatures he needs.

B. STOLBERG, *The Story of the CIO*, Viking, New York, 1938, p. 116

26. *Nevertheless, by the end of 1937 most of the automobile and steel industries were unionized and it was becoming progressively more difficult for the surviving moguls to resist. Walter Galenson sums up the position at the end of the thirties.*

For the first time, American trade unions began to work systematically at the precinct level within the framework of the established political parties. For the first time they tasted the fruits of electoral victories for which they could fairly claim credit, and these fruits, in the form of greatly enhanced legislative influence, were sweet indeed. The AFL of Samuel Gompers was a humble supplicant before the Congress of the United States on a very limited range of matters. The AFL of William Green, and the CIO of John L. Lewis and Philip Murray, were constant visitors in the halls of Congress, and it required the shock of the Taft–Hartley Act in 1947 to bring them to the realization that labor's political millennium had not yet arrived. Nonpartisanship in 1932 meant that the labor movement was at liberty to present its views to the national conventions of the Democratic and Republican parties, and to have those views generally disregarded. Nonpartisanship in 1940 meant a voice in the selection of many state and local candidates, invitations to meet publicly with the President of the United States and his Republican challenger, nationwide radio broadcasts by labor leaders, and attendance at trade union conventions by the highest officials of the nation, including the President himself.

In part, of course, the increased political influence of organized labor was a function of its numerical growth and its greater financial resources. But beyond this, there had come about an awareness by even the most old-fashioned of the AFL leaders of the augmented role of the federal government in the labor market, and the consequent acceptance of the need for institutionalizing the means of influencing government decisions. Political action had become a necessity, and in the light of what the two parties stood for, this implied pro-Democratic partisanship. A few staunch Republicans in the top leadership of the AFL managed for a while to ensure the preservation of the old Gompers slogans as official AFL policy, but in reality, the AFL, together with the rest of the labor movement, ceased to be neutral after 1936. The New Deal has effectively, and seemingly permanently, destroyed the possibility of an American labor party constructed on the British model, but only at the expense of bringing about a basic alteration in the nature of the Democratic Party.

The CIO Challenge to the AFL, Harvard University Press, 1960, pp. 609–10

VII

The Roosevelt Recession

*In his second Inaugural address Roosevelt placed his emphasis on the un-
finished tasks facing the nation. Much still remained to be done in the way of
recovery as well as reform, but the President's second term saw little advance
on either front. The Supreme Court furore and the violent trade union conflicts had unsettled the country and strengthened the anti–New Deal elements
in Congress so that in spite of his huge majorities Roosevelt found it difficult,
if not impossible, to carry his legislation. Moreover, the very policies which
had won the election had also almost totally alienated the leadership of
industry. Then in August 1937 began the 'Roosevelt Recession' which not
only wiped out the last two years of economic progress but raised grave doubts
about the New Deal's capacity ever to restore permanent prosperity in America.
Roosevelt's reaction to the crisis was hesitant in the extreme. It was not until
April 1938 that he agreed to unbalance the Federal budget still further and
use the government's spending powers to help set the economy back on an even
keel. At the same time, he instituted the fiercest attack of his administration on
the big business interests which he and many of his lieutenants were convinced
had conspired to bring on the recession. This was one interpretation, but it did
not really answer the great question of why after five years in power the New
Deal had failed to solve so many of America's economic problems. The chapter
closes with some alternative views.*

1. *The theme of Roosevelt's second Inaugural was unfinished business.*

. . . Our progress out of the depression is obvious. But that is not all
that you and I mean by the new order of things. Our pledge was not
merely to do a patchwork job with second-hand materials. By using
the new materials of social justice we have undertaken to erect on the
old foundations a more enduring structure for the better use of future
generations. . . .

. . . To hold to progress today, however, is more difficult. Dulled
conscience, irresponsibility, and ruthless self-interest already reappear.
Such symptoms of prosperity may become portents of disaster! Prosperity already tests the persistence of our progressive purpose . . .

... I see a great nation, upon a great continent, blessed with a great wealth of natural resources. Its hundred and thirty million people are at peace among themselves; they are making their country a good neighbor among the nations. I see a United States which can demonstrate that, under democratic methods of government, national wealth can be translated into a spreading volume of human comforts hitherto unknown, and the lowest standard of living can be raised far above the level of mere subsistence.

But here is the challenge to our democracy: In this nation I see tens of millions of its citizens – a substantial part of its whole population – who at this very moment are denied the greater part of what the very lowest standards of today call the necessities of life.

I see millions of families trying to live on incomes so meager that the pall of family disaster hangs over them day by day.

I see millions whose daily lives in city and on farm continue under conditions labeled indecent by a so-called polite society half a century ago.

I see millions denied education, recreation, and the opportunity to better their lot and the lot of their children.

I see millions lacking the means to buy the products of farm and factory and by their poverty denying work and productiveness to many other millions.

I see one-third of a nation ill-housed, ill-clad, ill-nourished.

It is not in despair that I paint you that picture. I paint it for you in hope – because the Nation, seeing and understanding the injustice in it, proposes to paint it out. We are determined to make every American citizen the subject of his country's interest and concern; and we will never regard any faithful, law-abiding group within our borders as superfluous. The test of our progress is not whether we add more to the abundance of those who have much; it is whether we provide enough for those who have too little.

The Public Papers and Addresses of Franklin D. Roosevelt, ed. S. Rosenman, Macmillan, New York, 1941, vol. vi, pp. 2–5

2. *Harry Hopkins, in an article published not long after, also dwelt on the dangers of complacency.*

We have had unusual opportunities in these recent years. Our entire population has, to a varying degree, been shaken out of its complacency.

Even the rich and powerful were rudely awakened from their smug acceptance of the complete and fundamental rightness of every element of the existing order. Insecurity brought them a vision of doubts and uncertainty which are normally the lot of the poor. Middle-class people especially gained a new, if temporary perspective, as the stability of their jobs, their homes and their savings trembled beneath them and disappeared. New ideas and new solutions to old problems seemed less alarming under such circumstances. Economic and social theory was no longer ignored or despised as a remote classroom boondoggle. Moreover, in the individual insecurity of the depression, people of all classes began to look to collective action as a way out. This took many forms, but instinctively it involved a looking to the government. Business men looked to the government for relief from the pressure of their debts and the excesses of competition, farmers for a fair price for their produce, workers for a decent wage and the right to work together collectively for better conditions, the unemployed for some minimum of security, a livelihood, a job.

So in the depression we had the exceptional situation of a people looking to their government for relief from problems with comparatively little regard to the form this relief should take. But with the first flush of recovery, many of those who enjoy its benefits find themselves weary of their contingent responsibilities. The very conception of change appears suddenly dangerous and radical. They are once again consecrated to the recapture of the *status quo*. They are bored with the poor, the unemployed and the insecure. They are relieved to cast off the unacceptable burden that the depression has too long saddled on their conscience. They are tired as well of the government, except in so far as they are willing to devote their energies to the task of returning government to its historic role as policeman and guardian for vested interests. Take the government out of business, they say, and let business take its profits undisturbed! Take the government out of relief and let the unemployed return to the old tradition of looking out for themselves! Let not the historic role of the propertied be modified by regulation or taxation; let not the self-respect and initiative of the jobless be undermined by governmental mollycoddling! The fact that many business men do not share these attitudes is encouraging.

If we are to be honest with ourselves, we must face recovery with the realization that many of our basic problems are still unsolved, and that a powerful minority of our population is no longer in a mood to solve them. On the other hand there are evidences that the larger and less articulate section of our population demands action on these problems. The election is the best possible evidence of that fact. The vitality of the labor and farm movement is another. The apparent support from many sources for a continued relief program is another.

'The Future of Relief', *New Republic*, 10 February 1937, pp. 8–9

3. Hopkins was right about the revived confidence in laissez-faire. This is what the Lynds found in 'Middletown'.

... It is still true in 1936 that, to Middletown, such things as poverty or a depression are simply exceptions to a normally good state of affairs; and anything that goes wrong is the fault of some individuals (or, collectively, of 'human nature') rather than anything amiss with the organization and functioning of the culture. The system is fundamentally right and only the persons wrong; the cures must be changes in personal attitudes, not in the institutions themselves. Among these personal cures for its social woes are the following six basic qualities needed for a better world outlined in a local address: 'faith, service, cooperation, the Golden Rule, optimism, and character'. 'The typical citizen,' says an editorial approvingly, 'discounts the benefits of the political and economic New Deal and says that common sense is the answer to the depression.... He thinks hard work is the depression cure.'

[*As a local banker put it:*]

'All these big plans they're making in Washington look well, read well–but they just won't work. They're Utopian, and we don't live and try to do business in a Utopia! By what God-given right do these fellows in Washington think they can do a job so big? It's the very immensity of national planning that makes it impossible. The old law of supply and demand can't be repealed or amended. It applies to labor and materials, raw and finished. Roosevelt's like a general who sits at the top and hands down orders from man to man till they get to the privates sweating under a sixty-pound pack–and he's the fellow that carries out the order.

'You can't make the world all planned and soft. The strongest and best survive–that's the law of nature after all–always has been and always will be.'

Middletown in Transition, Constable, London, 1937, pp. 493, 500

4. *In short, government and business were still at odds and both believed they alone had the key to the future. In August 1937 these assumptions received a shattering blow when the United States plummeted into a recession more severe than anything experienced since the worst days of the Hoover régime. Who was to blame? Business blamed the New Deal and many New Dealers, including the President himself, blamed business, as Henry Morgenthau, the Secretary of the Treasury, discovered on 8 November.*

. . . Roosevelt was depressed. Fascism, he said, was making gains throughout the world, as the Rome–Berlin–Tokyo Pact suggested. Brazil was veering that way. Take the situation in the United States, he said. Four or five people might get together, talk it over, and decide they had to have their own man in Washington. Even though he said every so often that he wanted business to make a profit and that he believed in property rights, business did not believe him. The President thought there were about two thousand men who had reached the conclusion they had to block the New Deal, to go on strike against government.

J. M. BLUM, *From the Morgenthau Diaries*, Houghton Mifflin, Boston, 1959, p. 393

5. *At the same time the administration was in the throes of what was to prove a highly consequential debate over the proposed remedy for the slump, between the advocates of deficit spending on the part of the government, which Keynes and others like Marriner Eccles had been urging for years, and those like Morgenthau who were determined on achieving a balanced Federal budget. This is how Morgenthau felt.*

Morgenthau disagreed completely with the whole drift of Eccles's thinking. Constant or increasing deficits, he believed, would impair the government's credit, force Congress to start the printing presses, precipitate runaway inflation and national disaster. Progress toward a balanced budget, on the other hand, would protect the value of government securities, win the confidence of private enterprise, and result in an upturn of private investment that would sustain a new prosperity. So Morgenthau had thought on taking office; so he believed in 1936; so, indeed, he still believed in 1959. He would not relax in caring for the needy unemployed, but he would not relax his purpose of balancing the national budget precisely as he balanced the budget on his farm. [*On 20 October he was threatening resignation.*]

'I won't stay and knowingly and consciously have an unbalanced budget in order to correct the mistakes made by other people. . . . We have come to a crossroad. The crossroad is when private business needed the money which the Government has been taking up to this time, and we are at that crossroad now. I don't see why we can't use those words. . . . The time has come. And the only person around here who is not in line is Wallace [Secretary of Agriculture] and Wallace wants private industry to do it. . . . The President wants private industry to do it. . . . And it's not balancing the budget which is putting the stock market down. Then why the hell should we unbalance the budget to cover up the mistakes of other people? For four years we have carried the burden of mistakes made by other Departments.'

Ibid., pp. 280, 388–9

6. *The President was basically in sympathy with his Secretary of the Treasury. He had called for a balanced budget in 1932 and his attitude had changed little since this homily to the National Emergency Council in January 1934; to prove it he had drastically reduced Federal spending in the summer of 1937.*

There is one thing that should be worked in, and that is that they should be told all the different things the government cannot do. That doesn't appear here at all. You know, we are getting requests practically to finance the entire United States. There are individuals who want $500 to start raising chickens, and from there up to the corporation that wants to borrow money to meet its payroll; from there up to the railroad that has to refund its bonds coming due; from there up to the municipality that says the wicked banks won't let us have any money; and from there down to the individual who says he is entitled to work, the white collar man, from the individual all the way up the scale. There is a general feeling that it is up to the government to take care of everybody, financially and otherwise – the artists, musicians, painters, and brass bands. One brass band asked to be financed on a trip around the country. These directors are going to be asked to lend their support to tapping the Treasury of the United States in some way. I think somebody in one of these sessions should present a manual of don'ts to the various directors to tell them what the government can't and won't do.

One very simple illustration is CWA, which is so popular and successful that the letters and telegrams are coming in from the Governor of

New York down to the humblest citizen demanding that CWA continue on at least an equal scale, and possibly on a greater scale, all the way through the summer. If we continue CWA through the summer, it is going to cost seven or eight million dollars, and secondly, it will become a habit with the country. We want to get away from CWA as soon as we can. The CWA ends the end of April, and next winter, if there is still a great deal of relief needed, the matter can be taken up again. But they must know that it is going to end this year at the end of April. We cannot carry CWA through the summer. We all agree there has got to be a limit to CWA and the people must look forward to the time when it will have ended. We have got to assume more or less that things are going to straighten themselves out. We must not take the position that we are going to have permanent depression in this country, and it is very important that we have somebody to say that quite forcefully to these people. . . . Nobody is going to starve during the warm weather.

New Deal Mosaic, eds. L. G. Seligman and E. E. Cornwell Jr., Oregon University Press, 1965, pp. 75–6

7. *Besides a new injection of Federal spending, several members of the administration demanded a full-blooded attack on business, in the old progressive tradition. On 6 December Harold Ickes wrote in his diary:*

. . . I do not think that we will get anywhere trying to conciliate business. Big business wants all or nothing and if we give all, it will mean that we will be running the country into grave danger. . . . Jackson, Hopkins and I are all in agreement that the President ought to get into this fight since his Administration has been made an issue. We believe that if he does not fight and do it pretty soon, we are going to find ourselves in a bad way.
[*In the last week of December, Ickes and his colleagues took it upon themselves to make their attacks. Ickes described his own contribution.*]
It was frankly an attack on great agglomerations of capital. I raised the monopoly issue, pointing out that the struggle in this country was now, as it had been in the past, one of democracy and monopoly. I pointed out that if the latter won, it meant a fascist state with an end to our liberties. I singled out certain great business tycoons like Ford, the du Ponts, Girdler, and Rand, but except for the mention of their names, my speech was not personal.

145

The *Secret Diary of Harold L. Ickes*, Weidenfeld and Nicolson, London, 1955, vol. ii, pp. 262, 283

8. Yet at his press conference on 4 January, the President was urging co-operation with business which, in spite of his protestations, sounded remarkably like a revival of NRA.

Don't write the story that I am advocating the immediate reenactment of NRA. But the fact remains that in quite a number of the code industries under NRA it was perfectly legal for the heads of all the companies in a given industry to sit down around a table with the Government, and, from their own statistics and the statistics of their own trade associations and the statistics given them by the Government, figure out much more clearly than they ever had before, as an industry, what the probable demand of the country would be for a period of six months or a year ahead. In other words, they could make a more intelligent group estimate as to the purchasing power of the country and the inventories of the particular article necessary for the immediate future.

Now, done that way, it is a perfectly legitimate thing for them to do – sitting there, with the Government, and trying honestly to find out what the needs are going to be for the next six months or a year, so that they won't overproduce. It is legitimate just so long as it is done without any attempts at price-fixing or driving competitors out of business or things like that as a result of the conference.

There is a question today whether a meeting of that kind, around a table, is legal under the anti-trust laws. A lot of people are afraid of it. I would very much favor making it a completely legal thing to do: to meet around a table to find out, with the help of the Government, what the demands are, what the purchasing power of the country is, what the inventories are.

The Public Papers and Addresses of Franklin D. Roosevelt, ed. S. Rosenman, Macmillan, New York, 1941, vol. vii, pp. 33–4

9. It was not until April 1938 that Roosevelt took action and committed the government to a spending policy. Here is part of his recommendations to Congress, sent on 14 April.

The prosperity of the United States is of necessity a primary concern of Government. Current events, if allowed to run undisturbed, will continue to threaten the security of our people and the stability of our economic life. The National Administration has promised never to stand idly by and watch its people, its business system and its national life disintegrate. It is because the course of our economics has run adversely for half a year that we owe it to ourselves to turn it in the other direction before the situation becomes more definitely serious.

. . . the Congress and the Chief Executive can ill afford to weaken or destroy great reforms which, during the past five years, have been effected on behalf of the American people.

At this time we suffer from a failure of consumer demand. The hoped for reemployment of this spring is not proceeding fast enough to create an economic upturn.

Therefore the problem calls for action both by the Government and by the people.

Ibid., vol. vii, pp. 221–2, 225–6

10. *At the same time the President took up the old anti-monopoly battle-cries with the call for a full-scale investigation into big business practices. Here is part of the recommendations sent to Congress on 29 April.*

Private enterprise is ceasing to be free enterprise and is becoming a cluster of private collectivisms: masking itself as a system of free enterprise after the American model, it is in fact becoming a concealed cartel system after the European model. . . .

A discerning magazine of business has editorially pointed out that big business collectivism in industry compels an ultimate collectivism in government.

The power of a few to manage the economic life of the nation must be diffused among the many or be transferred to the public and its democratically responsible Government. . . .

. . . Those people, in and out of the halls of government, who encourage the growing restriction of competition either by active efforts or by passive resistance to sincere attempts to change the trend, are shouldering a terrific responsibility. Consciously, or unconsciously, they are working for centralized business and financial control. Consciously, or unconsciously, they are therefore either working for control of the Government itself by business and finance or the other alternative– a growing concentration of public power in the government to cope with such concentration of private power.

The enforcement of free competition is the least regulation business can expect. . . .

Once it is realized that business monopoly in America paralyzes the system of free enterprise on which it is grafted, and is as fatal to those who manipulate it as to the people who suffer beneath its impositions, action by the government to eliminate these artificial restraints will be welcomed by industry throughout the nation.

Ibid., vol. vii, pp. 308, 313, 320

11. *What Roosevelt expected to get from the anti-monopoly crusade is not clear. Broadus Mitchell provides an appropriately sardonic comment.*

. . . The whole episode of attempted reversion to competition was not only futile from the first, but was hypocritical on the part of the government, in view of the recent public sanction of business collaboration in NRA, preceded by increasing tolerance of these practices over a long period. Further, repentance for official intrigue with business endured only briefly, for the defense program and the country's progressive involvement in World War II signalized such use of industrial consolidations as had never been known before.

Depression Decade, Rinehart, New York, 1947, p. 229

Post-Mortem

12. *So the thirties in America were ending on a desperately low note. Malcolm Muggeridge caught the mood at the close of the decade.*

Until a concern for production and consumption became irrelevant in the light of a deeper concern—a concern for life itself rather than for the means of life, for the very continuance of any existence at all, whether over-producing or under-consuming, the machinery whereby commodities were produced and exchanged was subjected to a minute scrutiny and much criticism. A variety of suggestions, mild and drastic, were made for improving its working, or for replacing it altogether; many had their say on the subject, some at great length. There were advocates of currency reform, others who thought salvation lay in overhauling the banks; public works were not forgotten, and President Roosevelt's New Deal had its admirers. . . .

... Here, bedded in the earth, it was frequently pointed out, were raw materials, and here machines capable of transforming them into useful or pleasurable commodities; here were hands eager to extract these raw materials and work these machines, and here desire for what they would produce. Might not materials, machines, hands and desire be brought together, and the health, wealth and happiness of mankind greatly increased thereby? It seemed not. They would not come together, despite the ingenuity and labour devoted to that end; only came together when the resultant, instead of health, wealth and happiness, was death, destruction and misery. Derelict factories and shipyards continued idle until war spurred them into renewed activity; in peace they were paralysed, but the threat, and then the reality, of war brought back their life—like an indolent giant who cannot summon up the energy to move his huge limbs except to kill.

The Thirties, Hamish Hamilton, London, 1940, pp. 119–20

13. *The editors of the* New Republic, *looking back over Roosevelt's second term at about the same time, also laid their final emphasis on the sense of failure.*

The New Deal, even in its second term, has clearly done far more for the general welfare of the country and its citizens than any administration in the previous history of the nation. Its relief for underprivileged producers in city and country, though inadequate to the need, has been indispensable. Without this relief an appalling amount of misery would have resulted, and a dangerous political upheaval might have occurred. Since the expenditure of money for relief—even the insufficient amounts recently appropriated—has been the principal target of the administration's conservative enemies, this accomplishment alone would be sufficient reason for support of the New Deal. The assertion of the reactionaries that if the federal budget were balanced by cutting expenses, business would revive sharply enough to absorb the unemployed and make relief expenditures unnecessary, is incapable of proof and seems highly improbable.

In addition, the New Deal in this second period has accomplished much of permanent benefit to the nation. ... It is improbable that these changes will be or even can be destroyed by any new administration.

All these extraordinary accomplishments must be remembered when we speak of the points at which the New Deal has been disappointing in its second phase. The most important of these is of course its failure to discover or apply a genuine remedy for the stagnation of our economy, and for unemployment. These years have seen no return to the conditions of 1932 or 1933, to be sure, but on the other hand no great or permanent improvement in national income, production or employment above the level already achieved in 1936. Nor have they seen the adoption of any important new means of bringing about such improvement. The President has apparently been hoping continually that business and investment would gain momentum of their own accord, while business spokesmen have been blaming what they call the hostile attitude of the New Deal for a lack of confidence which they charged with responsibility for retarding advance. It is doubtful, however, whether they are right about this, in the view of economists who have studied the problem intensively. . . .

. . . The President's failure to make more progress in tackling the central problem of our economy is probably due mainly to two things – the strengthening of the conservative opposition, especially since the 1938 election, and concentration on the European situation. The country is weaker, whether for war or for peace, because of this slackening of pace in the New Deal. If our foreign policy can avoid involvement in the war, we shall be fortunate. But in any case we should not rely on war, whether we are in it or not, to do for us the domestic job that remains. If the New Deal is to deserve our support in the future, it must not rest on what it has already done, great as that is, but tell us how it is going to finish the task.

'The New Deal in Review 1936–1940', *The New Republic*, 20 May 1940, pp. 705–8

14. *Even after six years, as Michael Harrington points out, many sectors of American society were still outside the pale of the New Deal.*

Some of those who advanced in the thirties did so because they had unique and individual personal talents. But for the great mass, it was a question of being at the right point in the economy at the right time in history, and utilizing that position for common struggle. Some of those who failed did so because they did not have the will to take advantage of new opportunities. But for the most part the poor who were left behind had been at the wrong place in the economy at the wrong moment in history.

These were the people in the unorganizable jobs, in the South, in the minority groups, in the fly-by-night factories that were low on capital and high on labor. When some of them did break into the economic mainstream—when, for instance, the CIO opened up the way for some Negroes to find good industrial jobs—they proved to be as resourceful as anyone else. As a group, the other Americans who stayed behind were not originally composed primarily of human failures. Rather, they were victims of an impersonal process that selected some for progress and discriminated against others.

Out of the thirties came the welfare state. Its creation had been stimulated by mass impoverishment and misery, yet it helped the poor least of all. Laws like unemployment compensation, the Wagner Act, the various farm programs, all these were designed for the middle third in the cities, for the organized workers, and for the upper third in the country, for the big market farmers. If a man works in an extremely low-paying job, he may not even be covered by social security or other welfare programs. If he receives unemployment compensation, the payment is scaled down according to his low earnings.

One of the major laws that was designed to cover everyone, rich and poor, was social security. But even here the other Americans suffered discrimination. Over the years social security payments have not even provided a subsistence level of life. The middle third have been able to supplement the Federal pension through private plans negotiated by unions, through joining medical schemes like Blue Cross, and so on. The poor have not been able to do so. They lead a bitter life, and then have to pay for that fact in old age.

The Other America, Macmillan, New York, 1962, pp. 8–9

15. *As W. E. Leuchtenburg has remarked, the prevailing feeling at the end of the thirties was one of unfinished business.*

The New Deal left many problems unsolved and even created some perplexing new ones. It never demonstrated that it could achieve prosperity in peacetime. As late as 1941, the unemployed still numbered six million, and not until the war year of 1943 did the army of jobless finally disappear. It enhanced the power of interest groups who claimed to speak for millions, but sometimes represented only a small minority. It did not evolve a way to protect people who had no such spokesmen, nor an acceptable method for disciplining the interest groups. In 1946,

President Truman would resort to a threat to draft railway workers into the Army to avert a strike. The New Deal achieved a more just society by recognizing groups which had been largely unrepresented – staple farmers, industrial workers, particular ethnic groups, and the new intellectual–administrative class. Yet this was still a halfway revolution; it swelled the ranks of the bourgeoisie but left many Americans – share-croppers, slum dwellers, most Negroes – outside of the new equilibrium.

Some of these omissions were to be promptly remedied. Subsequent Congresses extended social security, authorized slum clearance projects, and raised minimum-wage standards to keep step with the rising price level. Other short-comings are understandable. The havoc that had been done before Roosevelt took office was so great that even the unprecedented measures of the New Deal did not suffice to repair the damage. Moreover, much was still to be learned, and it was in the Roosevelt years that the country was schooled in how to avert another major depression. Although it was war which freed the government from the taboos of a balanced budget and revealed the potentialities of spending, it is conceivable that the New Deal measures would have led the country into a new cycle of prosperity even if there had been no war. Marked gains had been made before the war spending had any appreciable effect. When recovery did come, it was much more soundly based because of the adoption of the New Deal program.

Roosevelt and the New Dealers understood, perhaps better than their critics, that they had come only part of the way. Henry Wallace remarked: 'We are children of the transition – we have left Egypt but we have not yet arrived at the Promised Land.' Only five years separated Roosevelt's inauguration in 1933 and the adoption of the last of the New Deal measures, the Fair Labor Standards Act, in 1938. The New Dealers perceived that they had done more in those years than had been done in any comparable period in American history, but they also saw that there was much still to be done, much, too, that continued to baffle them. 'I believe in the things that have been done,' Mrs Roosevelt told the American Youth Congress in February, 1939. 'They helped but they did not solve the fundamental problems. . . . I never believed the Federal government could solve the whole problem. It bought us time to think.'

Franklin D. Roosevelt and the New Deal 1932–1940, Harper and Row, New York, 1963; Torchbook edn, pp. 346–8

16. *What, then, had caused the enduring stagnation of the thirties in the United States, so frighteningly emphasized by the depression of 1937–38? There were many attempts to explain it. E. Carey Brown, using a telling array of statistics, lays the blame on the government's cautious fiscal policy.*

The trend of the direct effects of fiscal policy on aggregate full-employment demand is definitely downward during the 'thirties. For recovery to have been achieved in this period, private demand would have had to be higher out of a given private disposable income than it was in 1929. Fiscal policy, then, seems to have been an unsuccessful recovery device in the 'thirties–not because it did not work, but because it was not tried. . . .

2. The federal government's fiscal action was more expansionary throughout the 'thirties than it was in 1929. . . . In 1929, its fiscal action resulted in a substantial net drag on demand. But this changed sharply in 1931 to an expansionary effect. . . . Expansion continued throughout the period except for the sharp drop in 1937, which represented a shift in demand of over $2\frac{1}{2}$ per cent of GNP [Gross National Product] in one year. It was followed by expansionary activity on a fairly large scale, but not of sufficient size to approach that of 1934–36.

3. State and local governments' fiscal policy was expansionary through 1933, but decreasingly so. By 1934, it had fallen clearly below 1929 and remained in an almost neutral position throughout the rest of the period. The federal government's policies were little more than adequate in most years of the 'thirties to offset these contractive effects of state and local governments. Indeed, if we take the seven years from 1933 on, in only two was the federal share significantly enough to offset state and local shrinkages.

4. The primary failure of fiscal policy to be expansive in this period is attributable to the sharp increase in tax structures enacted at all levels of government. Total government purchases of goods and services expanded virtually every year, with federal expenditure especially marked in 1933 and 1934. But full-employment tax yields more than kept pace. Our rough estimates show that in 1929, a year of full employment, all governments combined had a deficit (federal surplus and state and local deficit), while 1933 to 1939, except for 1936, were years of surplus or approximate balance at full employment.

The changes made in the tax structure in this period were marked, but their quantitative impact has been masked by the sharp fall in total income and tax yields. The federal Revenue Act of 1932 virtually doubled full employment tax yields and essentially set the tax structure for the entire period up to the second world war. . . .

. . . Since the highly deflationary impact of this law has not been fully appreciated, some of its major provisions are briefly noted here.

The Revenue Act of 1932 pushed up rates virtually across the board, but notably on the lower- and middle-income groups. The scope of the act was clearly the equivalent of major wartime enactments. Personal income tax exemptions were slashed, the normal-tax as well as surtax rates were sharply raised and the earned income credit equal to 25 per cent of taxes on low incomes was repealed. Less drastic changes were made in the corporate income tax, but its rate was raised slightly and a $3,000 exemption eliminated. Estate tax rates were pushed up, exemptions sharply reduced, and a gift tax was provided. Congress toyed with a manufacturers' sales tax, but finally rejected it in favor of a broad new list of excise taxes and substantially higher rates for the old ones. While some of these excises were later repealed, most remained throughout the decade. Somewhat later in the 'thirties, processing taxes made further temporary inroads on demand, and the social security taxes began in 1937 to exert a profound effect.

State and local government were also active in new revenue legislation throughout this period. The major changes were to find the state governments moving heavily into general sales and excise taxation, personal and corporate income taxes, and the gasoline tax.

In brief, then, it took the massive expenditures forced on the nation by the second world war to realize the full potentialities of fiscal policy. Until then, the record fails to show its effective use as a recovery measure. Indeed, the general expansionary policy seems stronger in the early part than in the later part of the decade.

'Fiscal Policy in the Thirties: a reappraisal', *American Economic Review*, 1956, pp. 863, 866–9

17. *J. Steindl ascribed the crisis to inexorable developments within capitalism itself. See also Appendix I, Table 5.*

. . . The accumulation of capital shows a definite pattern: *Rise– Decline–Stagnation.*

Is it really necessary to go back so far into history to understand the events which are still vivid in our memory? Indeed, it is only after these data have become available that we can clearly appreciate even the meaning of stagnation. In terms of capital accumulation the decade of the great depression stands out from all the preceding ones as historically unique. In this period the system of highly developed capitalism worked under conditions to which it was never subject before. And it is only now that we can realize equally clearly how futile an attempt would be to deal with the events between the wars in isolation. Stagnation did not come over-night. Preceding it there had been a long process of secular change, which passed almost unnoticed, because memories are short and comparisons over long periods are difficult to make. Hardly anybody during the 'New Era' [the 1920s] was aware of the fact that the annual rate of growth of business capital then was only half of what it had been thirty years earlier!

. . . already towards the end of the last century–in the 1890's–the American economy had undergone a transition which gave considerable weight to the oligopolistic pattern in the total economy. This transition had raised profit margins at that time. . . . As a consequence there should have been a fall in utilisation below the previous level. We might regard the big depression in the middle of the 'nineties as the signal of these difficulties arising from an increase in profit margins, and consequent fall in effective demand in relation to capacity. The decline in the average long-run level of utilization would then be the explanation for the falling off in the rate of growth of capital.

One might prefer slightly more complicated explanations starting from the same point. The growth of oligopoly should have resulted in a redistribution of profits as between competitive and oligopolistic industries. This in itself should have tended to weaken the incentive to invest on the average, if we assume that a certain marginal volume of profits calls forth less addition to investment in an oligopolistic than it does in a competitive industry. This hypothesis is justified by the consideration that oligopolistic industries have to be much more afraid of excess capacity than others, as they cannot as easily hope to make room for themselves at the expense of competitors. The shift in profits to oligopolistic industries may thus equally well explain the primary decline in the growth of capital.

While the speculative character of this theory has been stressed, there is no reason to hide what it can claim as an advantage. It does not, on the face of it, contradict any well-established facts. At the same time, the explanation does not lead back to causes which are in themselves puzzling and mysterious problems, like the development of technology and the trend of population, but it leads back to a very plain and well-known fact, the explanation of which is not too difficult: the growth of oligopoly at a certain stage of capitalist development.

Maturity and Stagnation in American Capitalism, Blackwell, Oxford, 1952, pp. 166, 191–2

18. *One of the most prominent believers in the causes dismissed by Steindl is the American Keynesian, Alvin Hansen. At the time of the 1938 recession he wrote this.*

Many reasons have been assigned for the currently low level of new investment. There are those who are convinced that the basic cause goes very deep: that it is to be sought in a fundamental change which it is believed our social order is undergoing. It is said that we are passing through a transition period – the implications and significance of which history alone can appraise – a transition from a free economy to a controlled economy. The framework in which private enterprise is permitted to function is becoming more narrowly circumscribed. It is said that business chafes in the new 'harness'; that like a 'bucking bronco' it refuses to function until its old freedoms are restored. Thus, it is alleged, we are confronted with an irreconcilable conflict between business and government. Private enterprise, operating in a free market, can, it is said, function with a high order of efficiency and even with reasonably full employment. At the opposite extreme it is conceded that a highly centralized collectivism could command and direct the productive resources. But a hybrid economy, an economy which is neither free nor regimented, cannot, it is argued, function at anything like full employment. This limping hybrid system continues to rely on private enterprise, yet the motivating and energizing forces are dampened down and at times almost wholly suppressed. From this point of view, there can be no escape from a deadlock which can be broken only by driving on toward a completely authoritarian state. The present recession is thus regarded as only a preliminary demonstration that a hybrid society, half-free and half-controlled, can succeed only to a very limited degree. Such a society, it is said, quickly gets all snarled up in its own processes. Every attempt at a solution involves it in a maze of contradictions. Every artificial stimulant saps its inner strength. Every new measure conjures out of the ground a hundred new problems. . . .

[*But to Hansen, the advocate of precisely such a mixed economy, the reasons for decline had to be found in external factors such as the difficulty of obtaining*

investment outlets, the slower growth of population and the emergence of a
sophisticated technology.]

Adequate investment outlets are necessary to sustain full employment and a satisfactory income level. But investment outlets are more
difficult to find in a non-expanding economy. We are living in a
period which is in several important respects distinctly different from
that of the nineteenth century. It was one thing to find adequate investment outlets in a century quite unique in the world's history–a
century with vast, rich areas inviting occupation and large capital out-
lays on housing, manufacturing and transportation equipment. In such
an expanding economy investment outlets were easy to find and indeed
the main difficulty was a shortage of capital and man-power. Now all
this has been changed and we are confronted with an economy with no
large, rich areas to be occupied anywhere in the entire globe ... and
with a practically stationary population in the industrial countries. It
is a plain fact that a perfectly enormous amount of capital was absorbed
in the nineteenth century for no other reason than the tremendous rate
of population growth. England's population quadrupled in a hundred
years; the whole of Europe's tripled and ours increased fifteenfold in a
single century.

... The nineteenth century witnessed not only the widening of
capital (to use Hawtrey's phrase) incident to an expanding demand, but
also a deepening of capital, the use of more and more capital per unit of
output. A capitalistic economy with a machine method of production
has taken the place of a handicraft economy with its direct production
processes. The transformation of a rural economy into a capitalistic
one is something distinctly different from the further evolution of
a society which has already reached the status of a fully-developed
machine technique. It is true that we are still engaged in making labor-
saving inventions. Extremely important, however, is the question:
Are these new labor-saving techniques likely to be preponderantly
capital-using or neutral with respect to the use of capital?

I do not make any forecast; but it is a grave question whether inventions and innovations are not likely in the future to be less capital-
using than in the nineteenth century. In contrast, while we were in
process of changing over from a direct method of production to an
elaborate capitalistic technique, as in the last century, innovations per-
force had to be capital-using in character.

Full Recovery Or Stagnation? Black, London, 1938, pp. 283–4, 312–15

19. Steindl may be said to represent the left, Hansen the centre. One of the most formidable spokesmen for the right was the economist J. A. Schumpeter who saw the answer in the New Deal's hostility to business.

. . . Opportunities for technological or organizational or commercial innovation cannot be thought of as vanishing (if they are vanishing) except very gradually. If there actually be a tendency toward decline in capital absorption, it can assert itself only in time, though shocks to individual industries may be both sudden and serious. The rate of increase in population declines imperceptibly per year. The call of entrepreneurial adventure is too deep-seated to cease dramatically *of itself.* And so on. Such tendencies . . . may affect contour lines over time and bend them downward. But they cannot explain the weakness of any given prosperity, and they look absurd in the role of explaining factors of a sudden slump. . . .

. . . our task reduces to substituting for unconvincing reasons why investment opportunity should be vanishing, a more convincing one.

. . . The analysis of Chap. XIV, Sec. B supplies it: capitalism produces by its mere working a social atmosphere – a moral code, if the reader prefer – that is hostile to it, and this atmosphere, in turn, produces policies which do not allow it to function. There is no equilibrating apparatus to guarantee that this atmosphere or these policies should develop in such a way as to prevail in the fullness of time, *i.e.*, when the capitalist process will have really spent its force or be spending it. Whenever they prevail sooner, there is danger of deadlock, by which we mean a situation in which neither capitalism nor its possible alternatives are workable. This is what, to a certain extent and presumably not yet for good, has happened in this country.

It might be replied that anticapitalist attitudes are also, like the tendencies adduced by the theory of vanishing investment opportunity in its usual acceptance, a matter of slow growth and hence, similarly open to the objections raised against the theory above. But we are able to do in this case what cannot be done for those tendencies, *viz.*, to show when, and how, that attitude came *suddenly* to a head and suddenly acquired dominating importance. And anticapitalist policies, unlike attitudes, may be dated. The coincidence in time between them and disappointing performance of the economic engine is indeed striking.

At least since 1932 the burden of direct taxation imposed upon that part of the national revenue which goes to the higher and highest brackets was undoubtedly high enough to affect 'subjective' investment opportunity or, as we have previously expressed it, to shift the water-shed between 'to do and not to do'. No other than direct or mechanical effects need, however, be attributed to this burden until roughly 1933–34, because the increase in taxation was then accepted as a sacrifice to be made in a national emergency, as it had been during the war. But from the revenue act of 1934 on, this was no longer so. Permanence of the burden for reasons unconnected with emergency, involving a transfer or redistribution of wealth which in the highest brackets amounted to the socialization of the bulk of private income, and in some cases taxation for taxation's sake and regardless of insignificance of results for the Treasury, then became part of an established policy, the general drift of which was not reversed in 1938. . . .

. . . The antisaving theories and the *ressentiments* of the day found a very characteristic expression in the special surtax on undistributed corporate income (undivided profits tax), which ranged from 7 to 27 per cent. . . . The actual presence of accumulated 'reserves', and the possibility of accumulating them quickly, strengthens the position of a concern with respect to the risks and chances of innovation and expansion which it confronts. One of the causes of the efficiency of private business is that, unlike the politician or public officer, it has to pay for its mistakes. But the consequences of having to do so are very different according to whether it risks owned or borrowed 'funds', or whether a loss will only reduce surpluses or directly impinge upon original capital. Adequate book reserves are as necessary a requisite as adequate stocks of material, and in their absence, or with reduced facilities of acquiring or replenishing them, an entirely different and much more cautious business policy would impose itself. In prosperity, investment opportunities would be seen in a perspective of reduced proportions; in depression, firms would have to bow more readily to the storm. In the latter case, in particular, the important class of considerations–pure business considerations among them–that used to induce many firms 'to make a stand' for some time, even at considerable immediate loss, would tend to vanish from the businessman's mind. . . .

As regards what we have called industrial policies unfavorable to investment opportunity . . . two instances will sufficiently illustrate what we mean. First, we have seen reasons to expect that developments in the field of public utilities would be a leading feature of the current. . . . We have also seen that, barring federal enterprise, that expectation was not fulfilled. The writer does not see how it could possibly be denied that in this case existing investment opportunity was prevented from having its normal effect, not so much by what was actually done, but by the blanket threat behind it. Expected competition from federal or municipal power plants was a factor in some sectors. The Public Utilities Holding Company Act endangered the American solution of the fundamental problem of power finance. But the decisive element of the situation was that indefinite threat: executives and investors would have had to be completely blind to the political forces that were being marshaled against them, if they had been prepared to take the responsibility for, or to cooperate in, new investment on a large scale. The case thus serves to show not only how unrealistic any theory of investment opportunity is which leaves the political factor out of account, but also how easily the latter may acquire an importance compared with which that of any decline of investment opportunity for reasons inherent to the capitalist process would be negligible, even if it did occur at a significant rate per year.

Second, there is nothing surprising in the fact that under the circumstances the no less old hostility against 'monopoly power' should have asserted itself again all over the industrial field. But 'monopoly' really means any large-scale business. And since the economic 'progress' in this country is largely the result of work done within a number of concerns at no time much greater than 300 or 400, any serious threat to the functioning of these will spread paralysis in the economic organism to a much greater degree than a similar threat to the corresponding number of concerns would in any other country. . . . That hostility propelled or facilitated the fiscal and labor policies which we have glanced at above. Beyond these very little was actually done; but much was foreshadowed at various times, even before the monopoly investigation, recently instituted. This may have meant nothing or everything, according to whether or not the threats–no doubt, again indefinite– were taken seriously by those whose decisions they could have influenced. But it should be observed how very much like 'liquidity preference owing to vanishing investment opportunity' the behavior would look which would result if they were. . . .

. . . Real or supposed drifts and trends may count as much as or more than facts, threats as much as actions, indefinite threats more than specific ones, in creating the psychic environment in which the nation's work has to be done. *We* know that behind those measures, administrative acts, and anticipations there is something more fundamental, *viz.*, an attitude hostile to the industrial bourgeoisie which is no ephemeral composite of individual circumstances and political exigencies of the

day but the product of the same social process that created that bourgeoisie. Businessmen presumably do not hold that theory. But they
need not hold any in order to realize that there is in those measures and
programs more than there would have been in similar measures and
programs 30 years ago. They *are* not only, but they *feel* threatened.
They realize that they are on trial before judges who have the verdict
in their pocket beforehand, that an increasing part of public opinion is
impervious to their point of view, and that any particular indictment
will, if successfully met, at once be replaced by another. . . .

. . . To deny that this impairs the efficiency of the economic engine
or, if we retain the slogan, reduces investment opportunity, would
seem to the writer unreasonable.

Business Cycles, McGraw-Hill, New York, 1939, vol. ii, pp. 1036,
1038–44, 1046, 1049

VIII

The Approach of War

The political deadlock evident since 1937 persisted throughout the next two years. In the mid-term elections of 1938 Roosevelt tried to break it by campaigning vigorously against Democrats hostile to the New Deal, but this attempt to purge the party of its reactionaries was yet another humiliating defeat for the President. Southern Democrats and like-minded conservative Republicans continued to form a solid coalition against reform. The situation was made even more difficult for Roosevelt by the fact that from this point onwards he was, to all intents and purposes, a 'lame duck' President who would leave office in January 1941; hardly anyone anticipated he would seek a third term. Moreover, the mounting European crisis leading to the Second World War was having its impact on the American scene and there is some evidence that Roosevelt was gradually forced to abandon reform at least partly in exchange for support for a more internationalist foreign policy. At all events in his speech to Congress of January 1939 Roosevelt effectively bade farewell to the New Deal and closed its six-year history. Yet if the onset of war put paid to reform, there is little doubt that it brought the complete recovery America had sought in vain for a decade. The measures of April 1938 may well have succeeded given time but, from the autumn of 1938 on, the main stimulus to the United States' economy came from the development of a war machine geared to supply the needs of the European powers. As the statistics show, in 1941, the year of America's own entry into war, by one of the great ironies of history, the country was more prosperous than ever before.

1. By 1938, as the mid-term elections approached, the Democrats were in disarray. The Economist had forecast trouble ahead as early as November 1936, straight after the election.

Not since the Civil War have the Republicans fallen to such low representation, and only once, just after the war, were the Democrats reduced to so pitiful a handful. The danger of this result is obvious. The majority is too large for efficient service. It is bound to deteriorate into factionalism. And as the Solid South sent 101 representatives to the lower house, most of whom cannot by wild exaggeration be described as New Dealers, they will constitute an immediate conservative influence.

The public so far has not paid much of a price for the new doctrine of unionization. If strikes and riots and, later on, gross inconvenience to the public become the order of the day, Mr Roosevelt may topple from his place as labour's Messiah. He may have to treat labour more 'objectively' than he did on occasion during the last four years. And once he has chilled the enthusiasm of his labour following, his second honeymoon will have ended. If he loses labour he may spoil the dream of a long series of Democratic victories. To make a permanently liberal party composed both of labour and the South would be a feat. President Roosevelt is more enviable to-day, before his inauguration, than he is likely to be a year hence.

The Economist, 21 November 1936, p. 357

2. *In the elections Roosevelt did make a bid to transform the Democrats into 'a permanently liberal party'. Speaking against Senator George of Georgia on 11 August 1938 he said this.*

To carry out my responsibility as President, it is clear that if there is to be success in our Government there ought to be co-operation between members of my own party and myself–co-operation, in other words, within the majority party, between one branch of Government, the Legislative branch, and the head of the other branch, the Executive. That is one of the essentials of a party form of government. It has been going on in this country for nearly a century and a half. The test is not measured, in the case of an individual, by his every vote on every bill –of course not. The test lies rather in the answer to two questions: first, has the record of the candidate shown, while differing perhaps in details, a constant active fighting attitude in favor of the broad objectives of the party and of the Government as they are constituted today; and secondly, does the candidate really, in his heart, deep down in his heart, believe in these objectives? I regret that in the case of my friend, Senator George, I cannot honestly answer either of these questions in the affirmative.

The Public Papers and Addresses of Franklin D. Roosevelt, ed. S. Rosenman, Macmillan, New York, 1941, vol. vii, pp. 469–70

3. In a radio address on election eve he set the struggle in an international context.

As of today, Fascism and Communism—and old-line Tory Republicanism—are not threats to the continuation of our form of government. But I venture the challenging statement that if American democracy ceases to move forward as a living force, seeking day and night by peaceful means to better the lot of our citizens, then Fascism and Communism, aided, unconsciously perhaps, by old-line Tory Republicanism, will grow in strength in our land. . . .

. . . The modern independent industrial and agricultural society which we live in is like a large factory. Each member of the organization has his own job to perform on the assembly line, but if the conveyor belt breaks or gets tangled up, no one in the factory, no matter how hard he tries, can do his own particular job. Each of us—farmer, business man or worker—suffers when anything goes wrong with the conveyor belt.

If our democracy is to survive it must give the average man reasonable assurance that the belt will be kept moving.

Dictators have recognized that problem. They keep the conveyor belt moving—but at a terrible price to the individual and to his civil liberty.

The New Deal has been trying to keep those belts moving without paying such a price. It does not wish to run or manage any part of our economic machine which private enterprise can run and keep running. That should be left to individuals, to corporations, to any other form of private management, with profit for those who manage well. But when an abuse interferes with the ability of private enterprise to keep the national conveyor belt moving, government has a responsibility to eliminate that abuse.

We do not assume for a minute that all we have done is right or all that we have done has been successful, but our economic and social program of the past five years has definitely given to the United States of America a more stable and less artificial prosperity than any other nation in the world has enjoyed in that period.

Ibid., vol. vii, pp. 586–8

4. But Roosevelt lost his battle and from now on considerations of war overshadowed everything else. In the view of Rexford Tugwell, this was to exert a critical influence on the New Deal. Here he writes about the aftermath of the Ludlow resolution which called for a national referendum before America involved itself in war. The vote on the resolution was taken in January 1938.

The Republicans mostly voted for consideration. This was expected partisanship. But it was actually the southern Democrats who defeated it. They had had a well-developed coalition with Republicans in opposition to all domestic administration measures–with a few exceptions–but on foreign policy they were to be counted on as solid support against isolationism.

If he had not sensed before that something like this was developing, Franklin knew it now. The chief strength of the opposition to his foreign policy came from the sources he counted on to uphold his domestic measures. It looked as though he might have to choose between them. It amounted to this: he could risk collective security to get domestic reform, or he could risk domestic reform to get an acceptable foreign policy. As the months passed and he considered this dilemma, he was gradually forced to the conclusion, especially after the Munich results became evident and Hitler was again on the move, that the world crisis was paramount. Reform must be sacrificed. . . .

. . . If 1938 had been disappointing in domestic matters, 1939 threatened to be downright disastrous. Franklin would face his now familiar dilemma with its alternatives made more disagreeable. The North and West would support reform but not collective security. The South would support collective security but not reform. He would have to confirm the choice he had begun to make in 1938: sacrifice of the New Deal for foreign policy. And the price demanded would be higher, perhaps much higher than his most pessimistic calculations had forecast before the elections.

The Democratic Roosevelt, Doubleday, New York, 1957, pp. 470–1, 476

5. *Mrs Roosevelt lends some weight to this interpretation in this extract from her memoirs.*

I also remember wanting to get all-out support for the anti-lynching bill and the removal of the poll tax, but though Franklin was in favour of both measures, they never became 'must' legislation. When I would protest, he would simply say: 'First things come first, and I can't alienate certain votes I need for measures that are more important at the moment by pushing any measure that would entail a fight.' And as the situation in Europe grew worse, preparation for war had to take precedence over everything else. That was always 'must' legislation, and Franklin knew it would not pass if there was a party split.

This I Remember, Hutchinson, London, 1950, p. 132

6. *Certainly the valedictory tone of Roosevelt's message to Congress on 4 January 1939 made it seem that he regarded the New Deal as a closed chapter.*

In meeting the troubles of the world we must meet them as one people –with a unity born of the fact that for generations those who have come to our shores, representing many kindreds and tongues, have been welded by common opportunity into a united patriotism. If another form of government can present a united front in its attack on a democracy, the attack must and will be met by a united democracy. Such a democracy can and must exist in the United States. . . .

Our nation's program of social and economic reform is therefore a part of defense, as basic as armaments themselves.

Against the background of events in Europe, in Africa and in Asia during these recent years, the pattern of what we have accomplished since 1933 appears in even clearer focus.

For the first time we have moved upon deep-seated problems affecting our national strength and have forged national instruments adequate to meet them.

Consider what the seemingly piecemeal struggles of these six years add up to in terms of realistic national preparedness.

We are conserving and developing natural resources–land, water, power, forests.

We are trying to provide necessary food, shelter and medical care for the health of our population.

We are putting agriculture–our system of food and fiber supply–on a sounder basis.

We are strengthening the weakest spot in our system of industrial supply–its long smouldering labor difficulties.

We have cleaned up our credit system so that depositor and investor alike may more readily and willingly make their capital available for peace or war.

We are giving to our youth new opportunities for work and education.

We have sustained the morale of all the population by the dignified recognition of our obligations to the aged, the helpless and the needy.

Above all, we have made the American people conscious of their interrelationships and their interdependence. They sense a common destiny and a common need of each other. Differences of occupation, geography, race and religion no longer obscure the nation's fundamental unity in thought and in action.

We have our difficulties, true – but we are a wiser and tougher nation than we were in 1929, or in 1932. . . .

. . . We have now passed the period of internal conflict in the launching of our program of social reform. Our full energies may now be released to invigorate the processes of recovery in order to preserve our reforms, and to give every man and woman who wants to work a real job at a living wage.

But time is of paramount importance. The deadline of danger from within and from without is not within our control. The hour-glass may be in the hands of other nations. Our own hour-glass tells us that we are off on a race to make democracy work, so that we may be efficient in peace and therefore secure in national defense.

The Public Papers and Addresses of Franklin D. Roosevelt, ed. S. Rosenman, Macmillan, New York, 1941, vol. viii, pp. 4–5, 7

7. *These were brave words, but the New Deal had still not banished the spirit of uncertainty that had weighed on America for nearly a decade. Hadley Cantril comments on the panic-stricken reaction to Orson Welles's radio adaptation of* The War of the Worlds, *broadcast on 30 October 1938.*

. . . Particularly since the depression of 1929, a number of people have begun to wonder whether or not they will ever regain any sense of economic security. The complexity of modern finance and government, the discrepancies shown in the economic and political proposals of the various 'experts,' the felt threats of Fascism, Communism, prolonged unemployment among millions of Americans – these together with a thousand and one other characteristics of modern living – create an environment which the average individual is completely unable to interpret. Not only do events occur that he is unable to understand, but almost all of these events seem to be completely beyond his own immediate control, even though his personal life may be drastically affected by them. He feels that he is living in a period of rapid social change, but just what direction the change should take and how it may be peacefully accomplished he does not know. For the most part, the potential consequences of forthcoming events are unpredictable.

This situation is not something known only to the public official, the big businessman, or the social scientist. The masses of people themselves know all this most poignantly. The material consequences of a disturbed economic order are not difficult for anyone to recognize. And most important for our purposes are the psychological consequences in terms of personal anxieties, ambitions, and insecurities of this awareness that all is not right with the world.

H. CANTRIL, H. GAUDET, and H. HERTZOG, *Invasion from Mars*, Princeton University Press, 1940, pp. 379–80

8. *Evidence of distress was still all too plentiful. A week after Roosevelt's message to Congress, the* New York Times *published this report about the sharecroppers of Missouri, themselves in part the victims of New Deal agricultural policy.*

New Madrid, Mo., Jan. 11.–Huddled tonight around flickering roadside campfires, hundreds of Southeast Missouri sharecropper families, demonstrating against a low economic status, defied probable rain or snow, shrinking food supplies and the danger of disease.

Many of the ragged army of more than 1,000 men, women and children, most of them Negroes, were ill-prepared to face the predicted inclement weather.

Tents and improvised shelters of bed clothing offered little protection from the chilly wind which ushered in their second night in the open air.

The march to the highways was called as a protest against the growing movement in the cotton country to abandon sharecropping in favor of the employment of day laborers. Leaders of the demonstration contended that some landowners had evicted their renters to avoid sharing crop benefit payments with them.

Various landowners in the 'bootheel' area blamed the situation on Missouri's tremendous gain in farm population in recent years, restricted cotton acreage, the shift from manual labor and mule power to modern motorized farming, and losses suffered by some operators under the sharecropper system.

Many former croppers, 'day hands' during the recent cotton season, were in the groups whose camps were scattered along 150 miles of United States Highways 60 and 61.

Will Travers, leader of a group at Hayti, said all of his followers had been day laborers on farms in Pemiscot County, 'but we can't live on 75 cents a day.'

New York Times, 12 January 1939

9. *With the coming of war, however, the situation changed rapidly, as the major economic indices in Appendix I testify. Broadus Mitchell comments.*

Economic revival in the United States dated from the outbreak of war in Europe in September, 1939. Progress, except for a brief lapse, was accelerating. Every force of degeneration gave way to concerted effort; dejection was jolted into alertness, which became purpose and system. Fatigue was replaced by high national morale which developed private and public economic inventiveness. It was like watching blood drain back into the blanched face of a person who had fainted. Problems remained before recovery would be full, but all had obviously been placed in the way of solution.

Depression Decade, Rinehart, New York, 1947, p. 371

10. *Theodore Saloutos and John D. Hicks point to the effect on the Chicago cereals market.*

. . . Within a matter of a few days after the outbreak of hostilities, grain prices on the Chicago market soared as high as government and exchange rules would permit them to go. 'Trading came to a standstill. Rules which have been put into effect the past six years to curb runaway speculative markets met their first real test. Because they prohibited prices from going any higher than the daily limits amounting to 5 cents in wheat and rye, 4 cents in corn and 3 cents in oats, they throttled trade.' Buyers with orders to buy millions of bushels were unable to fill them because there were few sellers who wanted to dispose of their holdings at the maximum prices. Only a few sales took place, the first time in exchange history that anything like this had happened. Late in 1939 the Chicago market was described as 'a seething cauldron' that 'bubbled over with the greatest flood of orders it has had to digest in months as prices skyrocketed in the wheat, rye and soy bean pits'.

Agricultural Discontent in the Middle West 1900–1939, Wisconsin University Press, 1951, p. 537

11. *An inscription on the Works Projects Administration's building at the New York World's Fair in 1939 served to point up the irony.*

The foundation upon which this nation stands is the dignity of man as an individual ... his right to free expression in politics and religion, and in the labor by which he builds his way of life. Work is America's answer to the need of idle millions. . . . Work, not charity ... peaceful work, not regimentation to build the machines of war ... useful public work, to benefit us all.

s. f. charles, *Minister of Relief*, Syracuse University Press, 1963, p. 128

Part Two
HISTORIOGRAPHY

I

Roosevelt

At the time of his nomination as Democratic candidate in 1932, few people suspected that Franklin Roosevelt would be given a place in the pantheon of great Presidents together with Washington, Jackson, and Lincoln. But his enthusiasm for compromise, then and later so bitterly criticized, was as much a source of strength as of weakness in that he saw the Presidency as a unique force for reconciling conflicting interests within the nation; and his apparent superficiality concealed a highly developed instinct for power. Before long he had established himself as a formidable popular leader who towered above both his party and his political opponents. So much so, indeed, that he was soon being accused of reaching for dictatorship, and the hectic international background of the 1930s lent a disquieting plausibility to these charges. Fears of a presidential dictatorship, however, have been a staple theme of American history since the time of Washington, and there can be little doubt that for most democrats Roosevelt was the outstanding champion of their cause in the struggle with totalitarianism. Much of this admiration, of course, stems from his leadership in the war years which lie outside the scope of this book, and Roosevelt's achievements appear a good deal less impressive if one examines his position in 1939. Yet even then he had the stature to make a successful bid for a third term of office and to take his country into a second world war. In spite of his several failures, Roosevelt never lost the confidence of a majority of the American people.

Character

1. *In 1932 Governor Franklin Delano Roosevelt did not appear, to Walter Lippmann at least, to have presidential qualities.*

. . . Franklin D. Roosevelt is an amiable man with many philanthropic impulses, but he is not the dangerous enemy of anything. He is too eager to please. . . . Mr Roosevelt is, as a matter of fact, an excessively cautious politician. . . . Franklin D. Roosevelt is no crusader. He is no tribune of the people. He is no enemy of entrenched privilege. He is a pleasant man who, without any important qualifications for the office, would very much like to be President. . . . It would not be denied that men less fitted than he have served acceptably as Presidents of the United States. Nevertheless, the judgement exists, and has grown more firm, that he has not the grasp of the issues or the disinterestedness or the resolution that a President must have in time of great emergency. No mathematical proof in support of such a judgement can be offered. But that it is the judgement of observers who have no axes to grind, that it is the judgement of men who have very considerable personal liking for him, is certain. All the appearances of the fit candidate he possesses. All the instinctive prejudices run in his favor. It is in spite of his attractiveness, in spite of his unquestioned personal integrity, in spite of his generous sympathies, that this judgement has formed itself among large numbers of discerning people that here is a man who has made a good Governor, who might make a good Cabinet officer, but who simply does not measure up to the tremendous demands of the office of President.

Interpretations 1931–1932, Macmillan, New York, 1932, pp. 261–2, 273

2. *Raymond Moley, writing at the same time, had a first-hand opportunity to observe Roosevelt's charm and his unacademic mental processes. These are extracts from a letter to his sister, written in April 1932.*

. . . You ask what he is like and it isn't easy to answer because I haven't had the chance to confirm a lot of fleeting impressions. One thing is sure – that the idea that people get from his charming manner – that he is soft or flabby in disposition and character – is far from true. When he wants something a lot he can be formidable – when crossed he is hard, stubborn, resourceful, relentless. I used to think on the basis of casual observation that his amiability was 'lord-of-the-manor'–'good-to-the-peasants'-stuff. It isn't that at all. He seems quite naturally warm and friendly – less because he genuinely likes many of the people to whom he is pleasant (although he does like a lot of people of all sorts and varieties) than because he just enjoys the pleasant and engaging role, as a charming woman does. And being a born politician he measures such qualities in himself by the effect they produce on others. He is wholly conscious of his ability to send callers away happy and glowing and in agreement with him and his ideas. And he particularly enjoys sending

174

people away who have completely forgotten (under his spell) the thing they have come to say or ask. On the whole, his cordiality and his interest in people is, to all appearances, unfeigned. . . .

. . . The man's energy and vitality are astonishing. I've been amazed with his interest in things. It skips and bounces through seemingly intricate subjects and maybe it is my academic training that makes me feel that no one could possibly learn much in such a hit or miss fashion. I don't find that he has read much about economic subjects. What he gets is from talking to people and when he stores away the net of conversation he never knows what part of what he has kept is what he said himself or what his visitor said. There is a lot of autointoxication of the intelligence that we shall have to watch. But he gets a lot from talking to people who come in. A typical approach to a big problem is 'so-and-so was telling me yesterday'. Another is 'now *we* found in dealing with the *State* so-and-so that we had to deal with such-and-such'.

This quality seems to give Tugwell some worries because he wants people to show familiarity with pretty elementary ideas. But I believe that his [Roosevelt's] complete freedom from dogmatism is a virtue at this stage of the game. He will stick to ideas after he has expressed them, I believe and hope. Heaven knows Hoover is full of information and dogmas but he has been imprisoned by his knowledge and God save us from four more years of that! If we can't get a President with a fluid mind we shall have some bad times ahead.

After Seven Years, Harper, New York, 1939, pp. 10, 11

3. *Many were struck by the apparent complexity of Roosevelt's character, for example, Robert Sherwood.*

Being a writer by trade, I tried continually to study him, to try to look beyond his charming and amusing and warmly affectionate surface into his heavily forested interior. But I could never really understand what was going on in there. His character was not only multiplex; it was contradictory to a bewildering degree. He was hard and he was soft. At times he displayed a capacity for vindictiveness which could be described as petty, and at other times he demonstrated the Christian spirit of forgiveness and charity in its purest form. He could be a ruthless politician, but he was the champion of friends and associates who for him were political liabilities, conspicuously Harry Hopkins, and of causes which apparently competent advisers assured him would constitute political suicide. He could appear to be utterly cynical, worldly, illusionless, and yet his religious faith was the strongest and most mysterious force that was in him. Although he was progressive enough and liberal enough to be condemned as a 'traitor to his class' and 'that Red in the White House', he was in truth a profoundly old-fashioned person with an incurable nostalgia for the very 'horse-and-buggy era' on which he publicly heaped so much scorn.

The White House Papers of Harry L. Hopkins, Eyre and Spottiswoode, London, 1948, vol. i, p. 10

4. *To Sir Arthur Salter, who saw a good deal of Roosevelt during the Second World War, his impenetrability was the result of his struggle with the poliomyelitis which had crippled him for life in 1921.*

Roosevelt fought his inner fight and won. He pursued the most public of careers, and with a concentration helped by exemption from the normal distractions of youth. His dynamic personality, his passionate will, his inexhaustible nervous energy, seemed even to draw extra strength from a sublimation of his physical infirmity. So far from falling back upon the meditative, introspective mood of the recluse, his manner became that of an exuberant extrovert, easily accessible, informally friendly, frankly enjoying wit and humour (even the least subtle– perhaps especially the least subtle), welcoming any contest with his peers with a warrior's zest. His will was hardened and tempered by his inner struggle; his political instinct sharpened by concentration of interest on the political environment. Having fought and won the hardest fight of all, why should he fear anything which a human foe or fate itself could threaten?

If any sign remained of the inner conflict, it was not in any weakening but in a certain exaggeration of the qualities he displayed. Sometimes one seemed to detect a forced and unnatural note in his exuberance and gaiety–not so much that the mood was at the moment unreal but that it had been induced by previous effort. His apparent enjoyment of an anecdote was often more than it merited. In his easy accessibility to many who had little to offer he guarded his strength too little for what he alone could accomplish. One had, too, the impression that his manner of generous familiarity was perhaps a screen for an inner, and untouchable, reserve and an inner loneliness. Few men perhaps have

been on Christian-name terms with so many and yet had so few intimate friends. The lined and laughing face was perhaps a mask worn
for so long that it had become part of himself.

Personality in Politics, Faber and Faber, London, 1947, pp. 176–7

5. *For Rexford Tugwell, however, Roosevelt's character was elementally
simple.*

Many of those who have written about this second presidential
Roosevelt have said that his was an unusually complex nature. I have
never thought this an illuminating characterization; but I could understand why Frances Perkins, for instance, said so. There was always much
that was hard to explain, many actions that seemed inconsistent, many
things begun and apparently abandoned. It was impossible to develop
a highly recognizable simple personality from the known facts, one
exactly typed and reduced to rule. It did seem complex. But that, I
think, was because so much of it was hidden.

No historic figure ever lent himself less well to preconceived patterns
of behavior than Franklin Roosevelt. His most ardent partisan has to
explain embarrassing lapses from the strict code he himself accepted,
and his most malevolent critics find themselves losing their prolonged
struggle to prove him a spendthrift–if not a traitorous–leader with an
over-mastering mania for power. He was consistently neither a puritan
nor an unscrupulous schemer. Approaching the development of his
character and the history of his behavior in this polarized fashion will
not explain what posterity needs to know about so consequential a
career. But that he was not really more complex than most of us I am
fully convinced: he may well have been less so. He believed in an external guidance not all of us accept as a reality, and he was certain of a
commanding destiny most of us have no reason to anticipate. He considered himself appointed to be a leader, but that was because there was
work to be done which he judged he could do. If these controlling
forces operated on his nature more powerfully than is normal, there
is ample explanation in his environment and in the encouragement
flowing in upon him from every side.

There is something beyond all this, something internal to be understood. . . . It cannot be located specifically in intelligence, in attractiveness, or in any other quality of temperament or character. It consists in
an impulsive urge so deeply seated and so primitively energized that it

activates and controls every other impulse. Looking back on the Roosevelt career, I find its most persistent as well as its most astounding feature is this fierce flame burning at its core. The head of steam it generated allowed its containing vessel no rest even in invalidism, much less in seeming defeat; it drove his turbines with a merciless impatience. Its source was certainly an original force which is shared very unequally among men. . . .

. . . I have tried to show . . . how the deep volcanic pressure had its way with the individual, how his mind coped with the responsibilities it brought him, how he rose to the occasions of national crisis, how he sometimes dodged and temporized in the interest of eventual victory, and how the obligations he felt, as well as the lessons he learned, controlled his actions. The force within him always demanded and got some kind of response, although it was often masked by falsification of intentions or concealment of objectives. But, as we must also see, he could, when necessary, hold the pressure in check and wait his time with extraordinary patience. This often misled opponents and associates alike who thought he had quit when he was only waiting the right moment.

The Democratic Roosevelt, Doubleday, New York, 1957, pp. 11–13

6. *His wife believed that religious faith was his prime source of strength.*

I think he believed that he could meet the tremendous crisis the country was facing better than anyone else in the country. A man must have this confidence in himself or he could never undertake the heavy responsibilities of leading a nation. People used to comment to me on the egoism of my uncle, Theodore Roosevelt. I know many people felt that Franklin D. Roosevelt had the same quality. Undoubtedly he did to a certain extent; a man could not carry the burdens of the presidency otherwise.

I always felt that my husband's religion had something to do with his confidence in himself. As I have said, it was a very simple religion. He believed in God and in His guidance. He felt that human beings were given tasks to perform and with those tasks the ability and strength to put them through. He could pray for help and guidance and have faith in his own judgement as a result. The church services that he always insisted on holding on Inauguration Day, anniversaries, and whenever a great crisis impended, were the expression of his religious faith. I think this must not be lost sight of in judging his acceptance of responsibility and his belief in his ability to meet whatever crisis had to be met.

This I Remember, Hutchinson, London, 1950, p. 64

7. *Another great inspiration was his rapport with people, as Samuel Rosenman points out.*

I think that the great reason for Roosevelt's place in the hearts and heads of people was his ability to make them feel that he associated himself personally with each of them in each one's aspirations for something better in life. He did not seem to be someone far removed, fighting their battles in a rarefied atmosphere. He was right down in the sweaty arena with them, side by side, expressing what they were thinking, doing what they wanted, taking his strength and his boldness from their strength and their support—making them feel that he and they were all doing it together.

Working With Roosevelt, Hart-Davis, London, 1952, p. 499

8. *Farley, the campaign manager, noticed the same thing.*

... The successful man must demonstrate that the opportunity to rub elbows with other men is a real source of pleasure, not an irksome task to be put up with for what it brings. Roosevelt is successful in that respect because he so thoroughly enjoys campaigning and mixing with his fellow mortals. He rode for hours in the 1936 campaign in motor processions, waving constantly to people along the roadsides, shaking hands with hundreds, and delivering ten or even fifteen speeches a day. He never gave the impression of working hard; on the contrary he was stimulated and exhilarated. The husky voice and worn-down look was noticeable by its absence.

Behind the Ballots, Harcourt, Brace, New York, 1939, p. 318

Achievements

9. *Whether or not one agrees with his policies it is clear that Roosevelt enormously enhanced the office of President.*

Roosevelt's influence on the Presidency was tremendous. Only Washington, who made the office, and Jackson, who remade it, did more than he to raise it to its present condition of strength, dignity, and independence. I often wonder if Mr Eisenhower realizes how many of the powers and privileges he commands, and how much of the respect and assistance he enjoys, are a direct legacy from Franklin Roosevelt. The press conference, the Executive Office, the right to reorganize his administration, and the powers to protect industrial and financial peace are all parts of this legacy. Generals obey him, Congress defers to him, and leaders of other nations honor him far more readily than they would had Roosevelt not been so forceful a President. Like every such President he left his successor to reap the wild wind, and in at least one instance, the passage of the Twenty-second Amendment, the reaction to his high-riding incumbency was sufficiently angry to weaken the office permanently. Yet the verdict of history will surely be that he left the Presidency a more splendid instrument of democracy than he found it.

CLINTON ROSSITER, *The American Presidency*, Harcourt, Brace, New York, 1956, p. 119

10. *Some saw him turning this office into a personal dictatorship. Raymond Moley, turning away from Roosevelt more and more, was greatly perturbed by a conversation they had early in 1936.*

. . . Each 'attack' helped him, Roosevelt repeated.

That was as might be. But was *all* criticism of his administration to be construed as 'attack' upon him? I asked. Wasn't there a vital distinction? I, for instance, had been privately and publicly critical of the surplus tax sponsored by Oliphant. Did that mean that I was 'attacking' the administration as a whole and that, hence, I had become an enemy?

'I am not interested in talking about the tax proposal,' was the answer. 'You can have any opinion you want on that. That's a detail.' And then, impatiently, 'You seem to be interested in personalities and details. I am not interested in personalities. It's not what you say or think about an individual in the administration or about a specific issue. There's one issue in this campaign. It's myself, and people must be either for me or against me.'

After Seven Years, Harper, New York, 1939, p. 342

11. *Soon after Roosevelt's death, Dwight Macdonald, then on the far left, also deplored the tendencies to paternalistic dictatorship which he believed he detected in the late President.*

. . . Roosevelt had become the Father especially of the left-of-centre section of American society. This was an unhealthy state of affairs, both politically and psychologically, and would have been objectionable even had Roosevelt been a far wiser and more benevolent Father than he was. Rebellion against paternal authority is the road to maturity for society as for the individual; in this sense, while one naturally is sorry to see anyone die, one must regard Roosevelt's death as a gain.

He is often compared to Lincoln or Wilson, but there was in him little of that humanity which the former, for all his unscrupulous politicking, often showed, or of the genuine liberal idealism of the latter. In the last few years, he had even grown cynically weary of the pretence of humane and progressive aims, declaring that the New Deal was dead, and the Atlantic Charter was not taken seriously.

Yet when he died, he was mourned as a great humanitarian and the Father of the common people. The myth was still intact. By this, we may measure the deterioration of our politics in the last two generations.

The Responsibility of Peoples, Gollancz, London, 1957, pp. 185–6

12. *For such rabid critics as John T. Flynn it was impossible to say anything good of him, even in death.*

The figure of Roosevelt exhibited before the eyes of our people is a fiction. There was no such being as that noble, selfless, hard-headed, wise and farseeing combination of philosopher, philanthropist and warrior which has been fabricated out of pure propaganda and which a small collection of dangerous cliques in this country are using to advance their own evil ends.

The Roosevelt Myth, rev. edn, Devin-Adair, New York, 1956, p. 419

13. *Some opponents even went so far as to compare Roosevelt with Hitler. Winston Churchill refuted them, in an article published late in 1934.*

To compare Roosevelt's effort with that of Hitler is to insult, not Roosevelt but civilization. The petty persecutions and old-world assertions of brutality in which the German idol has indulged only show their smallness and squalor compared to the renaissance of creative effort with which the name of Roosevelt will always be associated. . . .

However we may view the Presidency which has reached half its natural span, it is certain that Franklin Roosevelt will rank among the greatest of men who have occupied that proud position. His generous sympathy for the underdog, his intense desire for a nearer approach to social justice, place him high among the great philanthropists. His composure combined with activity in time of crisis class him with famous men of action. His freeing of the United States from prohibition and the vigour of his administrative measures of relief and credit expansion proclaim him a statesman of world renown. He has known how to gain the confidence and the loyalty of the most numerous and the most ebullient of civilized communities, and all the world watches his valiant effort to solve their problems with an anxiety which is only the shadow of high hope.

Great Contemporaries, Reprint Society edn, London, 1941, pp. 336, 343–4

14. *G. W. Johnson, an American commentator, also exploded this notion.*

Both had risen to power on the crest of a wave of protest set in motion by the same sort of grievances. Both took over countries economically in a state of collapse and virtually disintegrating socially. Both faced the problem of putting millions of idle men back to work immediately, and the even more urgent problem of putting some spirit into an apathetic and despairing people.

There were other similarities. In Germany, as in America, the people were not so much aflame with enthusiasm for the new leader as inflamed with wrath against the old ones. In Germany, as in America, the gravamen of the old leaders' offence was not so much what they had done as what they had failed to do. In Germany, as in America, the indictment of the old leaders included a multitude of counts, but there as here they may all be summed up as failure to obey the injunction of the Constitution of the United States 'to provide for the general welfare'. Finally, in Germany as in America, the new leader, largely because he was new, was given *carte blanche* to do what he thought best.

If we came out with the New Deal and the Germans came out with Nazism, the main reason is because we had chosen the author of the Commonwealth Club speech and the Germans had chosen the author of *Mein Kampf*. There is at least this much in the 'leadership principle'.

Roosevelt: An American Study, Hamish Hamilton, London, 1942, p. 211

15. *Roosevelt, of course, was anything but a radical, as Frances Perkins pointed out.*

I knew Roosevelt long enough and under enough circumstances to be quite sure that he was no political or economic radical. I take it that the essence of economic radicalism is to believe that the best system is the one in which private ownership of the means of production is abolished in favour of public ownership. But Roosevelt took the *status quo* in our economic system as much for granted as his family. They were part of his life, and so was our system; he was content with it. He felt that it ought to be humane, fair, and honest, and that adjustments ought to be made so that the people would not suffer from poverty and neglect, and so that all would share.

The Roosevelt I Knew, Hammond, London, 1947, p. 265

16. *Broadus Mitchell agreed.*

Enough admirers and antagonists have attributed to President Franklin Roosevelt an economic philosophy. The variety of these imputed systems suggests that in truth he had no reasoned design founded in analysis and issuing in deliberate articulated actions. If anything, he moved less with the fervor of an innovator than with the assurance of a conservative. He had the Tory tolerance for change. Accustomed all his life to the power bestowed by position, earned by ability, and exercised unselfishly, he knew the difference between shallow opportunism and hopeful experiment. Possessed of tradition, its dogmas did not awe him. Rules, for him, were the result of reasonable assent of society; if they no longer served, or required to be reinterpreted, they could be set aside or modified in the same way in which they had been formed.

Depression Decade, Rinehart, New York, 1947, p. 124

17. *Above all, in the eyes of Isaiah Berlin, he was the champion of western democracy.*

Over this vast seething chaos presided a handsome, charming, gay, very intelligent, very delightful, very audacious man, Mr Franklin Delano Roosevelt. He was accused of many weaknesses. He had betrayed his class; he was ignorant, unscrupulous, irresponsible. He was ruthless in playing with the lives and careers of individuals. He was surrounded by adventurers, slick opportunists, intriguers. He made conflicting promises, cynically and brazenly, to individuals and groups and representatives of foreign nations. He made up, with his vast and irresistible public charm, and his astonishing high spirits, for lack of virtues considered as more important in the leader of the most powerful democracy in the world–the virtues of application, industry, responsibility. All this was said and some of it may indeed have been just. What attracted his followers were countervailing qualities of a rare and inspiring order: he was large-hearted and possessed wide political horizons, imaginative sweep, understanding of the time in which he lived and of the direction of the great new forces at work in the twentieth century–technological, racial, imperialist, anti-imperialist; he was in favour of life and movement, the promotion of the most generous possible fulfilment of the largest possible number of human wishes, and not in favour of caution and retrenchment and sitting still. Above all, he was absolutely fearless.

He was one of the few statesmen in the twentieth or any other century who seemed to have no fear at all of the future. He believed in his own strength and ability to manage, and succeed, whatever happened. He believed in the capacity and loyalty of his lieutenants, so that he looked upon the future with a calm eye, as if to say, 'Let it come, whatever it may be, it will all be grist to our great mill. We shall turn it all to benefit.' It was this, perhaps, more than any other quality, which drew men of very different outlooks to him. In a despondent world which appeared divided between wicked and fatally efficient fanatics marching to destroy, and bewildered populations on the run, unenthusiastic martyrs in a cause they could not define, he believed in his own ability, so long as he was at the control, to stem this terrible tide. He had all the character and energy and skill of the dictators, and he was on our side. He was, in his opinions and his public action, every inch a democrat.

'Roosevelt through European Eyes', *The Political Quarterly*, 1955, pp. 338–9

18. *For Rexford Tugwell, he was a democrat in the best possible sense of the word.*

As I have worked at this book I have always been aware of writing about a man who attempted to do much more than he was able to carry through. I became quite certain also that he was finally conscious of his role and had a clear focus on his aims. When he fell short, moreover, he knew better than anyone else the extent and significance of the failure. He was a political man, a democrat; he believed in getting things done with full, if not always with complete, consent. Getting this approval often required compromise. He took what he could for what he had to give. He thus subordinated the important to the necessary, trusting his judgment to yield a public profit. If there was a residue of hatred from those who were beyond the margins of compromise, he accepted it. He did not like it, but it was inevitable and it did not unduly worry him.

When he died our society was measurably farther forward in every respect than when he became President. He grasped leadership when we were economically paralyzed and socially divided. The nation was a giant in chains of its own forging. He loosened the chains by relieving the paralysis of fear; he reduced the divisions by attacking poverty; and he began a reconstruction. His reconstructive plans had to be postponed because of first the prospect and then the fact of war. But there were clear indications . . . that he would have come back to them if he had lived. He did not think himself a failure; he was simply not finished.

When he is criticized—and he still is, and bitterly—the criticism comes either from those who dissented from his conception of the future or those who would have had him get there by different means. But no one who believes in the democratic method can honestly say that he did not earn the right to define the future or to choose the means for approaching it. He was an elected leader, not one who had his power from force or from unauthorized chicanery. Some critics may not agree that what he wanted was sufficient, others may not agree that what he wanted was desirable, and neither may admire the methods he used; but none of them can claim that he did not take expert advantage of our complex and peculiar way of doing things. As we look back, it is more and more apparent that a political genius of a rare and effective sort was at work. He accepted both problems and conditions for their solution and found his own answers. Usually a majority approved, and approved emphatically.

To accomplish his aims he adopted–or perhaps he always had–the same view of the presidency as his most effective predecessors. He used the office as an instrument to enhance the well-being of all the people and to maintain the securities of the nation itself. It was his view that as President he had powers co-ordinate with and equal to those of the Congress. They were derived from the same source. The President, he believed, was much better equipped to understand national needs and to define the means for satisfying them than the legislative branch; and so he must be a leader. On the whole, it can be said that no President before him grasped more completely or met more fully the responsibilities of his office. He made the presidency an instrument more commensurate with its obligations than he found it because he saw so clearly what those obligations were and because it was his natural bent to accept and carry out public duties.

We are a lucky people. We have had leaders when the national life was at stake. If it had not been for Washington we might not have become a nation; if it had not been for Lincoln we might have been split in two; if it had not been for this later democrat we might have succumbed to a dictatorship.

The Democratic Roosevelt, Doubleday, New York, 1957, pp. 10–11

19. *By the close of the thirties the New Deal had lost much of its impetus, and yet Roosevelt still retained an astonishing popularity. As Max Lerner remarked, he seemed to have outshadowed his programme.*

. . . Roosevelt has not been effective on the crucial question of unemployment, which is America's dynamite dump. Nothing can be clearer than his failure to translate his own deepening perceptions into a working program. I need not spell out that fact here. What needs, however, to be said is that while Roosevelt will no doubt be linked in history with the pragmatic and piecemeal reforms of the New Deal, he is at once smaller and bigger than the New Deal. Smaller because the New Deal is not one man's creation but the product of mass aspirations. Bigger in the sense that his personal stature has survived the relative failure of the New Deal and the scattering of its battalions. It may not be rational but it is true that many would vote for Roosevelt who would reject most of his works. His Presidential tenure offers an uncanny perspective: here is a man who lost and had to compromise on most of his goals, yet he has emerged with prestige and popular appeal probably as great as ever.

Ideas for the Ice Age, Viking Press, New York, 1941, p. 403

20. *In part this was due to the American people's response to the Roosevelt charisma, in part to Roosevelt's almost mystical view of the Presidency as the embodiment of the nation. Speaking in October 1934 he had said this.*

. . . a true function of the head of the Government of the United States is to find that unity of purpose that is best for the nation as a whole. This is necessary because government is not merely one of the many co-ordinating groups in the community of the Nation, but is essentially the outward expression of the unity and the leadership of all groups. . . . Government by the necessity of things must be the leader, must be the judge of the conflicting interests of all groups in the community.

The Public Papers and Addresses of Franklin D. Roosevelt, ed. S. Rosenman, Random House, New York, 1938, vol. iii, p. 436

21. *Tugwell, observing him at about the same time, remarked on this feeling of Roosevelt's with a baffled admiration.*

He saw the nation, as none of the others did, whole; he saw part working with part, all functioning together; the men in the cities, the men on the farms, the men at sea, all working for each other as they worked for their families. And he was the centring point. He could not make the nation over. He could not make it other than it was. He could only make it more superbly what it was.

'The Experimental Roosevelt', *Political Quarterly*, 1950, p. 264

22. *As Arthur Schlesinger points out, Roosevelt's was a large vision.*

. . . Each ideological system, as he must have felt it, described certain aspects of American reality, each missed out on certain vital features, and effectiveness might therefore most probably lie not in taking one or the other but in combining and applying both to meet the needs of a particular situation.

Though Tugwell and the others believed in experimentation, Roosevelt was at bottom a far more consistent experimentalist. They were ready to experiment *within* their systems. But Roosevelt transcended systems for the sake of a more complex vision of America, which included elements of coordination and of decentralization, of nationalism and of internationalism, and thus also included means of preventing any system from being pushed to logical–and probably destructive–extremes.

The Coming of the New Deal, Houghton Mifflin, Boston, 1959, pp. 193–4

23. *In short, Roosevelt, like the other major political figures of this decade, seemed to have attained the status of a mythological hero. Thurman Arnold puts this view.*

. . . A governmental program . . . must proceed on the assumptions of current mythology. In other words, we lack a religion of government which permits us to face frankly the psychological factors inherent in the development of organizations with public responsibility. Governmental effort based on such factors is considered Machiavellian, and contrary to proper principles. We tolerate such an attitude on the part of politicians as a necessary evil. . . .

. . . Yet all the signs today point to the fact that a new creed, which can reconcile itself to the facts of human organization, is about to be born. It as yet has no formulas. It is represented vaguely by the personality of Roosevelt who has become the symbol for a political attitude which cannot yet be put into words. The fact that Roosevelt has become the symbol of a new attitude is shown by the fact that so many of those who support him are hostile or else indifferent to the particular measures he advocates.

Many commentators express surprise at this. How can specific measures advocated by Roosevelt be so unpopular with groups of people who still keep faith with him? Hostile editors, observing the failure of some Roosevelt policy, are puzzled over the continuing Roosevelt support. They attribute it to his charming smile, his radio voice, and whatnot. The answer to the problem of Roosevelt's popular support in spite of the defeat of so many of his plans has little to do with his personal characteristics. Institutions which express in concrete form the vague aspirations of any group always arouse that kind of allegiance.

Never has this been expressed in a more striking way than by the parade of intellectuals who testified against the Roosevelt Supreme Court plan before the Senate Committee. These individuals stated that they disapproved of the majority decisions of the Court on national affairs, yet they considered it essential to the nation that the Court continue in power over national affairs. For these persons, composed of radicals and conservatives alike, the Court represented the supremacy of intellect and reason. Hence they were for it, no matter what it did. To attribute this to Hughes's charming manner or Sutherland's public personality is to make the same mistake about the influence of the Supreme Court which is being made about the present Roosevelt influence.

What Roosevelt represents to the great majority of the electorate cannot be so easily formulated because no authoritarian literature has developed (as it has with respect to the Court) to explain him as a symbol. Yet he expresses for a majority of the public the current distrust of old myths and the belief that the Government has a new rôle to play in providing for security of individuals in their jobs and in the distribution of goods. The position of a living man as such a symbol has always been precarious, because dead men are much safer in such niches than the living. Nevertheless, the writer believes that Roosevelt will continue to fill this symbolic need until something else is substituted. . . .

. . . Individuals can become symbols only in unstable times. Lincoln would never have been the great myth of national unity had it not been for the Civil War. He came to represent a new conception of the State. Roosevelt has a less secure place because the aspirations which he represents are less concrete. Nevertheless, the mental pictures of a society which are first—in times of confusion—represented by an individual, inevitably become part of the folklore later. And in that process comes stability.

Roosevelt will lose his present symbolic importance when the attitude toward government which he represents has become expressed in an inspirational literature which is generally accepted as a sort of backlog of fundamental principles. In this highly organized age, attitudes toward the function of government must be redefined, and until that process is complete a personality will take the place of a philosophy.

The Folklore of Capitalism, Yale University Press, 1937, pp. 389–92

II

The New Deal

Interpretations of the New Deal are legion, but they fall into four broadly recognizable categories: the critics of the right, the left, centre-right, and centre-left.

For the right wing the New Deal is a betrayal, a betrayal of laissez-faire or of the pre-1917 tradition of liberal reformism. In many instances, of course, the two lines of thinking became synonymous when old-style reformers identified themselves more and more with the business ethic. Hoover, after all, had professed his belief in Federal regulation before the New Deal pushed him farther across to the right; in the case of the First New Dealer Moley, this metamorphosis had taken place by 1936. Yet, whatever their background, all these men were convinced that Roosevelt had brought socialism, if not communism, to the United States and begun the 'twenty years of treason' denounced by Republicans in the 1952 election campaign. Moley, it is worth noting, worked for Goldwater in 1964.

The left, like the right, has seen the New Deal as a betrayal, but here because it betrayed the hopes for a radically new order of things which the depression had engendered. In this view the New Deal had failed America because it shied away from government planning and government intervention on a large scale. At bottom, these commentators argue, this was due to the ideological inconsistency of the administration, personified by the President himself. In other words, the New Deal lacked the courage to make a complete break with the liberal past and establish a coherent new view of the future. The result was half-measures and a dismally inadequate degree of recovery.

Responding to these attacks, the partisans of the New Deal fall into two main divisions, centre-left and centre-right. The centre-left admit the element of failure, but stress the novel aspects of the New Deal which in their opinion made it amount to a revolution in American history, destroying the world of the twenties once and for all. The New Deal, they say, was revolutionary because it was a response to a catastrophe never before experienced in the United States, because it answered the needs of groups hitherto unrepresented in American politics, revolutionary in its mood and in its methods, revolutionary in effect if not at times in intention.

The centre-right, on the other hand, have chosen to emphasize the continuity between the New Deal and the historical tradition of radical liberal protest in the United States, and their view is sometimes ruefully shared by the left. The New Deal, so these historians say, was the embodiment of an essentially pragmatic liberalism and it was a positive virtue that it should have steered clear of the rigid ideologies of both right and left and sought its solutions in familiar, American terms. Its failures, according to this argument, are infinitely less important than its achievement in restoring the morale of liberal democracy in general at a desperate and critical time. The political and economic success of this 'middle way' in western liberal democracy since the Second World War no doubt helps to explain the current predominance of this particular view.

The Problem Posed

1. *The problem for America in the 1930s was whether it could preserve the values of a liberal society and at the same time regain its economic prosperity. Here are three statements of that problem, one by an English Communist and two by Liberals, one English, one American. We open with John Strachey, at the time of writing (1935) still a believer in Marxist solutions.*

The inability of capitalist economist science as such to consider the existence of crises at all, and the consequent embarrassment of capitalist economists in discussing them, does not, however, make the question any less important for the rest of us. In particular, it is urgently necessary for us to make up our minds as to whether the occurrence of crises is accidental to or inherent in the capitalist system. This is the master question. For upon the answer to it must necessarily depend our attitude to existing society. If we come to the conclusion that catastrophic crisis are accidental to capitalism, then we shall certainly work for their elimination by appropriate reforms. For who would be so mad as to recommend the scrapping of the system itself if the catastrophes which it is bringing upon us were remediable? If it were possible so to reform capitalism that it would provide us with an epoch of peaceful, steady, even if gradual, social progress, then none but those who objected to the system upon ethical grounds would work for its abolition. And even they, no doubt, would seek its abolition as the result of a series of cumulative reforms.

Indeed, if it were possible so to reform capitalism that it would maintain human civilization even at the level of the last fifty years; if it were possible to avert the onset of ever worsening crises, with their tremendous train of political and military consequences, then, however bitterly we might detest the system, such a reformed and stabilized capitalism would probably survive indefinitely. If it becomes inescapably apparent, however, that capitalism must in future fail, not merely to provide us with a basis for social progress, but to maintain even our recent level of civilization; if it becomes apparent that capitalism must certainly plunge us into a series of ever deepening crises, and that these crises can only bring international and civil war in their train; then not only those who have always had good cause to detest capitalism but all reasonable men will find themselves impelled to work for the overthrow of the existing system of society.

The Nature of Capitalist Crisis, Gollancz, London, 1935, pp. 17–18

2. John Dewey, the American philosopher, saw the crisis in these terms.

The crisis in liberalism . . . proceeds from the fact that after early liberalism had done its work, society faced a new problem, that of social organization. Its work was to liberate a group of individuals, representing the new science and the new forces of productivity, from customs, ways of thinking, institutions, that were oppressive of the new modes of social action, however useful they may have been in their day. The instruments of analysis, of criticism, of dissolution, that were employed were effective for the work of release. But when it came to the problem of organizing the new forces and the individuals whose lives they radically altered into a coherent social organization, possessed of intellectual and moral directive power, liberalism was well-nigh impotent. The rise of national polities that pretend to represent the order, discipline and spiritual authority that will counteract social disintegration is a tragic comment upon the unpreparedness of older liberalism to deal with the new problem which its very success precipitated.

But the values of freed intelligence, of liberty, of opportunity for every individual to realize the potentialities of which he is possessed, are too precious to be sacrificed to a régime of despotism, especially when the régime is in such large measure merely the agent of a dominant economic class in its struggle to keep and extend the gains it has amassed at the expense of genuine social order, unity and development. Liberalism has to gather itself together to formulate the ends to which it is devoted in terms of means that are relevant to the contemporary situation. The only form of enduring social organization that is now possible is one in which the new forces of productivity are coöperatively controlled and used in the interest of the effective liberty and the cultural development of the individuals that constitute society. Such a social order cannot be established by an unplanned and external convergence of the actions of separate individuals, each of whom is bent on personal private advantage. This idea is the Achilles heel of early liberalism. The idea that liberalism cannot maintain its ends and at the same time reverse its conception of the means by which they are to be attained is folly. The ends can now be achieved *only* by reversal of the means to which early liberalism was committed. Organized social planning, put into effect for the creation of an order in which industry and finance are socially directed in behalf of institutions that provide the material basis for the cultural liberation and growth of individuals, is now the sole method of social action by which liberalism can realize its professed aims.

Liberalism and Social Action (1935), Capricorn Books, New York, 1963 edn, pp. 53–5

3. *John Maynard Keynes believed that liberalism could make the adaptation of which the others spoke.*

. . . the result of filling in the gaps in the classical theory is not to dispose of the 'Manchester System', but to indicate the nature of the environment which the free play of economic forces requires if it is to realize the full potentialities of production. The central controls necessary to ensure full employment will, of course, involve a large extension of the traditional functions of government. Furthermore, the modern classical theory has itself called attention to various conditions in which the free play of economic forces may need to be curbed or guided. But there will still remain a wide field for the exercise of private initiative and responsibility. Within this field the traditional advantages of individualism will still hold good.

Let us stop for a moment to remind ourselves what these advantages are. They are partly advantages of efficiency – the advantages of decentralization and of the play of self-interest. The advantage to efficiency of decentralization of decisions and of individual responsibility is even greater, perhaps, than the nineteenth century supposed; and the reaction against the appeal to self-interest may have gone too far. But, above all, individualism, if it can be purged of its defects and its abuses, is the best safeguard of personal liberty in the sense that, compared with any other system, it greatly widens the field for personal choice. It is also the best safeguard of the variety of life, which emerges precisely from this extended field of personal choice, and the loss of which is the greatest of all the losses of the homogeneous or totalitarian state. For this variety preserves the traditions which embody the most secure and successful choices of former generations; it colours the present with the diversification of its fancy; and, being the handmaid of experiment as well as of tradition and of fancy, it is the most powerful instrument to better the future.

Whilst, therefore, the enlargement of the functions of government, involved in the task of adjusting to one another the propensity to consume and the inducement to invest, would seem to a nineteenth-century publicist or to a contemporary American financier to be a terrific encroachment on individualism, I defend it, on the contrary, both as the only practicable means of avoiding the destruction of existing economic forms in their entirety and as the condition of the successful functioning of individual initiative.

The General Theory of Employment, Interest and Money (1936), Macmillan, London, 1960 paperback edn, pp. 379–80

Liberalism Betrayed

4. *Herbert Hoover, for obvious reasons, had to convince posterity that Roosevelt's presidency had been a disaster.*

The reasons for this failure of the United States to recover were obvious. The first was the setback caused by the wholly unnecessary bank panic. More important than this temporary blow was the whole New Deal collectivism. There is no middle road between any breed of collective economy and our American system. . . .

The American system is based upon the confidence, hopes and the judgment of each man in conducting his business affairs upon his judgment. He determines his prices in relation to demand, supply and competition. His policies are based upon endless chains of contracts and agreements. If only one link be touched, the whole chain weakens and the expected results are frustrated. Also, under 'planned economy' the actions of government and bureaucrats are unpredictable. At once men become hesitant and fearful. Every time the planners inject their dictation into some region of private enterprise, somehow, somewhere, men's minds and judgments become confused. Initiative and enterprise slacken; production and consumption slow down. At once unemployment is increased, and every fear is accelerated. Then more drastic powers and more government agencies are demanded by the planners. And thus the cancer of power over men grows by creating its own emergencies.

. . . By the time Roosevelt took office the fears from abroad had disappeared. A new line of domestic fears was created. They came from tinkering with currency and credit, from creeping fascist dictation to industry, labor, and agriculture. We entered areas of socialism through government production and distribution. We witnessed great centralization of power with a huge bureaucracy. We began a vast increase in government expenditures and debt. We witnessed great forces of moral corruption and intellectual dishonesty. We saw the legislative arm reduced to a rubber stamp, and the Supreme Court subjugated. We saw the development of class hatred at the hands of the government. There was ample reason to fear, to hesitate, and to postpone commitments.

It has been the technique of all collectivist leaders to single out some element of the community for concentrated hate. Lenin directed hate toward the 'bourgeoisie'; Hitler, toward the Jews; Mussolini, toward the Communists and democrats; Mr Roosevelt concentrated his denunciation on a generalized class which he called 'economic royalists.' Whatever the merit of this technique may have been politically, its result is the discouragement of good men and slowing up of the economy of the nation.

. . . The recognition of Russia on November 16, 1933, started forces which were to have considerable influence in the attempt to collectivize the United States, particularly through the labor unions. We saw government conducted by 'emergencies,' purges, propaganda, bureaucracy, hate, the turmoil of class conflict—all of collectivist pattern. We saw an era of the deepest intellectual dishonesty in public life. We saw the growth of executive power by the reduction of the legislative arm, with few exceptions, to a rubber stamp. We saw the subjection of the Supreme Court to the collectivist ideas of the executive. We saw the independence and responsibility of the states undermined by huge Federal subsidies directly to the citizens.

Thus the four great pillars of free men were weakened. As a result of eight years of the New Deal, there was not more but less liberty in America. And, unique among the nations of the world free of collectivism, we had not ended the Great Depression. Its vast unemployment and its huge numbers on relief were only ended by war.

The Memoirs of Herbert Hoover. The Great Depression 1929–1941, Hollis and Carter, London, 1953, pp. 475, 476, 478, 484–5

5. *John T. Flynn, a former Communist, was the spokesman of the right-wing Roosevelt-haters.*

. . . many good people in America still cherish the illusion that Roosevelt performed some amazing feat of regeneration for this country. They believe he took our economic system when it was in utter disrepair and restored it again to vitality; that he took over our political system when it was at its lowest estate and restored it again to its full strength. He put himself on the side of the underprivileged masses. He transferred power from the great corporate barons to the simple working people of America. He curbed the adventurers of Wall Street, and gave security to the humble men and women of the city. And above all he led us through a great war for democracy and freedom and saved the civilization of Europe.

But none of these claims can be sustained. He did not restore our economic system to vitality. He changed it. The system he blundered us into is more like the managed and bureaucratized, state-supported system of Germany before World War I than our own traditional order. Before his regime we lived in a system which depended for its expansion upon private investment and private enterprise. Today we live in a system which depends for its expansion and vitality upon the government. . . .

. . . No, Roosevelt did not restore our economic system. He did not construct a new one. He substituted an old one which lives upon permanent crises and an armament economy. And he did this not by a process of orderly architecture and building, but by a succession of blunders, moving one step at a time, in flight from one problem to another, until we are now arrived at that kind of state-supported economic system that will continue to devour a little at a time the private system until it disappears altogether.

He did not restore our political system to its full strength. One may like the shape into which he battered it, but it cannot be called a repair job. He changed our political system with two weapons–blank-check congressional appropriations and blank-check congressional legislation. In 1933, Congress abdicated much of its power when it put billions into his hands by a blanket appropriation to be spent at his sweet will and when it passed general laws, leaving it to him, through great government bureaus of his appointment, to fill in the details of legislation.

These two baleful mistakes gave him a power which he used ruthlessly. He used it to break down the power of the states and to move that power to Washington and to break down the power of Congress and concentrate it in the hands of the executive. The end of these two betrayals–the smashing of our economic system and the twisting of our political system–can only be the Planned Economic State, which, either in the form of Communism or Fascism, dominates the entire continent of Europe today. The capitalist system cannot live under these conditions. Free representative government cannot survive a Planned Economy. Such an economy can be managed only by a dictatorial government capable of enforcing the directives it issues. The only result of our present system–unless we reverse the drift–must be the gradual extension of the fascist sector and the gradual disappearance of the system of free enterprise under a free representative government.

There are men who honestly defend this transformation. They at least are honest. They believe in the Planned Economy. They believe in the highly centralized government operated by a powerful executive. They do not say Roosevelt saved our system. They say he has given us a new one. That is logical. But no one can praise Roosevelt for doing this and then insist that he restored our traditional political and economic systems to their former vitality.

The Roosevelt Myth, rev. edn, Devin-Adair, New York, 1956, pp. 413–15

6. *For Moley, Roosevelt had abandoned the best traditions of progressivism.*

Time makes its own inexorable estimates, and they cannot be prejudged. But it would be dishonest for me not to end this seven years' story on a note of deep regret.

The great surge toward orderly and progressive economic reform that gained impetus during the sixty years following the War between the States has had few parallels in modern times, except perhaps the movements for political reform in England and the sweep of republicanism on the Continent after the Napoleonic wars. Like those movements, progressivism in the United States grew out of the efforts of thousands of disassociated, dissimilar individuals and groups. There were reform administrations in cities and states. There were scores of local legislative experiments. There were numberless political preachers. There were teachers and books that gave a new cast to people's thinking about economic questions. By the onset of the depression millions of Americans realized that economic civilization, as we had known it, was not and need not be an eventual absolute. Millions wanted to see it made more equitable, more efficient, more productive.

It was Roosevelt's special fortune that he became President when, in economic calamity, progressivism at last won the adherence of a majority of our people. In that sense he was handed a torch that had been carried by others for generations. He was the trustee of a magnificent tradition. That he was able to go so far in so short a time was in large part the result of the accumulated force of what had been so long denied fulfillment.

Roosevelt's administration has achieved much. It has outlawed many abuses. It has readjusted some of our lopsided economic relationships. It has established firmly in the nation's consciousness the principle of economic interdependence. There will remain, after Roosevelt has left office, a vastly changed philosophy of business enterprise, an improvement in the methods of social-welfare activities. Many of the New Deal measures, even those that have failed, have had an important educational value, for they have shown what will not work. These gains are incontestable.

But it is difficult to reconcile them with what they have cost. It is not alone that immense treasure has been spent for economic rehabilitation that has not materialized, that, after seven years, investment remains dormant, enterprise is chilled, the farmers' problem has not yet been solved, unemployment is colossal. It is that thousands of decent men and women who felt, as sincerely as Roosevelt, that we must redefine the aims of democratic government in terms of modern needs, have been alienated. They asked only that the repair work done upon the structure of policy follow a consistent pattern of architecture. They pointed out that unskillful combinations of Gothic, Byzantine, and Le Corbusier defy the law of gravity, and invite ultimate collapse.

After Seven Years, Harper, New York, 1939, pp. 398–9

The Revolution Lost

7. For the left the failures of the New Deal were the result of the unwillingness of liberalism in general to adopt a planning ideology. The Oxford academic, Richard Crossman, wrote this in 1938.

The uncertainty and lack of direction which we have noticed in democratic thought up till 1914 continued till 1931: indeed, it may be urged that it continues today. And yet I believe that 1931 was a dividing point both in England and in America. Far more thoroughly than the Great War, the Great Slump impressed upon the Anglo-Saxon peoples the insecurity of the foundations on which freedom and prosperity were based, and the rise of Fascism and of Fascist imperialism has only deepened that impression. England is now a country, not, as before 1931, living blindly on the traditions of the past, but groping towards a new philosophy both of domestic and of international affairs. The post-1918 effort to apply the principles of Lockeian Liberalism to the building of a machinery of international order has failed as decisively as the Conservative struggle to return to pre-War 'normalcy'. The belief in national governmental organization as the instrument of positive good is also undermined. In short, the economic and social conditions which rendered Liberalism so palatable have gone, and we are at last aware that they are gone. For the first time since the era of Hobbes we are faced by problems which demand a radical solution, and which cannot be shelved by kindly compromise and 'muddling through'. At last we too have reached a crisis where the only practical course open to us is to become philosophers and undertake a radical analysis of the fundamental postulates of our society.

Planning for Freedom, Hamish Hamilton, London, 1965, p. 30

8. The chief count in the left-(and right-)wing indictment of the New Deal was inconsistency. Roosevelt was well aware of this, as he stated in the general introduction to his collected public addresses.

In these volumes those who seek inconsistencies will find them. There were inconsistencies of methods, inconsistencies caused by ceaseless efforts to find ways to solve problems for the future as well as for the present. There were inconsistencies springing from the need for experimentation. But through them all, I trust that there also will be found a consistency and continuity of broad purpose.

Consistently I have sought to maintain a comprehensive and efficient functioning of the representative form of democratic government in its modern sense. Consistently I have sought through that form of government to help our people to gain a larger social justice.

The Public Papers and Addresses of Franklin D. Roosevelt, ed. S. Rosenman, Random House, New York, 1938, vol. i, p. xiii

9. *The sense of a confusion of purpose was there from the beginning. Edmund Wilson writes about Washington in 1933.*

. . . For the first time it is becoming possible to fill in the whole American picture. Yet this is not being done in any coördinated fashion. The different departments know different facts, and they propose to deal with them in different ways – different people in the same department propose to deal with the same facts in different ways. There is no real over-all policy for reassembling the broken-down competitive mechanism. The opponents of the President do not know quite what to do; and his liberal supporters are baffled. And then there is the group of Progressives, the President's liberal opponents. At the moment, the needle of the compass seems to quiver between the opposite attractions of reaction and further reform.

And the President himself is still handling things so suavely, still showing himself so accomplished a politician that it is hard to tell how firmly he grasps the problems involved in the experimentation which constitutes the New Deal.

The American Earthquake, Allen, London, 1958, pp. 564–5

10. *Moley was bewildered by the apparent chaos.*

That Roosevelt could look back over the vast aggregation of policies adopted between March, 1933, and November, 1936, and see it as the result of a single, predetermined plan was a tribute to his imagination. But not to his grasp of economics. One had only to review the heterogeneous origins of the policies he had embraced by the time of his re-election, the varying circumstances, impulses, beliefs that had produced them, to guess at their substantive conflict and contradiction. . . .

If this aggregation of policies springing from circumstances, motives, purposes, and situations so various gave the observer the sense of a certain rugged grandeur, it arose chiefly from the wonder that one man could have been so flexible as to permit himself to believe so many things in so short a time. But to look upon these policies as the result of a unified plan was to believe that the accumulation of stuffed snakes, baseball pictures, school flags, old tennis shoes, carpenter's tools, geometry books, and chemistry sets in a boy's bedroom could have been put there by an interior decorator.

Or, perhaps it would be more apt to say that the unfolding of the New Deal between 1932 and 1937 suggested the sounds that might be produced by an orchestra which started out with part of a score and which, after a time, began to improvise. It might all hang together if there were a clear understanding between the players and the conductor as to the sort of music they intended to produce. But nothing was more obvious than that some of the New Dealers believed that the theme was to be the funeral march of capitalism; others, a Wagnerian conflict between Good and Evil; and still others, the triumphant strains of the *Heldenleben*.

After Seven Years, Harper, New York, 1939, pp. 365–6, 369–70

11. *For one of the most recent commentators on the period, E. W. Hawley, the ambiguity of the New Deal represented not uncertainty but Roosevelt's masterly political awareness.*

The search in twentieth-century America . . . was for some solution that would reconcile the practical necessity with the individualistic ideal, some arrangement that would preserve the industrial order, necessarily based upon a high degree of collective organization, and yet would preserve America's democratic heritage at the same time. Americans wanted a stable, efficient industrial system, one that turned out a large quantity of material goods, insured full employment, and provided a relatively high degree of economic security. Yet at the same time they wanted a system as free as possible from centralized direction, one in which economic power was dispersed and economic opportunity was really open, one that preserved the dignity of the individual and adjusted itself automatically to market forces. And they were unwilling to renounce the hope of achieving both. In spite of periodic hurricanes of anti-big-business sentiment, they refused to follow the prophets that would destroy their industrial system and return to former simplicities. Nor did they pay much attention to those that would sacrifice democratic ideals and liberal traditions in order to create a more orderly and more rational system, one that promised greater security, greater stability, and possibly even greater material benefits. . . .

In a time of economic adversity . . . it would seem practically inevitable that the policy-making apparatus of a democracy should register both streams of sentiment. Regardless of their logical inconsistency, the two streams were so intermixed in the ideology of the average man that any administration, if it wished to retain political power, had to make concessions to both. It must move to check the deflationary spiral, to provide some sort of central direction, and to salvage economic groups through the erection of cartels and economic controls. Yet while it was doing this, it must make a proper show of maintaining competitive ideals. Its actions must be justified by an appeal to competitive traditions, by showing that they were designed to save the underdog, or if this was impossible, by an appeal to other arguments and other traditions that for the moment justified making an exception. Nor could antitrust action ever be much more than a matter of performing the proper rituals and manipulating the proper symbols. It might attack unusually privileged and widely hated groups, break up a few loose combinations, and set forth a general program that was presumably designed to make the competitive ideal a reality. But the limit of the program would, of necessity, be that point at which changes in business practice or business structures would cause serious economic dislocation. It could not risk the disruption of going concerns or a further shrinkage in employment and production, and it would not subject men to the logical working out of deflationary trends. To do so would amount to political suicide.

To condemn these policies for their inconsistency was to miss the point. From an economic standpoint, condemnation might very well be to the point. They were inconsistent. One line of action tended to cancel the other, with the result that little was accomplished. Yet from the political standpoint, this very inconsistency, so long as the dilemma persisted, was the safest method of retaining political power. President Roosevelt, it seems, never suffered politically from his reluctance to choose between planning and antitrust action. His mixed emotions so closely reflected the popular mind that they were a political asset rather than a liability.

The New Deal and the Problem of Monopoly, Princeton University Press, 1966, pp. 473–4, 475–6

12. James MacGregor Burns has dubbed this ambivalence of Roosevelt's 'broker leadership'. Here he describes its functioning–and its shortcomings.

Viewed as a matter of political leadership, Roosevelt's Grand Experiment took the form of what can be called broker leadership. During his first two years in office he seemed to conceive of his presidential role as one of dealing with and mediating among the leaders of organized groups, especially labor, farmers, and businessmen. If the economics of the broker state meant improvisation, a host of energetic and ill-assorted government programs, and economic betterment without real recovery, the politics of broker leadership brought short-term political gains at the expense, perhaps, of long-term strategic advance.

Roosevelt was no theorist. It is doubtful that he chose this course as a result of a well-defined political philosophy. It simply emerged, shaped only roughly by his underlying concept of the public good, from the day-to-day projects and improvisations of his regime. It probably never occurred to him that the NRA, with its functional representation of business and labor groups, and the AAA, dominated by the big farm groups, showed some likeness to the corporate state fashioned by Benito Mussolini, with its syndicates of workers and employers. But George Peek, AAA chief, saw that the power of special interest groups could not be separated from the state, even in a democracy. 'The truth is,' he said bluntly, 'that no democratic government can be very different from the country it governs. If some groups are dominant in the country, they will be dominant in any plan the government undertakes.'

. . . Such an approach had profound implications for Roosevelt's political leadership. It meant that he took the more passive method of responding to major political and economic pressures, rather than the more positive one of deliberately building up some voting alignment on the left or right that would recast the basic pattern of political power. It meant that he ignored the possibilities for the future of a voting alignment of great strength–one composed of less privileged farm groups, masses of unorganized or ill-organized industrial workers, consumers, Negroes, and other minority groups. It is significant that the President allowed consumers short shrift in NRA and AAA, that he failed to put pressure behind the food and drug bill that Tugwell had drawn up for the protection of consumers, that he allowed postponement of unemployment and old-age pension measures, that he showed little interest at first in Wagner's efforts to strengthen labor's right to organize, that he was hazy and cool on the subject of a pending anti-lynching bill.

Roosevelt: The Lion and The Fox, Harcourt, Brace, New York, 1956, pp. 197–8

13. *An English socialist, E. F. M. Durbin, found this intuitive method highly distasteful.*

. . . The general character of the action taken to meet the democratic demand arising out of a Trade Cycle depression is always the same. It is *called* 'planning'. It actually consists in the substitution of monopoly control for competition in all the markets and industries that it touches. Whether it is described as 'agricultural adjustment' in America, or 'agricultural planning' in England; whether it consists of processing taxes and restricted output in America or milk marketing schemes in Britain; whether it applies to pigs or to coal; the policy is one of organized monopoly and restricted production. The power of the State is used not to oppose and limit monopoly, but to create it. We move at a bewildering pace into a regime of State organized monopoly.

About this policy two things are to be noticed. First, it is in the interest of *all* the factors employed in the industries affected. It benefits labour as well as property. The policy is therefore not difficult to initiate, though it may be difficult to reverse. Secondly, it benefits both those groups at the expense of the community. Industries live by strangling each other. Benefits are gained for a section by starving, not by feeding, the whole of society. As the number of monopolized sections increases, even the sectional benefits diminish, as all prices rise against everybody. We come to live, not by taking in each other's washing, but by each man garrotting his neighbours. It is a policy of slow, suicidal, sectional restrictionism.

The Politics of Democratic Socialism, Routledge, London, 1940, pp. 100–1

14. *Looking back on events in May 1940 another British socialist, Harold Laski, saw the situation as an ideological failure on the part of liberalism.*

. . . I do not think it is an unfair comment upon liberal legislation during the past forty years to say that it was prepared to be forced to be generous where it was not prepared spontaneously to be just. It made concessions, now here and now there, some of them, I admit, big concessions. But it was never ready to undertake that wholesale re-examination of social foundations that was called for, because its votaries could not bring themselves to believe that it was, in very truth, the foundations that had been called into question.

. . . the evolution of social forces, particularly of economic forces, has made the major doctrines of liberalism the instrument of a system of vested interests, and . . . liberal procedures can only survive by adapting these major doctrines to a situation which, so far, the philosophers of liberalism have steadfastly refused to confront. No one is more convinced than I am of the value of these procedures. But conviction of their value is not the same thing as belief that they will be used. We have lived for two generations before the compulsion of the call for drastic change. We have met it either by casual and interstitial improvisation or, even worse, by the refusal to recognize its urgency. That is true in the economic field; it is true in the social, witness the twin problems of education and nutrition; it is true in the field of empire; it is, alas, tragically true in the field of international relations. Instead of the wholesale planning of our social order in terms of historic experience scientifically estimated, we have drifted to profound disunity at home and totalitarian conflict abroad. And the liberal answer to our situation has not been the revision of its basic concepts; it has been merely the emphasis, which no one denies until catastrophe is imminent, upon the value of its procedures.

'The Decline of Liberalism', in *Hobhouse Memorial Lectures 1930–1940*, Oxford University Press, London, 1948, pp. 16, 17–18

15. *Richard Hofstadter, reviewing the New Deal shortly after Roosevelt's death, was extremely bitter at what he saw as a lost opportunity.*

Among postwar statesmen, Herbert Hoover, who is not usually thought to have much in common with these men of the progressive era–and whose methods and temper, in fact, were quite different–still adhered to much the same premises and accepted the same goals. Like the progressives, he expected to see a brilliant and expansive future, but he expected to reach it along the traditional highway. Franklin D. Roosevelt stands out among the statesmen of modern American liberalism–and indeed among all statesmen since Hamilton–for his sense of the failure of tradition, his recognition of the need for novelty and daring. His capacity for innovation in practical measures was striking, and the New Deal marked many deviations in the American course; but his capacity for innovation in ideas was far from comparable; he was neither systematic nor consistent, and he provided no clearly articulated break with the inherited faith. Although it has been said repeatedly that we need a new conception of the world to replace the ideology of self-help, free enterprise, competition, and beneficent cupidity upon which Americans have been nourished since the foundation of the Republic, no new conceptions of comparable strength have taken root and no statesman with a great mass following has arisen to propound them. Bereft of a coherent and plausible body of belief–for the New Deal, if it did little more, went far to undermine old ways of thought–Americans have become more receptive than ever to dynamic personal leadership as a substitute. This is part of the secret of Roosevelt's popularity, and, since his death, of the rudderless and demoralized state of American liberalism.

The American Political Tradition (1948), Vintage Books, New York, 1957, p. vii

The Revolution Achieved

16. *For those left of centre, however, the New Deal was something positive, a radical new departure. One contemporary, Ernest Lindley, believed he sensed it at once.*

. . . Within sixty of those breath-taking days that followed March 4 [1933], the arrival of a revolution had been proclaimed by several discerning periodicals, and the curiosity of the world focused on the American Experiment. It was a bloodless revolution, to be sure. In fact, a completely peaceful revolution accomplished without an ounce of armed force, or the threat of its use, without a black shirt, a brown shirt, an underground organization. On the contrary, it was effected with the most scrupulous observance of the recognized processes of law-making and meticulous regard for the historic rights of free speech and free assemblage. Yet the word 'revolution' sprang naturally to the lips. No other word seems strong enough to describe a change so swift and fundamental. The United States had embarked on an experiment in new economic relationships of revolutionary audacity and magnitude. As an incident to this, President Roosevelt had been endowed with greater power than any American had possessed in peacetime since the adoption of the Constitution. Probably never before had a change so abrupt and far-reaching been wrought peaceably within the framework of democratic institutions. It was a revolution shaped by one man yet certainly impelled by mass forces. Although there were increasing cries of pain or fright from the old régime as a few hallowed economic shrines sank from view, it was, in its initial stages, almost a co-operative revolution.

The Roosevelt Revolution—First Phase, Gollancz, London, 1934, p. 10

17. *Walter Lippmann, too, felt a clean break with the past, but he did not attribute it exclusively to the New Deal. See also I, 23 and 24.*

The point is that a radically new conception of the functions of government was established in the autumn of 1929. The subsequent course of events becomes utterly unintelligible if we accept naïvely what the partisans of Mr Hoover and of Mr Roosevelt say today. Only those who have forgotten the inclusive and persistent experimentation before March, 1933, can, I think, fail to see that most of President Roosevelt's recovery program is an evolution from President Hoover's program; and that there is a continuity of principle; and that both programs are derived from the unprecedented doctrine that the government is charged with responsibility for the successful operation of the economic order and the maintenance of a satisfactory standard of life for all classes in the nation. After October, 1929, that doctrine was the major premise of the Hoover Administration. It is the major premise of the Roosevelt Administration. Never, except in time of war, has it been the major premise in the policies of any other President.

The New Imperative, Macmillan, New York, 1935, p. 13

18. *Arthur Krock, writing in 1938, agreed that the New Deal had changed the face of America.*

[The] end will be the disappearance of the New Dealers and the obscuration of their leader and his methods, though not of his ideas. By whom and by what will they be replaced? Ordinary reportorial wisdom cannot penetrate the future for a precise answer. But generally the prophecy can be made that the government will be taken over by some form of Liberals or by a species of Fascists. The seed of the right-wing Conservative is not disclosed in the womb of near time by any mental X-ray. He rests, sterile, with his theories and methods, in the grave of political history in America.

The political execution of the Conservative, who for so many years arrested the demands of growing social consciousness and of economic justice in the United States, is Mr Roosevelt's great contribution and that of his *régime*. Only an incredible catastrophe can cancel it by the popular acceptance of a Fascist state, long or brief of tenure. The President has risked the enduring status of his contribution by policies that make that cataclysm less inconceivable than otherwise it would have been – piling up debts and taxes in repetitions of defeated efforts to purchase recovery, softening the people with fond and foolish paternalisms designed to get votes, and conducting some branches of government in a low moral climate.

But still that disaster seems to lie on another road than the one the people are slowly forcing the President to take with them instead of following him to the end of his own course. And if it is avoided many of the richest fruits of the new American civilization will, when justice is done, be recognized as the products of the President's political horticulture.

'Washington, D.C.', in *We Saw It Happen*, eds. H. W. Baldwin and S. Stone, Simon and Schuster, New York, 1938, pp. 349–50

19. *Samuel Lubell saw the revolution in the New Deal in its popular backing.*

No matter what else had happened, the growing up of these children of the 13,000,000 immigrants who poured into the country between 1900 and 1914 was bound to exert a levelling pull on American society. As it was, the depression–striking when most of them had barely entered the adult world–sharpened all their memories of childhood handicaps. When Roosevelt first took office, no segment of the population was more ready for 'a new deal' than the submerged, inarticulate urban masses. They became the chief carriers of the Roosevelt Revolution.

The really revolutionary surge behind the New Deal lay in this coupling of the depression with the rise of a new generation, which had been malnourished on the congestion of our cities and the abuses of industrialism. Roosevelt did not start this revolt of the city. What he did do was to awaken the climbing urban masses to a consciousness of the power in their numbers. He extended to them the warming hand of recognition, through patronage and protective legislation. In the New Deal he supplied the levelling philosophy required by their sheer numbers and by the hungers stimulated by advertising. In turn, the big-city masses furnished the votes which re-elected Roosevelt again and again–and, in the process, ended the traditional Republican majority in this country. . . .

. . . Never having known anything but city life, this new generation was bound to develop a different attitude towards the role of government from that of Americans born on farms or in small towns. To Herbert Hoover the phrase 'rugged individualism' evoked nostalgic memories of a rural self-sufficiency in which a thrifty, toiling farmer had to look to the market place for only the last fifth of his needs. . . .

. . . In the city, though, the issue has always been man against man. . . . The wage earner had to look to the government to make sure that the milk bought for his baby was not watered or tubercular; he had to look to the government to regulate the construction of tenements so all sunlight was not blocked out. If only God could make a tree, only the government could make a park.

The Future of American Politics, Hamish Hamilton, London, 1952, pp. 28–9, 32–3

20. *For Whittaker Chambers, a former communist turned conservative, the New Deal's apparent moderation was deceptive; in reality it had recast the whole basis of American life. This revelation came to him after an interview with the former Brain Truster Adolf Berle on the night of 2–3 September 1939.*

I had noted its obvious features–its coalition of divergent interests, some of them diametrically opposed to the others, its divided counsels, its makeshift strategy, its permanently shifting executive personnel whose sole consistency seemed to be that the more it changed, the more it remained the most incongruously headed hybrid since the hydra. Now with a curiosity newborn of Berle, I saw how misleading those surface manifestations were, and tactically how advantageous, for they concealed the inner drift of this great movement. That drift was prevailingly toward socialism, though the mass of those who, in part directed, in part were carried along by it, sincerely supposed that they were liberals.

I saw that the New Deal was only superficially a reform movement. I had to acknowledge the truth of what its more forthright protagonists sometimes unwarily, sometimes defiantly, averred: the New Deal was a genuine revolution, whose deepest purpose was not simply reform within existing traditions, but a basic change in the social, and above all, the power relationships within the nation. It was not a revolution by violence. It was a revolution by book-keeping and lawmaking. In so far as it was successful, the power of politics had replaced the power of business. This is the basic power shift of all the revolutions of our time. This shift *was* the revolution. It was only of incidental interest that the revolution was not complete, that it was not made by tanks and machine guns, but by acts of Congress and decisions of the Supreme Court, or that many of the revolutionists did not know what they were or denied it. But revolution is always an affair of force, whatever forms the force disguises itself in. Whether the revolutionists prefer to call themselves Fabians who seek power by the inevitability of gradualism, or Bolsheviks who seek power by the dictatorship of the proletariat, the struggle is for power.

Witness, Deutsch, London, 1953, pp. 331–2

21. *Hofstadter, who appears to have moved across from left to centre-left in the decade after 1945, came to see the New Deal in revolutionary terms.*

. . . granting that absolute discontinuities do not occur in history, and viewing the history of the New Deal as a whole, what seems outstanding about it is the drastic new departure that it marks in the history of American reformism. The New Deal was different from anything that had yet happened in the United States: different because its central problem was unlike the problems of Progressivism; different in its ideas and its spirit and its techniques. Many men who had lived through Progressivism and had thought of its characteristic proposals as being in the main line of American traditions, even as being restoratives of those traditions, found in the New Deal an outrageous departure from everything they had known and valued, and so could interpret it only as an effort at subversion or as the result of overpowering alien influences. Their opposition was all too often hysterical, but in their sense that something new had come into American political and economic life they were quite right.

Consider, to begin, the fundamental problem that the New Dealers faced, as compared with the problems of the Progressives. When Theodore Roosevelt took office in 1901, the country was well over three years past a severe depression and in the midst of a period of healthy economic development. Its farmers were more prosperous than they had been for about forty years, its working class was employed and gaining in living standards, and even its middle class was far busier counting the moral costs of success than it was worrying about any urgent problems of family finance. When F.D.R. took his oath of office, the entire working apparatus of American life had gone to smash. The customary masters and leaders of the social order were themselves in a state of near panic. Millions were unemployed, and discontent had reached a dangerous pitch on the farms and in the cities.

Indeed, the New Deal episode marks the first in the history of reform movements when a leader of a reform party took the reins of government confronted above all by the problems of a sick economy. . . .

. . . The earlier American tradition of political protest had been a response to the needs of entrepreneurial classes or of those who were on the verge of entrepreneurship – the farmers, small businessmen, professionals, and occasionally the upper caste of the artisans or the working class. The goal of such classes had generally been to clear the way for new enterprises and new men, break up privileged business, big business and monopolies, and give the small man better access to credit. The ideas of this Progressive tradition, as one might expect, were founded not merely upon acceptance but even upon glorification of the competitive order. The Jeffersonians, the Jacksonians, and after them most of the Progressives had believed in the market economy, and the only major qualification of this belief they cared to make stemmed from their realization that the market needed to be policed and moralized by a government responsive to the needs of the economic beginner and the small entrepreneur.

. . . Even before F.D.R. took office a silent revolution had taken place in public opinion, the essential character of which can be seen when we recall how little opposition there was in the country, at the beginning, to the assumption of the New Dealers that henceforth, for the purposes of recovery, the federal government was to be responsible for the condition of the labor market as a part of its concern with the industrial problem as a whole. Nothing revolutionary was intended – but simply as a matter of politics it was necessary for the federal government to assume primary responsibility for the relief of the unemployed. And, simply as a matter of politics, if the industrialists were to be given the power to write enforceable codes of fair practice, labor must at least be given some formal recognition of its right of collective bargaining. Certainly no one foresaw, in the first year or two of the New Deal, that the immense infusions of purchasing power into the economy through federal unemployment relief would be as lasting or as vital a part of the economy of the next several years as they proved in fact to be. Nor did anyone in fact foresee how great and powerful a labor movement would be called into being by the spirit and promise of the New Deal and by the partial recovery of its first few years. But by the end of 1937 it was clear that something had been added to the social base of reformism. The demands of a large and powerful labor movement, coupled with the interests of the unemployed, gave the later New Deal a social-democratic tinge that had never before been present in American reform movements. Hitherto concerned with reforms of an essentially entrepreneurial sort and only marginally with social legislation, American political reformism was fated henceforth to take responsibility on a large scale for social security, unemployment insurance, wages and hours, and housing.

The Age of Reform (1955), Vintage Books, New York, 1961, pp. 303–5, 307–8

22. Looking back from the vantage point of the late 1950s, Carl N. Degler also believed that the basic impulse of the New Deal was revolutionary.

In the thirties, as now, the place of the New Deal in the broad stream of American development has been a matter of controversy. Historians and commentators on the American scene have not yet reached a firm agreement–if they ever will–as to whether the New Deal was conservative or radical in character, though it does appear that the consensus seems to lean toward calling it conservative and traditional. Certainly, if one searches the writings and utterances of Franklin Roosevelt, his own consciousness of conservative aims is quickly apparent. 'The New Deal is an old deal–as old as the earliest aspirations of humanity for liberty and justice and the good life,' he declared in 1934. 'It was this administration,' he told a Chicago audience in 1936, 'which saved the system of private profit and free enterprise after it had been dragged to the brink of ruin. . . .'

But men making a revolution among a profoundly conservative people do not advertise their activity, and above all Franklin Roosevelt understood the temper of his people. Nor should such a statement be interpreted as an insinuation of high conspiracy–far from it. Roosevelt was at heart a conservative, as his lifelong interest in history, among other things, suggests. But he was without dogma in his conservatism, which was heavily interlaced with genuine concern for people. He did not shy away from new means and new approaches to problems when circumstances demanded it. . . . In his pragmatic and common-sense reactions to the exigencies of the depression, Roosevelt, the easy-going conservative, ironically enough became the embodiment of a new era and a new social philosophy for the American people.

. . . Accent as heavily as one wishes the continuity between the re-forms of the Progressive era and the New Deal, yet the wide difference between the goals of the two periods still remains. The Progressive impulse was narrowly reformist: it limited business, it assisted agricul-ture, it freed labor from some of the shackles imposed by the courts, but it continued to conceive of the state as policeman or judge and nothing more. The New Deal, on the other hand, was more than a regulator–though it was that too, as shown by the SEC [Securities and Exchange Commission] and the reinvigoration of the antitrust division of the Justice Department. To the old goals for America set forth and fought for by the Jeffersonians and Progressives the New Deal appended new ones. Its primary and general innovation was the guaranteeing of a minimum standard of welfare for the people of the nation. WPA and the whole series of relief agencies which were a part of it, wages and hours legislation, AAA, bank deposit insurance, and social security, each illustrates this new conception of the federal government. . . .

But the guarantor state as it developed under the New Deal was more active and positive than this. It was a vigorous and dynamic force in the society, energizing and, if necessary, supplanting private enterprise when the general welfare required it. . . . To achieve that minimum standard of well-being which the depression had taught the American people to expect of their government, nothing was out of bounds.

But it is not the variety of change which stamps the New Deal as the creator of a new America; its significance lies in the permanence of its program. For, novel as the New Deal program was, it has, significantly, not been repudiated by the Eisenhower administration, the first Re-publican government since the reforms were instituted. Verbally, it is true, the Republican administration has had to minimize its actual commitments to the New Deal philosophy, and it tends to trust private business more than the New Dealers did–witness, for example, its elimination of the minor governmental manufacturing enterprises which competed with private firms. But despite this, the administration's firm commitment to the guaranteeing of prosperity and averting depression at all costs is an accurate reflection of the American people's agreement with the New Deal's diagnosis of the depression. Nor has the Republican party dared to repeal or even emasculate the legislation which made up the vitals of the New Deal: TVA, banking and currency, SEC, social security, the Wagner Act, and fair treatment of the Negro. The New Deal revolution has become so much a part of the American Way that no political party which aspires to high office dares now to repudiate it.

It may or may not be significant in this regard (for apothegms are more slippery than precise) but it is nonetheless interesting that Roosevelt and Eisenhower have both been impressed with the same single sentence from Lincoln regarding the role of the government. 'The legitimate object of Government,' wrote Lincoln, 'is to do for a community of people whatever they need to have done but cannot do at all or cannot do well for themselves in their separate or individual capacities.' Twice, in 1934 and again in 1936, F.D.R. in public addresses used this expression to epitomize his own New Deal, and Robert Donovan in his officially inspired book on the Eisenhower administration writes that this same 'fragment of Lincoln's writing . . . Eisenhower uses time and again in describing his own philosophy of government'. Between Lincoln and Eisenhower there was no Republican President, except perhaps Theodore Roosevelt, who would have been willing to subscribe to such a free-wheeling description of the federal power; in this can be measured the impact of the New Deal and the depression.

The conclusion seems inescapable that, traditional as the words may have been in which the New Deal expressed itself, in actuality it was a revolutionary response to a revolutionary situation. In its long history America has passed through two revolutions since the first one in 1776, but only the last two, the Civil War and the depression, were of such force as to change the direction of the relatively smooth flow of its progress. The Civil War rendered a final and irrevocable decision in the long debate over the nature of the Union and the position of the Negro in American society. From that revolutionary experience, America emerged a strong national state and dedicated by the words of its most hallowed document to the inclusion of the black man in a democratic culture. The searing ordeal of the Great Depression purged the American people of their belief in the limited powers of the federal government and convinced them of the necessity of the guarantor state. And as the Civil War constituted a watershed in American thought, so the depression and its New Deal marked the crossing of a divide from which, it would seem, there could be no turning back.

Out Of Our Past, Harper, New York, 1959, pp. 412–16

Liberalism Vindicated

23. *As Degler remarks, however, Roosevelt was always at pains to stress the elements of continuity in the New Deal. Here he looks back at the events of 1933.*

Millions of people . . . had begun to feel that the machinery of modern American economics and government had broken down so completely under the strain of the new demands placed upon it by modern civilization, that an entirely new type of mechanics for existence would have to be invented. They were not clear in their own minds as to what type they should seek; but their confidence and morale were so shaken that many of them would have been willing to accept any form of specious glittering guarantee of a chance to earn a livelihood. . . .

. . . On the occasion of the all-night session of the Democratic National Convention in Chicago, in 1932, I was at the Executive Mansion in Albany with my family and a few friends. . . . From . . . our desire to epitomize the immediate needs of the Nation came the phrase a 'New Deal,' which was used first in the acceptance speech and which has very aptly become the popular expression to describe the major objectives of the Administration.

The word 'Deal' implied that the government itself was going to use affirmative action to bring about its avowed objectives rather than stand by and hope that general economic laws alone would attain them. The word 'New' implied that a new order of things designed to benefit the great mass of our farmers, workers and business men would replace the old order of special privilege in a Nation which was completely and thoroughly disgusted with the existing dispensation. . . .

There would be no effort to circumscribe the scope of private initiative so long as the rules of fair play were observed. There would be no obstacle to the incentive of reasonable and legitimate private profit.

Because the American system from its inception presupposed and sought to maintain a society based on personal liberty, on private ownership of property and on reasonable private profit for each man's labor or capital, the New Deal would insist on all three factors. But because the American system visualized protection of the individual against the misuse of private economic power, the New Deal would insist on curbing such power.

A frank examination of the profit system in the spring of 1933 showed it to be in collapse; but substantially everybody in the United States, in public office or out of public office, from the very rich to the very poor, was as determined as was my Administration to save it. . . .

The task of reconstruction . . . did not call for the creation of strange values. It was rather finding the way again to old, but somewhat forgotten, ideals and values. . . . America was privileged to show the world in that year of crisis that democracy can find within itself the elements necessary to its own salvation.

The Public Papers and Addresses of Franklin D. Roosevelt, ed. S. Rosenman, Random House, New York, 1938, vol. ii, pp. 3, 4–5, 9–10

24. *As Moley points out, the measures used to deal with the banking crisis in 1933 were far from revolutionary.*

It cannot be emphasized too strongly that the policies which vanquished the bank crisis were thoroughly conservative policies. The sole departure from convention lay in the swiftness and boldness with which they were carried out. Those who conceived and executed them were intent upon rallying the confidence, first, of the conservative business and banking leaders of the country and, then, through them, of the public generally. Had Roosevelt turned, in those fateful days, to the type of adviser that ultimately came into prominence in his administration it is more than likely that questions of reform would have taken precedence over considerations of safety, with a resultant confusion and delay that would have wreaked incalculable damage upon our whole economic order. If ever there was a moment when things hung in the balance, it was on March 5 1933 when unorthodoxy would have drained the last remaining strength of the capitalistic system.

After Seven Years, Harper, New York, 1939, p. 155

25. *Lippmann, writing on 15 June 1934, saw the New Deal as the successor to old-established American reform traditions.*

. . . There is an old rule of thinking, known as Ockham's razor, which says that in effect you must not use a complicated explanation when a simpler one will do. Those who have been endeavoring to explain the New Deal in terms of communism or fascism have been violating this rule. It is ever so much simpler to interpret it in the light of the President's own traditions and of his majority in Congress. So far as Mr Roosevelt is concerned, he is plainly a believer not only in the American constitutional system but in the American social ideal; that is, in men who are secure, independent and free. If he has attacked certain practices of big business and high finance, he has done so for the traditional American reason that they made the property and livelihood of the average man less secure. Not to see the New Deal as the lineal descendant of the reforming enthusiasm of Theodore Roosevelt's New Nationalism and Woodrow Wilson's New Freedom, to try to see in it something that originates in Moscow, Rome, or Berlin, is to miss the whole point and to become completely bewildered.

Interpretations 1933–1935, Macmillan, New York, 1936, p. 258

26. *Many on the left naturally agreed that the New Deal was primarily traditionalist; for instance, Harold Laski.*

For something like the first few months of Franklin Roosevelt's first term it looked as though America would indeed have a New Deal in deeds as well as words. Had that occurred the United States might have experienced another revolution as profound as the Civil War.

But what occurred was in no sense a revolution. The Great Depression transformed America into a social service state such as Great Britain had become under the Liberal government of 1906–14. The incomes of the very wealthy were taxed at new levels. Social security, including pensions for the aged, was introduced. The federal government assisted the programme of housing, and came to the aid of the unemployed by providing them with work or relief in various forms. It secured a tighter control of the process of investment when it established the Securities and Exchange Commission. The Wagner Act pushed forward the status of trade-unionism to a level beyond even that which had been dreamed of by the Knights of Labor. Nor was it unimportant that the New Deal made the process of government interesting in a way that it had not previously been interesting as a career even in the great days of the Virginian presidents. But when all the results of the New Deal are added up, both ownership and control remained fundamentally in the same hands as before President Roosevelt entered the White House.

The American Democracy, Allen and Unwin, London, 1949, p. 177

27. *Tugwell, the planner, regretfully subscribed to this view.*

The New Deal was an incident in American history which arose out of the great depression; it was, indeed, part of a convulsive struggle to overcome the depression. Most of its characteristics, however, developed out of traditional progressivism and most of its devices were accepted items in a general armoury . . . it would almost be true to say that the New Deal of the thirties consisted of postponed items from Wilson's programme which had been abandoned in favour of preparation for war in 1916.

There is an actual continuity here too which is sometimes forgot. For President Roosevelt had been a very active and loyal member of the Wilson Administration; and he had been an admirer as well as a distant (fifth) cousin of Theodore Roosevelt. He could quite legitimately think of himself as the inheritor of a tradition. That this was a relationship he felt deeply all his close associates were aware. It is not perhaps surprising in view of all the circumstances, if he tended to respect the tradition rather literally, somewhat as generals are said to begin all new wars by using the tactics of the last one. . . .

. . . To the Governor of New York . . . most of the nation's ills quite naturally seemed to have come from not having carried out the progressive programme. . . . This was in fact the kind of programme President Roosevelt would have liked to carry out. It was the furniture of his mind down into 1932; and his mind was never entirely purged of these preferences. If what was done in the New Deal is examined, much of it will be seen to be consistent with this conclusion. There were, as time passed, many departures from the pattern. Some, indeed, of the measures adopted almost at once, in the haste of the crisis, were quite out of harmony with it, and obviously owed their origin to an entirely different tradition. But the President did not adopt the alternative ideology, perhaps never quite understood it; he was, in fact, inconsistent. . . . And sometimes the contemporary inconsistencies were so confusing that it was uncertain which side of the basic ideological struggle the President himself had chosen. But to the insiders of that day it was clear enough that the President could be persuaded away from the old progressive line only in the direst circumstances and then only temporarily or if he could make for himself a satisfactory rationalization.

'The Experimental Roosevelt', *The Political Quarterly*, 1950, pp. 239–40, 241, 242

28. *To some observers like Thurman Arnold the power of traditionalism in American affairs was a positive handicap to reform in any meaningful sense.*

There was something peculiarly medieval in the faiths which sustained the business government in America. In the first place, men, with that astonishing ability to shut out reality characteristic of group thinking, actually believed that it was not government at all. The American Telephone and Telegraph Company and the United States Steel Corporation were 'individuals' who 'owned' their industries. Such intangible things as morale, a trained personnel, institutional habits, public acceptance and good will, indeed all the elements which distinguished a going concern, were thought of as private property, owned by an intangible individual, just as it was once thought that the King of France 'owned' the State. The independent principalities of business were subject to the spiritual values dramatized by the National Government. But the rulers of these principalities of business thought of the National Government as something designed to preserve their 'freedom'. The fiction was carried so far that men thought of the employees as also 'free' to work when and where they pleased. This curious faith could be expressed by the Supreme Court, in violation of all the observed facts, and achieve acceptance, even when contradicted in dissenting opinions by members of the Court itself. . . .

. . . Of course, industrial government never lived up to its creed. That fact created the atmosphere which produced our so-called liberals who studied the creed and preached about the sins of business in violating it. Such 'attacks' on business organization did not hamper it because they did not propose organizational changes. Instead they strengthened the creed by showing that in it lay the way of salvation. When organizational changes began to appear after the depression, the liberals opposed the change and lost their identity as a group. This is characteristic of liberal movements in times of change. They always disappear, because they are symptoms of belief in established forms. They stand on the same fundamental truths as conservatives and immediately join forces with conservatives when new organizations appear to violate these truths.

So long as liberals preached against business sin, they offered a safety valve through which the explosive energy of discontent could escape.

Actually, as any observer may note, the disagreement between the preacher and his congregation is one of the things which keeps the church alive, so long as the minister is willing to confine himself to preaching and exhortation. Men like to hear about their sins. They love to have theological doctrine expounded which they do not have the faintest intention of following. And since the economists and lawyers of the day believed that it was more important to leave the temporal government alone than to have even sound theories forced upon it, they operated like preachers in all churches since time immemorial. The barons of the Middle Ages didn't follow the Bible, but they felt that it was a great book just the same.

The Folklore of Capitalism, Yale University Press, 1937, pp. 110–11, 112–13

29. *Believers in the pragmatic tradition like Louis Hartz, on the other hand, see it as a virtue which other countries were unlucky not to possess.*

Few constrasts are more striking, and indeed more misleading, than the contrast between the 'radical', aggressive mood of Liberal Reform in the American New Deal and the 'conservative', defensive mood of Liberal Reform in Western Europe during the 'thirties. . . . Everywhere in the Radical camp there is a heightening of the old philosophic turmoil and indecision, as the need for even more collective action becomes patent. The term 'Radical' becomes in many quarters a term of contempt, a symbol of shilly-shallying and the building of impossible halfway houses. How different is the tone of the American New Deal! Here there is a feeling of high adventure, a sense of iconoclasm, genuine 'radicalism'. The young men who in Europe become socialists and communists in America for the most part become New Dealers. Liberal Reform here has all the youth and energy that Marxism has across the Atlantic.

And yet, as we are sometimes told, youth and energy are matters of perspective. Of course there is a substantive issue here which cannot be blinked. America came late to positive social legislation, so that the New Deal might reasonably be said to reflect some of the radical excitement of Europe at the turn of the century. There is a good deal of truth in Helen Lynd's remark that the American experience is usually the English experience delayed by fifty years. Moreover in the context of a prior devotion to Horatio Alger, which Europe never had, any amount of Liberal Reform was bound to seem iconoclastic. But compared to the larger mechanics of the American world, these are actually minor points. What makes the New Deal 'radical' is the smothering by the American Lockian faith of the socialist challenge to it.

. . . what appeared . . . was that happy pragmatism which as usual refused to concern itself with moral issues at all. And this, in turn, permitted the American democrat to go about solving his problems without the serious twinges of conscience which would surely have appeared had he felt that his Lockian 'Americanism' was at stake. In one sense this put him, from the angle of experimental freedom, far ahead of the European Liberal reformers or even the European socialists. During the 'thirties it used to be the fashion to lament with Thurman Arnold the way in which folklore and fixed ideas stood in the way of social change. But the truth is, the age was much freer of fetish in America than it was in Europe where ideological categories reigned. Where in England or France or Germany could you find the freewheeling inventiveness typified by the NRA, the TVA, the REA, the WPA, the SEC, and all the other New Deal alphabetical combinations and recombinations? What Thurman Arnold failed to see was that the technical pragmatism he wanted was nourished by the very 'folklore' he blasted. An irreversible ethics made all problems technical.

The Liberal Tradition in America, Harcourt, Brace, New York, 1955, pp. 260, 270

30. *Adolf Berle, too, claimed the New Deal as a triumph for the moderates.*

. . . In a broad sense, the New Deal was an institutional revolution. It shifted the major centers of economic power from private to public institutions. President Roosevelt and his intellectual as well as political cohorts quite consciously chose not to make it a socialist revolution. Thereby the intellectuals around FDR incurred the lasting enmity of a small but vocal extreme left wing, who hoped—as some still hope—to work up a sort of class war in a country which neither needs nor provides adequate material for that grim adventure. Tugwell (as also this reviewer) at the climax of his career nevertheless was assaulted as a 'socialist' by right-wing forces of finance, business and their political representatives who were losing power. Simultaneously the left considered we had missed (or funked) a golden opportunity to force a class revolution, European-style.

Both charges had elements of truth. We certainly followed Franklin Roosevelt in his determination to take economic power from the financial rulers in New York and their satellites, and to place it for the time being in Washington. We certainly refused to take advantage of the economic collapse to set up state socialism (let alone Communism) or to intrigue within the government to prepare such a development. We did undertake through democratically adopted measures to redistribute the national income, steering more of it toward the least-favored among the population. We hoped for a better distribution of wealth. We did intend that the federal government should take over the ultimate controls of currency and credit (as it did), and the power, where necessary, to allocate capital resources as well. We did hope for the location of residual power over the economic system in the hands of the democratically-elected Congress and the United States government, while maintaining non-statist enterprise as the major method of production.

Most of this was achieved, and in doing so Franklin Roosevelt quite consciously made the decisions. Thereby he (and we) – literally – violated dogma right and left. All of us believed in democracy, not in dictatorship of 'the proletariat' (or indeed of anyone else), whereas neither the extreme left nor the extreme right really accepts democracy at all. For once in history, the pragmatic, socially-minded reformists were succeeding in doing what Mirabeau and the moderates attempted but failed to bring about in France between 1789 and 1793.

'Intellectuals and New Deals' (a review of B. Sternsher's *Rexford Tugwell and the New Deal*), *New Republic*, 7 March 1964, pp. 21, 24

31. *The arch-apologist for pragmatic liberalism in the United States is Professor A. M. Schlesinger Jr. Here, finally, is his assessment of the essence of the New Deal.*

The great central source of the New Deal lay precisely in the instinctive response of practical, energetic, and compassionate people to dogmatic absolutes. The compulsion to sacrifice reality to doctrine presented a profound challenge to the pragmatic nerve. Many Americans, refusing to be intimidated by abstractions or to be overawed by ideology, responded by doing things. The whole point of the New Deal lay in its belief in activism, its faith in gradualness, its rejection of catastrophism, its indifference to ideology, its conviction that a managed and modified capitalist order achieved by piecemeal experiment could combine personal freedom with economic growth. 'In a world in which revolutions just now are coming easily,' said Adolf Berle, 'the New Deal chose the more difficult course of moderation and rebuilding.' 'The course that the New Deal did take,' said Harold Ickes, 'was the hardest course. It conformed to no theory, but it did fit into the American system – a system of taking action step by step, a system of regulation only to meet concrete needs, a system of courageous recognition of change.' Tugwell, rejecting laissez-faire and collectivism, spoke of the 'third course'. . . .

. . . Why did the New Deal have the pragmatic commitment? Why, under the impact of depression, was it not overborne by dogma as were most other governments in the world? The answer to this lies, I suspect, . . . in the suggestion that the New Deal represented, not just a response to depression, but also a response to pent-up frustrations and needs in American society – frustrations and needs which would have produced an activist, practical mood had there been no depression at all. The periodic demand for affirmative government in American politics, the periodic breakthrough of new leadership – these were already in the works before the depression. Depression, therefore, instead of catching a nation wholly unprepared, merely accelerated tendencies toward change already visible in the national community. The response to depression, in short, was controlled by the values of experimentalism, rather than by those of ideology. The New Deal, rejecting formalism and dogma, was thus able to conduct a fight against economic collapse without destroying the continuities which held American life together.

'The Sources of the New Deal', from *Paths of American Thought*, eds. A. M. Schlesinger Jr., and Morton White, Houghton Mifflin, Boston, 1963, pp. 389–91

Conclusion

Much of the domestic history of the United States since Roosevelt's sudden death in 1945 has been a vindication of the New Deal. During his twelve years in the White House the country had reached a new equilibrium well to the left of anything hitherto conceivable, and most Americans seemed happy with the results. Popular acceptance was underscored by the fact that even when a Republican régime at last came to power in 1953, it would not contemplate more than a marginal revision of the New Deal's achievements. Perhaps the ultimate accolade came on 31 December 1965 when Time magazine put Keynes on its cover and acknowledged him as the prophet of the new economics.

Yet the new dispensation was not short of critics. Irreconcilables on the far right of the Republican party still thought of 1933–53 as 'twenty years of treason' and in the decade after Roosevelt's death they made a determined bid to brand the Roosevelt administration as a halfway house to communism. Left of centre, meanwhile, younger liberals chafed at the stagnation of a society which appeared to believe it had solved all its problems, and sought to re-create the excitement of the New Deal but by means relevant to their own generation. Both sides, however, found it impossible to capture the nation. Kennedy was elected by a mere hair's breadth in 1960 and his 'New Frontier' made very little headway; Goldwater's attempt to return to the grand simplicities of rugged individualism in 1964 met with a devastating rebuff from the electorate. It took the trauma of Kennedy's assassination to create the opportunity for his successor to push through a mass of long-needed reforms in the shape of the 'Great Society' legislation.

Needless to say, Johnson's Great Society confronts formidable obstacles. To begin with, the Congressional opponents of reform, silenced by the 1964 la-dn slide, are now reasserting themselves and could seriously hamper progress once again. Then besides the purely political forces of opposition, long-term problems must be faced in several fields. In spite of spectacular economic expansion since 1961, great areas of poverty persist in backward rural districts and in the slums of the cities. Progress for American Negroes in particular remains agonizingly slow and most of them, despite Federal intervention, are still debarred from the many privileges of white society. The result has been an increasing turn towards the violence endemic in American life, an admission of the failure of democratic solutions. Moreover, one must remember that since

1939 several regions of the United States have been seriously dependent on a war economy for their prosperity, and the war in Vietnam has, of course, deepened this dependence as well as diverting precious funds from social welfare programmes. There may well be a heavy domestic price to pay for America's conception of its responsibilities as a great world power. Finally, the implementation of the numerous Great Society statutes has imposed such a burden on the administrative structures set up by the New Deal as to bring them dangerously close to collapse. What is now needed is a whole new set of relationships between governments at all levels and the people they govern. Under Lyndon Johnson, Roosevelt's protégé, the United States may have come to the end of one of its greatest experiments and be on the point of a new departure as dramatic and as far-reaching as the New Deal itself.

1. In 1940 John Dewey defined America's future role as follows:

The conflict as it concerns the democracy to which our history commits us is *within* our own institutions and attitudes. It can be won only by extending the application of democratic methods, methods of consultation, persuasion, negotiation, communication, co-operative intelligence, in the task of making our own politics, industry, education, our own culture generally, a servant and an evolving manifestation of democratic ideas. . . .

. . . An American democracy can serve the world only as it demonstrates in the conduct of its own life the efficacy of plural, partial and experimental methods in securing and maintaining an ever-increasing release of the powers of human nature, in service of a freedom which is co-operative and a co-operation which is voluntary.

Freedom and Culture, Allen and Unwin, London, 1940, pp. 175–6

2. Roosevelt realized the need to carry through the work of the New Deal after the Second World War was over. At his press conference of 28 December 1943 he said this.

. . . how did the New Deal come into existence? It was because there was an awfully sick patient called the United States of America, and it was suffering from a grave internal disorder – awfully sick – all kinds of things had happened to this patient, all internal things. And they sent for the doctor. And it was a long, long process – took several years before those ills, in particular that illness of ten years ago, were remedied. But after a while they were remedied. . . .

. . . And when victory comes, the program of the past, of course, has got to be carried on . . . it seems pretty clear that we must plan for, and help to bring about, an expanded economy which will result in more security, in more employment, in more recreation, in more education, in more health, in better housing for all our citizens, so that the conditions of 1932 and the beginning of 1933 won't come back again.

The Public Papers and Addresses of Franklin D. Roosevelt, ed. S. Rosenman, Harper, New York, 1950, vol. xii, pp. 570–2

3. A fortnight later, in his State of the Union address, he put it in more specific terms.

We have come to a clear realization of the fact that true individual freedom cannot exist without economic security and independence. 'Necessitous men are not free men.' People who are hungry and out of a job are the stuff of which dictatorships are made.

In our day these economic truths have become accepted as self-evident. We have accepted, so to speak, a second Bill of Rights under which a new basis of security and prosperity can be established for all—regardless of station, race, or creed.

Among these are:

The right to a useful and remunerative job in the industries or shops or farms or mines of the Nation;

The right to earn enough to provide adequate food and clothing and recreation;

The right of every farmer to raise and sell his products at a return which will give him and his family a decent living;

The right of every businessman, large and small, to trade in an atmosphere of freedom from unfair competition and domination by monopolies at home or abroad;

The right of every family to a decent home;

The right to adequate medical care and the opportunity to achieve and enjoy good health;

The right to adequate protection from the economic fears of old age, sickness, accident and unemployment;

The right to a good education.

All of these rights spell security. And after this war is won we must be prepared to move forward, in the implementation of these rights, to new goals of human happiness and well-being.

America's own rightful place in the world depends in large part upon how fully these and similar rights have been carried into practice for our citizens. For unless there is security here at home there cannot be lasting peace in the world.

Ibid., vol. xiii, p. 41

4. *Although Roosevelt did not live to see his vision fulfilled, the New Deal and the memory of the depression made a lasting impact on postwar American life, as the economist J. K. Galbraith remarked.*

Measured by its continuing imprint on actions and attitudes, the depression clearly stands with the Civil War as one of the two most important events in American history since the Revolution. For the great majority of Americans the Second World War, by contrast, was an almost casual and pleasant experience. Several millions found jobs who had doubted whether they might ever find jobs again. . . . Only a minority experienced the nagging homesickness, the fear, the physical suffering and the mutilation and death which is the less pleasant destiny of the fighting soldier in wartime. Because they were a minority the war left no lasting imprint. The depression which afflicted a great majority of the people did.

The depression not only contributed deeply to the insecurity with which Americans viewed their economy. It also had an important bearing on economic behaviour. In the years following the Second World War the fear of a recurrence of depression was without question a dominant factor in the calculations of a large proportion of all businessmen. The convention, so scrupulously observed by the business community, which bans the public expression of fear of economic collapse lest to express fear be to invite the fact, concealed much of this alarm. None the less, when *Fortune* magazine in 1946 asked some 15,000 leading business executives in confidence whether they expected an 'extended major depression with large-scale unemployment in the next ten years'—a phrasing that was not designed to minimize the scope of the contemplated disaster—fifty-eight per cent of those replying said they did. Of the remainder only twenty-eight per cent said they did not. In these same years labour was preoccupied with measures to maintain the level of employment and farmers with support prices that would provide shelter in a slump. Even the radicals had long ceased to talk about the inequality or exploitation under capitalism or its 'inherent contradictions'. They stressed only the utter unreliability of its performance.

American Capitalism: The Concept of Countervailing Power, Penguin, Harmondsworth, 1963 (rev. edn of 1956), pp. 78–9

5. *No major recession did come, however, and by the mid-fifties many commentators had come to feel that America had solved its basic economic problems. Here is Professor Sumner Slichter.*

. . . the community today does not have great economic problems that create the need for changes in institutions. There are, of course, plenty of economic problems – the tax system could stand much improvement, the farm program causes immense waste of valuable resources, venture capital is scarce especially for small enterprises, the country lacks an adequate program for developing the potentialities of talented young people, the problem of creeping inflation defies solution. All of these problems and others, too, are important, but they are not of first importance and they do not create the need for important changes in economic institutions.

Twenty-five years ago the situation was very different. At that time the economy had (or was thought to have) three great economic problems: (1) the great inequalities in incomes; (2) the problem of instability – business was subject to sharp ups and downs; and (3) the problem of stagnation – many people feared (quite erroneously but sincerely) that the economy lacked the capacity to develop an adequate demand for goods. All of these problems (real or imaginary) have been reduced to secondary importance or have been removed. The spread in the distribution of incomes has been greatly reduced through a stiffly progressive income tax, the development of large transfer payments (social security, public assistance, farm relief, grants to needy veterans), the passage of minimum wage laws, and the encouragement of powerful trade unions. Various changes, some of them planned and some the result of developments quite independent of plans, have tamed the business cycle. The planned changes include the reform of the banking system (especially the act of 1935), the Securities and Exchange Act of 1934, the social security program, the public assistance and farm programs, the introduction of long-term amortizable mortgages. Among the unplanned changes have been the increase in the number of important industries (increasing the chance that the response of the economy to any given upward or downward stimulus would be distributed over a longer period of time), the growth of long-range planning by managements, thus making investment expenditures less sensitive to short-term changes in business, the increase in tax rates tending to reduce the fluctuations in incomes after taxes, the great growth in the liquidity of the banking system as a result of the issuance of large amounts of short-term securities by the government during the war, and the increase in the relative importance of government expenditures which tend to dampen the business cycle because they move more or less independent of the short-run changes in business. The fears of stagnation have been eliminated mainly by the enormous expansion of technological research with the resulting gain in the capacity of the economy to create investment opportunities.

Economic Growth in the United States, Louisiana State University Press, 1961, pp. 189–91

6. *The political outcome, as Richard Hofstadter pointed out in 1955, was to make American liberalism respectable.*

Twenty years ago the dynamic force in American political life came from the side of liberal dissent, from the impulse to reform the inequities of our economic and social system and to change our ways of doing things, to the end that the sufferings of the Great Depression would never be repeated. Today the dynamic force in our political life no longer comes from the liberals who made the New Deal possible. By 1952 the liberals had had at least the trappings of power for twenty years. They could look back to a brief, exciting period in the mid-thirties when they had held power itself and had been able to transform the economic and administrative life of the nation. After twenty years the New Deal liberals have quite unconsciously taken on the psychology of those who have entered into possession. Moreover, a large part of the New Deal public, the jobless, distracted and bewildered men of 1933, have in the course of the years found substantial places in society for themselves, have become home-owners, suburbanites and solid citizens. Many of them still keep the emotional commitment to the liberal dissent with which they grew up politically, but their social position is one of solid comfort. Among them the dominant tone has become one of satisfaction, even of a kind of conservatism. Insofar as Adlai Stevenson won their enthusiasm in 1952, it was not in spite of, but in part because of the air of poised and reliable conservatism that he brought to the Democratic convention. By comparison, Harry Truman's impassioned rhetoric, with its occasional thrusts at 'Wall Street', seemed passé and rather embarrassing. The change did not escape Stevenson himself. 'The strange alchemy of time,' he said in a speech at Columbus, 'has somehow converted the Democrats into the truly conservative party of this country – the party dedicated to conserving all that is best, and building solidly and safely on these foundations.' The most that the old liberals can now envisage is not to carry on with some ambitious new program, but simply to defend as much as possible of the old achievements and to try to keep traditional liberties of expression that are threatened.

'The Pseudo-Conservative Revolt', from *The Radical Right*, ed. D. Bell, Anchor Books, New York, 1964 (first published 1963), pp. 75–6

7. The liberal wing of the Democratic party, however, wanted to break out of this mood of acceptance. Thus Professor A. M. Schlesinger Jr.

. . . One of the singular developments of the last decade was the rise of the notion that government was somehow the enemy. This was not George Washington's attitude toward government, nor Alexander Hamilton's, nor Andrew Jackson's, nor Abraham Lincoln's. The great American statesmen have all seen government as one means by which a free people achieves its purposes. But in the '50's we tended to suppose that a man engaged in making money for himself was in nobler work than a man serving the community (and that the more money he made, the greater his wisdom and virtue). That attitude will diminish in the '60's. Young men will go into public service with devotion and hope as they did in the day of T.R., Wilson and F.D.R. Government will gain strength and vitality from these fresh people and new ideas.

Of course, affirmative government *per se* can no more be a sufficient end for a good society than consumer goods *per se*. The object of strengthening government is to give force to the idea of public interest and to make possible the allocation of resources to necessary public purposes. There is no other way to meet the competition of communism. There is no other way to bring about a higher quality of life and opportunity for ordinary men and women.

This point—the quality of life—suggests the great difference between the politics of the '60's and the politics of the '30's. The New Deal arose in response to economic breakdown. It had to meet immediate problems of subsistence and survival. Its emphasis was essentially quantitative—an emphasis inevitable in an age of scarcity. But the '60's will confront an economy of abundance. There are still pools of poverty which will have to be mopped up; but the central problem will be increasingly that of fighting for individual dignity, identity, and fulfillment in an affluent mass society. The issues of the new period will not be those involved with refueling the economic machine, putting floors under wages, and farm prices, establishing systems of social security. The new issues will be rather those of education, health, equal opportunity, community planning—the issues which make the difference between defeat and opportunity, between frustration and fulfillment, in the everyday lives of average persons. These issues will determine the quality of civilization to which our nation aspires in an age of ever-increasing wealth and leisure. A guiding aim, I believe, will be the insistence that every American boy and girl have access to the career proportionate to his or her talents and characters, regardless of birth, fortune, creed, or color.

'The New Mood in Politics', in *The Politics of Hope*, Houghton Mifflin, Boston, 1962, pp. 91–2

8. *President Kennedy himself was anxious to move forward from the New Deal, as he proclaimed in a speech of 11 June 1962.*

. . . we cannot understand and attack our contemporary problems in 1962 if we are bound by traditional labels and wornout slogans of an earlier era. But the unfortunate fact is that our rhetoric has not kept pace with the speed of social and economic change. Our political debates, our public discourse—on current domestic and economic issues—too often bears little or no relation to the actual problems the United States faces.

What is at stake in our economic discussions today is not some grand warfare of rival ideologies which will sweep the country with passion but the practical management of a modern economy. What we need is not labels and clichés but more basic discussion of the sophisticated and technical questions involved in keeping a great economic machinery moving ahead. . . .

. . . How can we develop and sustain strong and stable world markets for basic commodities without unfairness to the consumer and without undue stimulus to the producer? How can we generate the buying power which can consume what we produce on our farms and in our factories? How can we take advantage of the miracles of automation with the great demand that it will put upon highly skilled labor and yet offer employment to the half million of unskilled school dropouts each year who enter the labor market, eight million of them in the 1960's?

How do we eradicate the barriers which separate substantial minorities of our citizens from access to education and employment on equal terms with the rest?

How, in sum, can we make our free economy work at full capacity – that is, provide adequate profits for enterprise, adequate wages for labor, adequate utilization of plant, and opportunity for all?

These are the problems that we should be talking about – that the political parties and the various groups in our country should be discussing. They cannot be solved by incantations from the forgotten past. But the example of Western Europe shows that they are capable of solution – that governments, and many of them are conservative governments, prepared to face technical problems without ideological preconceptions, can co-ordinate the elements of a national economy and bring about growth and prosperity – a decade of it.

Some conversations I have heard in our own country sound like old records, long-playing, left over from the middle thirties. The debate of the thirties had its great significance and produced great results, but it took place in a different world with different needs and different tasks. It is our responsibility today to live in our own world, and to identify the needs and discharge the tasks of the 1960's.

Public Papers of the Presidents of the United States. John F. Kennedy. Containing the Public Messages, Speeches and Statements of the President January 1 to December 31, 1962, United States Government Printing Office, Washington, D.C., 1963, pp. 473, 475

9. *Thea cceptance of the new status quo and, in particular, the rehabilitation of big business which it entailed, was also resisted by the right wing of American*

opinion where many trust-busters now found a home. This extract dates from the mid-fifties.

. . . the popular faith in competition–the historical bulwark against the pressure of private interests upon government–was somehow eroded. Public confidence in old-fashioned competition was shaken, and many came to regard industrial rivalry as wasteful, destructive, unstable, inefficient, and technologically obsolete. By contrast, bigness came to be endowed with the ultimate economic virtues: efficiency, productivity, expansion, technical progress, stability, social responsibility, welfare, and national security. Even the symbolic words of competitive economics–enterprise, initiative, freedom, and opportunity– were lifted out of context, clothed with new meaning and, by a process of semantic metamorphosis, applied to industrial giantism. Under this two-pronged attack on public opinion, people began to lose faith in competition, despair of its future, and regard efforts to preserve it as futile. Simultaneously, they came to develop an uncritical, worshipful, dependent attitude toward big business, admiring its productive power but oblivious to its dangers. While competition was bereft of its attractions, monopoly gradually lost its terror. And with public support for a vigorous antimonopoly policy progressively weakened, the federal government became an easier victim for pressure groups seeking special privilege. It could not, for lack of public support, resist their importunities or deny claims to promote the public welfare.

w. ADAMS and H. M. GRAY, *Monopoly in America*, Macmillan, New York, 1955, pp. 176–7

10. *In 1964 the far right had their chance with Senator Barry Goldwater as the Republican party's Presidential nominee. So far as the New Deal was concerned, they had learned nothing and forgotten nothing, as these extracts from their platform show.*

1. We Republicans shall first rely on the individual's right and capacity to advance his own economic well-being, to control the fruits of his efforts, and to plan his own and his family's future; and to assist the individual in surmounting urgent problems beyond his own power and responsibility to control. . . .

. . . In all such programmes where Federal initiative is properly involved to relieve or prevent misfortune or meet overpowering needs, it will be the Republican way to move promptly and energetically, and wherever possible to provide assistance of a kind enabling the individual to gain or regain the possibility to make his own way and to have a fair chance to achieve his own goals. . . .

In furtherance of our faith in the individual, we also pledge prudent, responsible management of the Government's fiscal affairs to protect the individual against the evils of spendthrift Government–protecting most of all the needy and fixed-income families against the cruellest tax, inflation–and protecting every citizen against the high taxes forced by excessive spending, in order that each individual may keep more of his earnings for his own and his family's use. For instance, we pledge:

. . . An end to chronic deficit financing, proudly reaffirming our belief in a balanced budget . . .

In furtherance of our faith in the individual, we also pledge the maximum restraint of Federal intrusions into matters more productively left to the individual. For instance, we pledge:

To continue Republican sponsorship of practical Federal–State–local programmes which will effectively treat the needs of the poor, while resisting direct Federal handouts that erode away individual self-reliance and self-respect and perpetuate dependency . . .

2. We Republicans shall vigorously protect the dynamo of economic growth–free, competitive enterprise–that has made America the envy of the world. For instance, we pledge: . . .

Assistance to small business by simplifying Federal and State tax and regulatory requirements, fostering the availability of longer term credit at fair terms and equity capital for small firms, encouraging strong State programmes to foster small business, establishing more effective measures to assure a sharing by small business in Federal procurement and promoting wider export opportunities;

An end to power grabbing regulatory actions, such as the reach by the Federal Trade Commission for injunctive powers and the ceaseless pressing by the White House, the Food and Drug Administration, and Federal Trade Commission to dominate consumer decision in the market place;

Returning the consumer to the driver's seat as the chief regulator and chief beneficiary of a free economy, by resisting excessive concentration of power, whether public or private;

. . . Improvement, and full and fair enforcement of the anti-trust statutes, coupled with long overdue clarification of Federal policies and interpretations relating thereto in order to strengthen competition and protect the consumer and small business;

Constant opposition to any form of unregulated monopoly whether business or labour . . .

. . . The redevelopment of an atmosphere of confidence throughout the Government and across the nation in which vigorous competition can flourish . . .

. . . In furtherance of our faith in the competitive system, we also pledge:

. . . Maximum reliance upon subordinate levels of government and individual citizens to meet the nation's need, in place of establishing even more Federal agencies to burden the people.

The Guardian, 17 July 1964

11. *In the event, however, the American electorate rejected these antique verities and chose instead the 'Great Society' of President Johnson. These extracts are from Johnson's celebrated speech of 22 May 1964.*

For a century we labored to settle and to subdue a continent. For half a century we called upon unbounded invention and untiring industry to create an order of plenty for all of our people.

The challenge of the next half century is whether we have the wisdom to use that wealth to enrich and elevate our national life, and to advance the quality of our American civilization.

Your imagination, your initiative, and your indignation will determine whether we build a society where progress is the servant of our needs, or a society where old values and new visions are buried under unbridled growth. For in your time we have the opportunity to move not only toward the rich society and the powerful society, but toward the Great Society.

The Great Society rests on abundance and liberty for all. It demands an end to poverty and racial injustice, to which we are totally committed in our time. But that is just the beginning.

The Great Society is a place where every child can find knowledge to enrich his mind and to enlarge his talents. It is a place where leisure is a welcome chance to build and reflect, not a feared cause of boredom and restlessness. It is a place where the city of man serves not only the needs of the body and the demands of commerce but the desire for beauty and the hunger for community.

It is a place where man can renew contact with nature. It is a place which honors creation for its own sake and for what it adds to the understanding of the race. It is a place where men are more concerned with the quality of their goals than the quantity of their goods.

But most of all, the Great Society is not a safe harbor, a resting place, a final objective, a finished work. It is a challenge constantly renewed, beckoning us toward a destiny where the meaning of our lives matches the marvelous products of our labor.

Public Papers of the Presidents of the United States. Lyndon B. Johnson. Containing the Public Messages, Speeches, and Statements of the President 1963–64. Book I. United States Government Printing Office, Washington, D.C., 1965, p. 704

12. *The implications of the Great Society, as Walter Lippmann explains, are revolutionary.*

. . . An affluent society is not simply a rich society; it is one which has mastered the new art of controlling and stimulating its own economic growth. To be sure, we are as yet only students and apprentices in the art. We have not yet fully mastered it. But we have a sufficiently promising start to justify our thinking that we have seen a breakthrough–that we are escaping from the immemorial human predicament of the haves and have-nots. This predicament has been based on the assumption that the size of the pie to be divided is fixed, and that therefore, if some have more, others must take less.

The assumption that this predicament exists has been the central idea of socialism and communism. However, it has also been the tacit assumption of recent reformist and welfare programs. We can see this in slogans like 'The New Deal' and 'The Fair Deal'. Both imply that there is always the same pack to be dealt.

The scientific breakthrough in modern economic theory was prepared in the years between the two world wars. But only recently, not until President Kennedy's proposal of a tax cut as part of a planned deficit, have the modern economists in the government service and in the great financial institutions been taken quite seriously. I will not say that they have moved into the driver's seat. But certainly they are in the seat next to the driver's, reading the signs and following the maps for him. The result of this change is a benign revolution which makes it possible that the costs of improving schools and colleges, of reducing poverty, of rebuilding slums, can be covered by calculated increases in the national output of wealth.

Newsweek, 18 January 1965, p. 11

13. *The scale of Johnson's achievement in getting his legislation through was equally momentous. Here is the columnist James Reston.*

The record of the 89th Congress shows what can happen in this country under the leadership of Lyndon Johnson and Barry Goldwater. They did not intend to cooperate but they have. Apart, they are insupportable, even insufferable; together invincible.

In combination, their unintended alliance has produced a torrent of social and economic legislation unmatched since the first Roosevelt Congress of 1933–34, and maybe not even then. It is an extraordinary, maybe even an unprecedented record, but one that could never have been enacted without the sharp ideological conflict between the populist President and his conservative opponent.

Washington and the country, of course, are still divided over whether the new education, health, conservation, civil rights and poverty laws are good or bad, but on the question of how these laws were passed, Conservatives and Liberals are in general agreement.

The Presidential election of 1964, giving the voters a clear ideological choice, produced the greatest popular landslide of this century, which weakened the Conservatives, strengthened the Liberals, broke the power of the Conservative Republican–Southern Democrat coalition in the House of Representatives, and created a majority for social and economic measures that had been blocked for a generation. In short, quite an 'echo'.

. . . The irony of the Goldwater challenge to the welfare state and planned economy is that, by losing so overwhelmingly, he brought in a Congress that enacted precisely the legislation he ran for the Presidency to oppose, and we are only now beginning to see the legislative consequences of his misadventure.

In its first 174 years, the Congress of the United States voted $5·8 billion in Federal funds for education; in 1965–66 alone, the 89th Congress voted $9·6 billion. The first 88 Congresses voted approximately $10 billion for health since the establishment of the Public Health Service in 1798; in the last two years the 89th Congress has voted $8·2 billion for health, including Medicare, almost as much as in the previous 168 years. And the record of most of the social and economic innovations of the 89th Congress follows the same pattern.

'The Goldwater Congress', *The New York Times International Edition*, 20 October 1966

14. *Many obstacles, of course, remain, before the Great Society can be fulfilled. One of the most dangerous is the reliance of large areas of the American economy on defence expenditure, as Emile Benoit pointed out–before the enormous involvement in Vietnam.*

Something less than one-tenth of the output of our economy is now devoted to defense–about $52 billion out of a total production or gross national product (G.N.P.) of $550 billion. A somewhat similar proportion of our employment is now absorbed in defense activities. Out of a total labor force of around 75 million, about 6·5 million people are employed directly or indirectly in defense work–roughly 2·5 million people in defense industry, some 3 million in the armed forces, and over 1 million as civilians in the Department of Defense and related agencies.

The big industrial concentration of defense production is now in the aerospace–electronics–nucleonics complex, which accounts for about four-fifths of all procurement. There is also a heavy geographic concentration of defense plants and installations, making such areas particularly vulnerable to the effects of disarmament. In Kansas, Washington, New Mexico, California and Connecticut, at least 20 to 30 per cent of all those employed in manufacturing work on defense projects. In Alaska, Hawaii, the District of Columbia and Virginia, one-tenth to one-quarter of all income is generated by military pay and allowances, or Defense Department civilian wages and salaries.

For individual communities and areas the problem may be even more acute. In a recent year, 82 per cent of all workers employed in manufacturing in San Diego worked in missiles and aircraft; the corresponding figure was 72 per cent in Wichita, 53 per cent in Seattle, and 27 per cent in the Los Angeles–Long Beach area.

The sudden termination of all this defense activity would obviously create quite a problem.

'Would Disarmanent Mean a Depression?' *The New York Times Magazine*, 28 April 1963

15. *Moreover, as Paul Johnson remarks here, poverty is still widespread in America. Early in 1965, according to the Department of Health, Education and Welfare, no less than 18 per cent of the population of the United States was living below the poverty line.*

. . . A generation ago, in *The Grapes of Wrath*, John Steinbeck described the fate of the Okies, driven by the dustbowl into the rich farming valleys of California. One reads the book as ancient history, something one associates in time with Hitler and Appeasement, with the age of Huey Long and the beginnings of the New Deal. In fact nothing fundamental has changed. The agricultural workers, be they poor whites, Mexican-Americans or Negroes, are still excluded from Federal Minimum Wage legislation and the unemployment insurance system. Most of them still live in hovels or work-camps. Indeed, the original camp described by Steinbeck is still in existence, though tarted up a little. Near Visalia, in the San Joaquin Valley, which is probably the richest agricultural land on earth, I visited a camp called the Linnell Farm Labour Centre, built as a temporary accommodation as part of the Federal Anti-Dustbowl programme in 1938. A quarter of a century later, it is still there, its tin huts crammed with Mexican-American labourers and their families. There are scores of such camps, some better, some worse. . . .

. . . In aggregate, the submerged classes . . . make up over one-fifth of the nation. Collectively, in the framework of a democratic system, they ought to be able to exert enormous leverage. In practice, their political influence is negligible. . . . The poor have votes, for the most part; but they lack the means and the organization to operate effectively in Washington–and, still more so, in the state capitals, where powerful local interests are often dominant.

When great masses of men and women are deprived of political expression by constitutional forms, a classic revolutionary situation comes into existence. What they are denied by law they will in time seize by force. But the operation of this historical maxim presumes a privileged minority denying power to the majority. In America today we have the reverse: 40 million dispossessed, crushed beneath the weight of a complacent and prosperous mass who enjoy a standard of living unprecedented in history. Even if we accept the view of the gloomier economists, that the poor in America constitute more nearly one-third to two-fifths of the population, the majority still have a strong vested interest in maintaining the status quo. Their numerical superiority rules out any possibility of a vast convulsive movement to change the existing structure by violence. . . .

. . . Thoughtful Americans are becoming disturbed by the accumulating evidence that their society–so glittering in achievement, so infinite in promise–is not functioning as it should. They are deeply ashamed of American poverty, appalled by its growing translation into violence . . .

But it is possible that America is entering an entirely new and thoughtful phase in its historical development. For nearly a quarter of a century, its immense national energies have been devoted almost exclusively to its new responsibilities as the paramount power in world affairs. . . . In the effort to become outward-looking, America has averted its eyes from the need for change within its own frontiers. Domestic problems have been treated with palliatives or neglected altogether. One consequence is poverty. Another is the political frustration that has bred the Goldwater movement.

But now the time is coming when Americans can once more afford to look inward. . . . The world is still a turbulent place, but American policy-makers now realize that there is a limit to their ability to reform it, and that they must rest satisfied with an uneasy thermonuclear peace. America is moving, I suspect, not so much towards isolationism, as towards self-scrutiny, and in the process a number of ancient shibboleths will be scrapped as ruthlessly as last year's car.

'America: The Sick Giant', *The New Statesman*, 17 July 1964, pp. 81–2, 83

16. *Finally there is the growing realization that the present administrative machinery which the United States inherited from the Roosevelt era is just not adequate to the tasks which the Great Society envisages. If it meets the challenge, America will have achieved a breakthrough comparable even to the New Deal. This, as James Reston makes clear, is one of the supreme issues confronting the coming generation.*

As President Johnson starts his fourth year in the White House, one fact is not only clear but undisputed: His Administration is poorly organized to administer the domestic programs he has introduced, and the administrative chaos of the state and local governments is even worse.

The reasons for this are fairly clear. The Administration has put through more social and economic programs in the last two years than it can absorb. The 89th Congress alone passed 21 new health programs, 17 new educational programs, 15 new economic development programs, 12 new programs for the cities, 17 new resource development programs, and 4 new manpower training programs.

These programs are administered by such a variety of different Federal agencies that, as Senator Robert Kennedy of New York remarked here this week, it is almost impossible for small town officials to know what money is available for what purposes or even where to go for information.

Senator Edmund S. Muskie of Maine, who is exploring this thicket, recently observed that Federal aid expenditures to the states and municipalities have risen from $1 billion in 1946 to $15 billion this year and are expected to go up to $60 billion by 1975. There are now, he noted, 170 different Federal aid programs on the books, financed by over 400 separate appropriations, and administered by 21 Federal departments and agencies aided by 150 Washington bureaus and over 400 regional offices empowered to receive applications and disburse funds.

This has created something almost unheard of here. Criticism of the system, cries of growing domination by the Federal Government, complaints about administrative confusion and waste are now coming not alone from the Administration's critics or from observers in the state capitals but from leading officials of the Johnson Administration itself.

'In almost every domestic program,' Secretary of Health, Education and Welfare John W. Gardner told the Muskie committee, 'we are encountering crises of organization. Coordination among Federal agencies leaves much to be desired. Communication between the various levels of government—Federal, state and local—is casual and ineffective. State and local government is in most areas seriously inadequate.'

Washington obviously cannot solve this problem by itself. There are now over 80,000 separate local governments in the United States, few of them large enough in population, area, or taxable resources to get adequate personnel or funds to apply modern methods in solving present and future problems.

Overlapping layers of local government, ineffective popular control, weak policy-making mechanisms, antiquated administrative machinery and underpaid and undertrained personnel—all these are keeping the state and local governments from forming an effective partnership with the Federal Government, which now provides 20 per cent of the total annual revenues of the states.

Yet it is probably unrealistic for Secretary Gardner to call on 'the American people' to correct these deficiencies. The remedy must begin in Washington. The interdepartmental committee system, designed to coordinate the activities of the various departments and agencies in the poverty program—to take just one example—has not worked.

'We have a President who is keenly interested in the problem,' Secretary Gardner told the Muskie committee. But we also have a President who is poorly organized himself, reluctant to delegate power over these home-front activities to the Vice-President or anybody else, and suspicious of political institutions of any kind.

He did not work easily with the Democratic caucus when he was in the Senate. He has not made an effective instrument out of the Cabinet or the National Security Council. He all but wrecked the Democratic National Committee after he got into the White House, and he is still trying to run the Presidency as if it were a Senator's office on Capitol Hill.

The problems, however, are monumental. They are getting bigger and more complicated all the time, and while the President talks about creating a new partnership with the states and municipalities and expounds on what he calls 'creative federalism,' the fact is that he has not created the machinery to carry this out. He has an administrative monstrosity on his hands, and even his own people are beginning to criticize it in public.

'Washington: Administrative Monstrosity', *The New York Times International Edition*, 24 November 1966

Appendix I: Statistics

Table 1

Gross National Product and its major components 1929–1942 and 1962 (in $ billion at 1954 prices)

	G.N.P.	Personal consumption expenditures	Gross private domestic investment	Government expenditure Federal	State and local
1929	181·8	128·1	35·0	2·9	15·6
1930	164·5	120·3	23·6	3·4	17·1
1931	153·0	116·6	15·0	3·7	17·9
1932	130·1	106·0	3·9	3·9	16·6
1933	126·6	103·5	4·0	5·3	14·6
1934	138·5	108·9	7·4	6·9	15·8
1935	152·9	115·8	16·1	6·7	16·3
1936	173·3	127·7	21·0	10·3	16·6
1937	183·5	132·1	27·0	9·6	16·4
1938	175·1	129·9	15·5	11·4	17·4
1939	189·3	137·3	21·6	11·0	19·1
1940	205·8	144·6	29·0	13·1	18·0
1941	238·1	154·3	36·7	30·7	16·9
1942	266·9	150·8	18·8	84·7	15·4
1962	474·8	317·6	65·2	49·0	41·2

Table 2

	Unemployed as percentage of labour force	Unemployed in millions	Millions employed by Federal government (from 1933) (numbers in December of any year)	Trade union membership (millions)	Federal surplus or deficit ($ billion, years ending 30 June)
1929	3·2	1·55	–	–	+0·73
1930	8·7	4·34	–	3·4	+0·74
1931	15·9	8·02	–	3·3	−0·46
1932	23·6	12·06	–	3·1	−2·74
1933	24·9	12·83	4·25	2·7	−2·60
1934	21·7	11·34	1·12	3·1	−3·63
1935	20·1	10·61	4·04	3·6	−2·79
1936	16·9	9·03	3·81	4·0	−4·43
1937	14·3	7·70	2·66	7·0	−2·78
1938	19·0	10·39	4·34	8·0	−1·18
1939	17·2	9·48	3·34	8·8	−3·86
1940	14·6	8·12	2·91	8·7	−3·92
1941	9·9	5·56	1·79	10·2	−6·16
1942	4·7	2·66	0·39	10·4	−21·49
1962	5·6	4·01	–	16·6	−6·38

Table 3

	Index of Manufacturing Production (1947–49 = 100)	Farm Price Index (1910–14 = 100)	Wholesale Price Index (1947–49 = 100)	Gross National Product per head ($ at 1954 prices)
1929	58	148	62	1492
1930	48	125	56	1336
1931	39	87	47	1232
1932	30	65	42	1041
1933	36	70	43	1007
1934	39	90	49	1095
1935	46	109	52	1201
1936	55	114	53	1352
1937	60	122	56	1423
1938	46	97	51	1347
1939	57	95	50	1445
1940	66	100	51	1558
1941	88	124	57	1784
1942	110	159	64	1979
1962	163 (1960)	243	120	2544

Source of Tables 1–3: U.S. BUREAU OF THE CENSUS, *Historical Statistics of the United States, Colonial Times to 1957* (Washington, D.C., 1960), pp. 143, 73, 200, 711, 409, 283, 117, 98. Figures for 1962 from U.S. BUREAU OF THE CENSUS, *Historical Statistics of the United States, Colonial Times to 1957; Continuation to 1962 and Revisions* (Washington, D.C., 1965), pp. 20, 14, 16, 96, 58, 43, 17, 20, 114. One billion dollars equals one thousand million dollars.

Table 4

Changes in Distribution of Family Personal Income 1929–1953

Fifths of population ranked by family personal income and top five per cent	Percentages of total				Percentage change	
	1929	1935–36	1941	1953	1929–41	1941–53
Lowest fifth	12·5 ⎫	4·1	4·1	4·9	+1·1 ⎫	+0·8
Second fifth	⎭	9·2	9·5	11·3	⎬	+1·8
Third fifth	13·8	14·1	15·3	16·6	+1·5	+1·3
Fourth fifth	19·3	20·9	22·3	22·5	+3·0	+0·3
Highest fifth	54·4	51·7	48·8	44·7	−5·6	−4·1
Top five per cent	30·0	26·5	24·0	19·9	−6·0	−4·1

Source: U.S. BUREAU OF THE CENSUS, *Historical Statistics of the United States, Colonial Times to 1957* (Washington, D.C., 1960), p. 166.

Table 5

Accumulation of capital in the United States 1869–1939

(Rates of growth in per cent per anum in dollar values at 1929 prices)

Decades 1 January to 1 January	Total reproducible wealth	Real estate improvements, equipment and inventories	Business capital	Population	Gainfully employed
1869–1879	4·1	4·4	3·9	2·3	3·0
1879–1889	4·9	5·2	4·8	2·2	3·0
1889–1899	4·9	4·7	4·5	2·0	2·2
1899–1909	4·2	4·0	3·9	1·9	2·5
1909–1919	3·5	3·0	2·8	1·4	1·3
1919–1929	2·8	2·6	2·2	1·5	1·4
1929–1939	0·2	0·3	−0·4	0·7	1·2

Source: J. STEINDL, *Maturity and Stagnation in American Capitalism* (Oxford, 1952), p. 160.

Appendix II: Biographies

THURMAN ARNOLD (1891–) Assistant Attorney-General in charge of the anti-trust drive begun in 1938 and concluded in 1943.

ADOLF BERLE (1895–) Member of the Brain Trust during the 1932 campaign; thereafter played a lesser role as special counsel to the Reconstruction Finance Corporation 1933–38.

HUGO BLACK (1886–) Senator for Alabama 1927–37. Roosevelt's first appointee to the Supreme Court. Did not retire at seventy.

LOUIS BRANDEIS (1856–1941) Doyen of the progressives of the Wilson school and one of the greatest advocates of his generation. Associate Justice of the Supreme Court 1916–39. Perhaps the greatest formative influence behind the so-called Second New Deal.

PIERCE BUTLER (1866–1939) One of the quartet of conservatives on the New Deal Supreme Court; Associate Justice 1923–39.

BENJAMIN CARDOZO (1870–1938) A Supreme Court liberal; Associate Justice 1932–38.

BENJAMIN COHEN (1894–) Protégé of Frankfurter (see below). Assisted in drafting a great deal of statute law, including the securities legislation of 1933 and 1934, and the Public Utilities Holding Company Act of 1935, in association with Corcoran (see below).

THOMAS CORCORAN (1900–) Protégé of Frankfurter (see below). Drafted much important legislation, including the Securities Exchange Act of 1934, and became one of Roosevelt's chief intermediaries with Congress. Most prominent 1935–38.

CHARLES COUGHLIN (1891–) Ordained Roman Catholic priest 1916. Pastor of the Shrine of the Little Flower, Detroit, from 1926 and there made his reputation as a broadcaster with an audience of millions. Fascist and anti-Semite. Founder of the extreme right-wing National Union for Social Justice.

HOMER CUMMINGS (1870–1956) An active Democrat from 1900. Attorney-General 1933–39.

MARRINER ECCLES (1890–   ) Banker from Utah and a prominent advocate of government spending. Governor of the Federal Reserve Board 1934–36.

JAMES FARLEY (1888–   ) Controller of the Democratic party machine as chairman of the Democratic National Committee 1932–40; sat in the cabinet as Postmaster-General 1933–40. Broke with Roosevelt over the issue of the third term.

FELIX FRANKFURTER (1882–1965) Brandeis's principal disciple and a great power behind the scenes, especially through pupils like Cohen and Corcoran whom he had placed in important positions in Washington. Associate Justice of the Supreme Court 1939–62.

WILLIAM GREEN (1870–1952) Old-style trade union leader and as President of the craft-dominated American Federation of Labour strenuously opposed the formation of industrial unions under the aegis of the Committee for Industrial Organization led by John L. Lewis (see below).

HARRY HOPKINS (1890–1946) Spent most of his early career as a welfare worker, mainly in New York. Appointed director of the Federal Emergency Relief Administration and the Civil Works Administration in 1933, then director of the Works Progress Administration from 1935 to 1938, handling massive Federal relief projects. Secretary of Commerce 1938–40. Roosevelt's most trusted lieutenant.

HERBERT HOOVER (1874–1964) A great technocrat and humanitarian destroyed by his steadfast commitment to laissez-faire. Chairman of the American commission for relief in Belgium 1915–19, Secretary of Commerce under Harding and Coolidge 1921–28. President of the United States 1929–33. Defeated by Roosevelt 1932.

CHARLES EVANS HUGHES (1862–1948) Chief Justice of the New Deal Supreme Court 1930–41 after an impressive career in law and politics. Governor of New York 1907–10, Associate Justice of the Supreme Court 1910–16, Republican candidate for President 1916 and only narrowly defeated by Wilson, Secretary of State 1921–25.

HAROLD ICKES (1874–1952) Came to prominence as an active municipal reformer in and around Chicago. A Republican Progressive but accepted the post of Secretary of the Interior from Roosevelt and held it 1933–46. Also director of the Public Works Administration, administering Federal relief, from 1933 to 1939.

ROBERT JACKSON (1892–1954) Liberal lawyer, Brandeisian, head of the Antitrust Division of the Department of Justice 1936–38. Solicitor-General 1938–39, Attorney-General 1940–41, Associate Justice of the Supreme Court 1941–54.

HUGH JOHNSON (1882–1942) Early career in U.S. Army 1903–19. Worked on the War Industries Board 1918. Member of the Brain Trust 1932. Administrator of the National Recovery Administration 1933–34.

JOHN L. LEWIS (1880–   ) President of the United Mine Workers of America 1920–60. Founder of the Committee for Industrial Organization in opposition to the craft unions' American Federation of Labour. Supported Roosevelt in 1936, broke with him in 1940.

HUEY LONG (1893–1935) Virtual dictator of the state of Louisiana, as Governor from 1928 to 1930 and as Senator from 1931 to 1935. The most serious political threat to Roosevelt within the Democratic party. Assassinated September 1935.

JAMES MCREYNOLDS (1862–1946) Another of the Supreme Court conservatives. Wilson's Attorney-General 1913–14; Associate Justice of the Supreme Court 1914–41.

RAYMOND MOLEY (1886–   ). One of the leading members of the Brain Trust in 1932. Assistant Secretary of State for a short time in 1933 until the failure of the London Economic Conference in July, then became a political journalist. Gradually turned against Roosevelt and finally ceased supporting him in 1936.

HENRY MORGENTHAU, JR. (1891–1967) Roosevelt's Secretary of the Treasury 1934–45. A staunch anti-Keynesian.

GEORGE PEEK (1873–1943) Administrator of the Agricultural Adjustment Administration May–December 1933. Special adviser to the President on foreign trade 1933–35.

FRANCES PERKINS (1882–1965) The first woman cabinet minister in the United States. Early career spent in work on social and labour problems in New York. Roosevelt's Secretary of Labour 1933–45.

OWEN ROBERTS (1875–1955) Associate Justice of the Supreme Court 1930–45 whose decision to side with the liberals on the Court converted the conservative majority into a minority.

ELEANOR ROOSEVELT (1884–1962) A cousin of Franklin Roosevelt whom she married in 1905. Lifetime spent in welfare work; keeper of the social conscience of the White House.

FRANKLIN DELANO ROOSEVELT (1882–1945) Member of the New York state Senate 1910–13. Assistant Secretary of the Navy 1913–20. Democratic nominee for Vice-President 1920. Crippled by poliomyelitis 1921. Governor of New York 1929–32. President of the United States 1933–45.

SAMUEL ROSENMAN (1896–) Counsel to Roosevelt when Governor of New York and one of his closest associates thereafter; editor of Roosevelt's *Public Papers*.

HARLAN STONE (1872–1946) Associate Justice of the Supreme Court 1925–41; Chief Justice 1941–46. Liberal supporter of the New Deal.

GEORGE SUTHERLAND (1862–1942) Senator for Utah 1905–17; Associate Justice of the Supreme Court 1922–38 and devout supporter of laissez-faire.

FRANCIS TOWNSEND (1867–1960) Medical practitioner. Founder of the Townsend old people's movement with its main strength in California and the states of the West. Briefly associated with the right-wing Union party in 1936, but broke with it before the election.

REXFORD TUGWELL (1891–) Member of the Brain Trust 1932. Assistant Secretary of Agriculture 1933, Under Secretary 1934, director of the Resettlement Administration set up to combat rural poverty 1935–37. Left politics at the end of Roosevelt's first term. Leading exponent of the policies of the First New Deal.

WILLIS VAN DEVANTER (1859–1941) One of the four Supreme Court conservatives; Associate Justice 1910–37. The first of Roosevelt's opponents to retire.

ROBERT WAGNER (1877–1953) Senator for New York 1927–49. Promoter of much important New Deal legislation, especially the Social Security Act and the National Labour Relations Act (the so-called Wagner Act) of 1935.

HENRY WALLACE (1888–1965). Member of a celebrated Iowa farming family and son of a Republican Secretary of Agriculture. Roosevelt's Secretary of Agriculture 1933–40, when he became Vice-President of the United States. Dropped from the vice-presidency in 1944, unsuccessful Progressive candidate for President in 1948.

Bibliography

These are some of the more important and useful books about the New Deal period. Most, but not all, can be obtained in Britain.

1. GENERAL HISTORIES

The best single-volume history of the New Deal is W. Leuchtenburg, *Franklin D. Roosevelt and the New Deal 1932–1940*, Harper and Row, New York, 1963. Still valuable, however, is D. W. Brogan, *The Era of Franklin D. Roosevelt*, Yale University Press, 1950. The definitive work is A. M. Schlesinger's *The Age of Roosevelt* of which three volumes have so far appeared covering the years up to 1936: *The Crisis of the Old Order 1919–1933*, *The Coming of the New Deal* and *The Politics of Upheaval*, Houghton Mifflin, Boston, 1957–60. An interesting pioneer work is B. Rauch, *The History of the New Deal 1933–1938*, Creative Age Press, New York, 1944. Roosevelt's biographer F. Freidel has written a useful pamphlet *The New Deal in Historical Perspective*, The American Historical Association, 1959. Other general histories are M. Einaudi, *The Roosevelt Revolution*, Harcourt, Brace, New York, 1959, D. Perkins, *The New Age of Franklin Roosevelt, 1932–45*, University of Chicago Press, 1957, and J. M. Woods, *Roosevelt and Modern America*, The English Universities Press, London, 1959. F. L. Allen, *Since Yesterday*, Hamish Hamilton, London, 1940, and D. Wecter, *The Age of the Great Depression 1929–1941*, Macmillan, New York, 1948, are vivid social histories. The relevant sections of C. Degler, *Out Of Our Past*, Harper and Row, New York, 1959, and R. Hofstadter, *The Age of Reform*, Knopf, New York, 1955, are particularly recommended, while at the other end of the political spectrum there is the conservative criticism of E. E. Robinson's *The Roosevelt Leadership 1933–1945*, Lippincott, New York, 1955, and the far-right vituperation of J. T. Flynn, *The Roosevelt Myth*, Devin-Adair, New York, 1956 (rev. edn). I. Leighton, ed., *The Aspirin Age 1919–1941*, Penguin Books, Harmondsworth, 1964 has some interesting essays on the period.

2. BIOGRAPHIES OF ROOSEVELT

The definitive biography is by F. Freidel and three volumes have so far appeared. The third, *Franklin D. Roosevelt: The Triumph*, Houghton Mifflin, Boston, 1956, covers the election of 1932. The best one-volume biography is R. Tugwell, *The Democratic Roosevelt*, Doubleday, New York, 1957. There is also the contemporary G. Johnson, *Roosevelt: Dictator or Democrat?* Hamish Hamilton, London, 1942, and the more recent J. M. Burns, *Roosevelt: The Lion and the Fox*, Harcourt, Brace, New York, 1956. Finally, there is the essay on Roosevelt in R. Hofstadter's *The American Political Tradition*, Vintage Books, New York, 1957, and a useful collection of miscellanea edited by J. Rosenau and entitled *The Roosevelt Treasury*, Doubleday, New York, 1951.

3. 'READINGS'

There are many books in this category, among them: F. Freidel, ed., *The New Deal and the American People*, Prentice-Hall, New Jersey, 1964; E. Rozwenc, ed., *The New Deal: Revolution or Evolution?* Heath, Boston, 1959; M. Keller, ed., *The New Deal: What Was It ?* Holt, Rinehart and Winston, New York, 1963; E. H. Merrill, ed., *Responses to Economic Collapse: The Great Depression of the 1930's*, Heath, Boston, 1964.

4. DOCUMENTARY AND STATISTICAL MATERIAL

Roosevelt's public statements have been compiled and edited by his aide Samuel Rosenman as *The Public Papers and Addresses of Franklin D. Roosevelt*. Those for the period 1928–39 have been published in eight volumes, 1928–36 by Random House, New York, 1938 and 1937–39 by Macmillan, New York, 1941. Many other contemporary documents are available in H. S. Commager, *Documents of American History*, Appleton-Century-Crofts, New York, 1963 (7th edn). The best general statistical source is U.S. Bureau of the Census, *Historical Statistics of the United States, Colonial Times to 1957*, United States Government Printing Office, Washington, D.C., 1960.

5. MEMOIRS AND BIOGRAPHIES

Many members of the inner circle of government in Washington have recorded their impressions of the New Deal era. Among the most valuable are E. Roosevelt, *This I Remember*, Hutchinson, London, 1950; F. Perkins, *The Roosevelt I Knew*, Hammond, London, 1947; S. Rosenman, *Working With Roosevelt*, Hart-Davis, London, 1952; H. L. Ickes, *The Secret Diary of Harold L. Ickes*, 2 vols, Weidenfeld and Nicolson, London, 1955; R. Moley, *After Seven Years*, Harper, New

York, 1939; J. Farley, *Behind the Ballots*, Harcourt, Brace, New York, 1938; H. Johnson, *The Blue Eagle from Egg to Earth*, Doubleday, New York, 1935; M. Eccles, *Beckoning Frontiers*, Knopf, New York, 1951. An edited version of Morgenthau's diaries is available edited by J. M. Blum and entitled *From the Morgenthau Diaries*, Houghton Mifflin, Boston, 1959. Hopkins's activities have been chronicled by S. F. Charles in *Minister of Relief*, Syracuse University Press, 1963. The memoirs of ex-President Hoover for this period are entitled *The Memoirs of Herbert Hoover. The Great Depression 1929–1941*, Hollis and Carter, London, 1953.

6. POLITICS AND PARTIES

One of the most stimulating analyses of the political scene in the 1930s is S. Lubell's *The Future of American Politics*, Hamish Hamilton, London, 1952. On Huey Long there is H. Kane, *Louisiana Hayride*, Morrow, New York, 1941, and on the American Liberty League G. Wolfskill, *The Revolt of the Conservatives*, Houghton Mifflin, Boston, 1962. For the far left, see D. Shannon, *The Socialist Party of America*, Macmillan, New York, 1955, and I. Howe and L. Coser, *The American Communist Party*, Houghton Mifflin, Boston, 1957.

7. THE ECONOMY

A standard economic history is B. Mitchell, *Depression Decade*, Rinehart, New York, 1947. Extremely helpful for the years 1929–33 is volume v of J. Dorfman's *The Economic Mind in American Civilization*, Viking Press, New York, 1959. The best book on the crucial monopoly issue is E. W. Hawley, *The New Deal and the Problem of Monopoly*, Princeton University Press, 1966. On farming there is T. Saloutos and J. Hicks, *Agricultural Discontent in the Middle West 1900–1939*, Wisconsin University Press, 1951. On the problem of economic stagnation see volume ii of J. Schumpeter, *Business Cycles*, McGraw-Hill, New York, 1939; A. Hansen, *Full Recovery or Stagnation?* Black, London, 1938, and J. Steindl, *Maturity and Stagnation in American Capitalism*, Blackwell, Oxford, 1952.

8. TRADE UNIONISM

There are several notable books on this topic, among them M. Derber and E. Young, eds., *Labor and the New Deal*. Wisconsin University Press, 1957; J. Morris, *Conflict within the AFL*, Cornell University Press, 1958; P. Taft, *The A. F. of L. from the Death of Gompers to the Merger*, Harper, New York, 1959; W. Galenson, *The CIO Challenge to the AFL*, Harvard University Press, 1960. I. Bernstein, *The Lean Years*,

Houghton Mifflin, Boston, 1960, gives an excellent account of the impact of the years 1929–33, while E. Ginzberg and H. Berman, *The American Worker in the Twentieth Century*, Collier-Macmillan, London, 1963, contains some fascinating first-hand material.

9. THE SUPREME COURT

A useful book of 'readings' is A. H. Cope and F. Krinsky, *Franklin D. Roosevelt and the Supreme Court*, Heath, Boston, 1952. A. T. Mason, *The Supreme Court from Taft to Warren*, Louisiana State University Press, 1958, has a good general account. Two pro-Roosevelt histories are E. S. Corwin, *Constitutional Revolution, Ltd.*, Claremont Colleges, California, 1941, and R. Jackson, *The Struggle for Judicial Supremacy*, Knopf, New York, 1941. The best summary of the debate is U.S. Senate, 75th Congress, 1st session: Committee on the Judiciary. *Hearings on the Reorganization of the Federal Judiciary*, United States Government Printing Office, Washington, D.C., 1937.

10. COMMENT

There is no better way of capturing the flavour of the period than by reading E. Wilson, *The American Earthquake*, Allen, London, 1958, and *The Shores of Light*, Farrar, Straus and Young, New York, 1952. In *Middletown in Transition*, Constable, London, 1937, the sociologists R. and H. Lynd give an interesting picture of the effects of the depression on a small town (Muncie, Indiana). W. Lippmann's *Interpretations 1931–1932* and *Interpretations 1933–1935*, Macmillan, New York, 1932 and 1936, also offer many penetrating insights. D. Aaron, *Writers on the Left*, Harcourt, Brace, New York, 1961, is a good guide to this sector of intellectual opinion, while M. Lerner, *Ideas for the Ice Age*, Viking, New York, 1941, and J. Wechsler, *The Age of Suspicion*, Random House, New York, 1953, also give the views of left-wing radicals. One of the most representative books of the decade, finally, is T. Arnold's *The Folklore of Capitalism*, Yale University Press, 1937.

Index